LEGACIES OF VIOLENCE

History, Society, and the State in Sardinia

The inhabitants of highland Sardinia celebrate a long history of resistance to outside authority. Many proudly declare that "not even the Roman Empire reached this far." Yet, since the late nineteenth century, the Italian government has made inroads into the mountain districts of the island, often through the use of force.

Antonio Sorge examines local understandings of this past and the effects that a history of violence exercises within a community. This history is particularly apparent among the shepherds of the island, and their practice of *balentia*, an ancient male code of honour ostensibly uncorrupted by the values of mainstream Italian society. A fascinating ethnography of a way of life that is disappearing as the inhabitants of the Sardinian highlands adopt a more mobile, cosmopolitan, and urban lifestyle, *Legacies of Violence* demonstrates how social memory continues to shape the present.

(Anthropological Horizons)

ANTONIO SORGE is an adjunct assistant professor in the Department of Anthropology at York University.

ANTHROPOLOGICAL HORIZONS

Editor: Michael Lambek, University of Toronto

This series, begun in 1991, focuses on theoretically informed ethnographic works addressing issues of mind and body, knowledge and power, equality and inequality, the individual and the collective. Interdisciplinary in its perspective, the series makes a unique contribution in several other academic disciplines: women's studies, history, philosophy, psychology, political science, and sociology.

For a list of the books published in this series see p. 195.

ANTONIO SORGE

Legacies of Violence

History, Society, and the State in Sardinia

UNIVERSITY OF TORONTO PRESS
Toronto Buffalo London

ISBN 978-1-4426-4989-7 (cloth)
ISBN 978-1-4426-2729-1 (paper)

Library and Archives Canada Cataloguing in Publication

Sorge, Antonio, 1975–, author
Legacies of violence : history, society, and the state in Sardinia /
Antonio Sorge.

(Anthropological horizons)
Includes bibliographical references and index.
ISBN 978-1-4426-4989-7 (bound).—ISBN 978-1-4426-2729-1 (pbk.)

1. Sardinia (Italy)—History.   2. Sardinia (Italy)—Social life and
customs.   3. Violence—Italy—Sardinia—History.   4. Collective memory—
Italy—Sardinia.   I. Title.   II. Series: Anthropological horizons

DG975.S31S67 2015   945'.9   C2015-900427-6

This book has been published with the help of a grant from the Federation for the
Humanities and Social Sciences, through the Awards to Scholarly Publications
Program, using funds provided by the Social Sciences and Humanities Research
Council of Canada.

University of Toronto Press acknowledges the financial assistance to its publishing
program of the Canada Council for the Arts and the Ontario Arts Council,
an agency of the Government of Ontario.

 Canada Council   Conseil des Arts
for the Arts   du Canada

 ONTARIO ARTS COUNCIL
CONSEIL DES ARTS DE L'ONTARIO
an Ontario government agency
un organisme du gouvernement de l'Ontario

University of Toronto Press acknowledges the financial support of the Government
of Canada through the Canada Book Fund for its publishing activities.

To my family

Contents

Preface   ix

Illustrations   xvii

1 Introduction   3

2 Landscape and History   23

3 On Barbarism   49

4 Anachronistic Men   71

5 Divergent Visions   100

6 Cohesion and Community   128

7 Conclusion   154

Notes   163

References   175

Index   191

Preface

Travelling south from the provincial capital of Nuoro on the Strada Provinciale 58 – one of the narrower secondary highways that lead into the heart of the Sardinian central highlands – we pass a junction near the 5-kilometre marker. To the east is the village of Oliena, while the monastery of Galanoli, whose Tuscan friars departed in the early 1990s, can be found to the west. The traveller wishing to continue onto Orgosolo will proceed past this junction and enter the Valley of Locoe. The semi-fertile soils of this valley bottom permit olive and almond trees to almost thrive, and vineyards can be kept with moderate success if spring rains are abundant. This is an enchanted, fragrant landscape in the springtime, when the orchards are in bloom, but asperous in midsummer with the blowing of the sirocco wind from North Africa. In the winter months, the northwesterly mistral leaves the air damp and the sky overcast. Regardless of season, from the Valley of Locoe we may catch a glimpse of Orgosolo in the distance, perched on the north slope of Monte Lisorgoni. Dwellings in the village are packed closely together. This is a classic Mediterranean nucleated highland settlement. In the surrounding countryside stillness prevails.

That stillness is only on the surface. The people of Orgosolo say that one is never alone in the countryside, and that any sense of solitude is merely an illusion. An outsider may be fooled, but once in Orgosolo proper he will soon realize his mistake. At 4,300 inhabitants this village may be pushing the upper limits of what anthropologists call a face-to-face community, but action and behaviour in Orgosolo cannot escape intense appraisal and evaluation by known social others. *Orgolesi* – the people of Orgosolo – know one another and can easily tell an insider from an outsider. Insiders know to conform to appropriate local expectations of hospitality, cooperation, cordiality, and most other behaviours based on shared notions of civility and subject to general scrutiny. All of this showcases the smooth operation of social intercourse, which can cloud realities of discord or disagreement, animosity or enmity, or divergent or contrasting ideals, values, world views, and conceptions of "the good life." Even within a small community uniformity or homogeneity in such matters should not be assumed. This may especially be the case today, as a plurality of messages is more readily available through mass media than ever before and ease and efficiency of communication and travel have increased individuals' opportunities to an extent previously unknown. This has, in itself, enabled a richer awareness of the world beyond the confines of any given locality – a world, it should be noted, that may be embraced or rejected to varying degrees. Indeed, contrary and ambiguous feelings are attached to all that encompasses the "traditional" or the "modern" in Orgosolo (both tangible or intangible). Points of reference vary, with some lauding the modernist ontologies represented by images of the outside world and others holding fast to a constellation of values and customary practices hostile toward forces that threaten to alter the mechanisms governing local life. My apprehension of this dynamic, which pervades social life in Orgosolo, was gradual, and took the form of an ethnographic encounter through which I set myself the task of disentangling its constituent strands.

The fieldwork upon which this study is based was of approximately fourteen months' duration, and was conducted largely in Orgosolo and, to a lesser extent, in surrounding towns and villages from January 2002 to May 2003, with a brief follow-up period in July 2008. An ethnographic engagement premised on deep cultural immersion proved indispensable to my acceptance within local networks so that I could establish social ties of my own. This was not always easy, for highland Sardinians' suspicion of outsiders is widely recognized, not least by Orgolesi themselves. Yet I would in time undergo a gradual metamorphosis from anonymous outsider to friend and neighbour.

I became a beneficiary of daily encounters with people who would open up wide vistas, allowing me to understand local realities that were initially obscure to me. The deep ties I established with my interlocutors, and the tone and temper of my interactions with them, helped shape my discoveries. So did a number of other factors. First, as a single male researcher in a community where men's and women's spheres are more or less clearly demarcated, I could not gain the same access to women's worlds as I could to men's worlds. The bias here is therefore towards men's roles in rural Sardinian society, although by no means does this suggest a neglect of women, women's lives, and women's problems, interests, aspirations, and views. In issues pertaining to gender, I have sought to provide a composite picture. Secondly, my foreignness was a source of consternation for some local people, especially in the early stages of my research, when my assurances of being a harmless anthropologist were not altogether convincing. To some of my interlocutors, especially young shepherds, I remained a figure of suspicion. In the early part of my fieldwork, many of my interactions with local men consisted of justifying my presence and, in some cases, responding to accusations (sometimes proffered light-heartedly, other times not) that I was a *poliziotto* (policeman) or *spia* (spy). My movements were well-known and discussed, which helped to explain why, on a regular basis, acquaintances I barely knew went out of their way to inform me of my own whereabouts, always with a mix of curiosity and amusement: "I saw you driving down the highway by Galanoli yesterday. Were you going to Mamoiada? Yes? And what's in Mamoiada?" "I saw you open the shades at ten o'clock this morning. You must have been up late!" Alternatively, "This morning I saw you in the distance jogging on the dirt road near Ventosu. You're trying to lose all the weight you've gained here, aren't you!" Or, "I saw your car parked outside of so-and-so's house yesterday! How's so-and-so doing?" It was only after several months that I was able to convince everyone, or almost, that I was not a covert agent of the state. Of course, such close scrutiny of my movements would eventually subside.

These anecdotes might convey an image of Orgosolo as closed, which some local folk, with a hint of pride, certainly do concede it to be. While there can be no community that is completely sealed from its wider social, economic, and political environment, the people of any locality may abide by self-definitions that stand in opposition to the outside world, usually for good reason. Orgosolo is one such place. I learned in the earliest days of my stay that there could be no other way to gain access to local worlds than by adopting a candid manner and suspending any expectations of how I would be received. In sum, I approached Orgosolo as an open social field, and let the ethnographic method of participant observation guide my research decisions. The final result is a partial – that is, partial in both senses of the term, necessarily incomplete and sympathetic to local concerns – account of highland Sardinian life and times. My theoretical interests before departing for the field did not unduly influence my attention in any specific direction and were not formative of my conclusions. Rather, I let my interlocutors' words and actions ultimately suggest the appropriate foci of inquiry, and I let myself be guided by the circumstances of the ethnographic encounter. Like Evans-Pritchard (1976:242), who let the Azande concern with witchcraft guide his research, and when with the Nuer became as "cattle-minded" as his hosts, I too let myself be guided by local concerns. Some of the dominant local concerns in Orgosolo, as I saw them expressed day to day, centred on the interrelated themes of masculinity, pastoral identity, and resistance to the outside world, which I would later contextualize within a theoretical framework encompassing questions of local history, violence, and the state. This was an exercise that required caution, and involved a need to address a comprehensive set of stereotypes long attached to Orgosolo in particular and central Sardinia in general. The mountain districts of this island have been reified in wider discourses that represent them as violent, isolated, and, indeed, *arretrati* (backward). This fact quickly became apparent to me. Acquaintances and interlocutors from larger Sardinian towns and cities often expressed amazement that a foreigner such as myself should decide to live in the highlands, "a place forgotten by man and by God," as one city-based acquaintance put it. Am I not afraid for my safety? No. Do you hear gunfire in the night? Sometimes. How do they treat you up there? Quite well. I could provide many anecdotes. Stereotypes abound regarding the ease with which highland Sardinians are moved to vengeance by the slightest personal offence. But these are stereotypes, and like so many other representations of various peoples of the rural Mediterranean, the hotheadedness of highland Sardinians is a common lay presupposition. Sensationalized mass media reports of arson, vandalism, manslaughter, and homicide provide an unflattering representation of an apparently violent population that has yet to be brought into mainstream Italian society. In this book I seek to address the origins of these views and how they are locally refracted, providing an account of the nuances of local life and of the changes that are affecting the village and district as a whole. In doing this, I adopt a historical perspective that brings into view the processes that have generated the realities of life on the Sardinian highlands over the *longue durée*, assuming that knowledge of the present can only be gained through an understanding of the past – in particular, how local people understand that past.

It goes without saying that the anthropological observer who wishes to comprehend social realities must resist any tendency to essentialize.

I argue that this is the whole point behind a comparative view of Mediterranean society. As Julian Pitt-Rivers (1977) pointed out, interest in an anthropological understanding of this region (understood not as a cultural area but as a concept of heuristic convenience) lies in how it may enable us to transcend the façades that make up official national images and permits an appreciation of how local realities, identities, and self-definitions depart from these imposed statist, national, and nationalist ideals. Beyond this, similarities and common themes, manifested through recurring patterns, reveal a certain "family resemblance" among the different societies of this region (Albera and Blok 2001:22-24; Horden and Purcell 2000:507). From the outset, highland Sardinia is considered part of this larger family, but it is also a region that bears the unmistakable imprint of the highland experience, most notably for its longstanding dissidence vis-à-vis the state. In sum, this is an account of a highly "emplaced" people, whose ties to a local territory, memory of historical belonging to a marginal collective, and sense of themselves as a distinct moral community are based on an idiom of opposition and latent hostility to the outside world. This social arena's local cultural formation presents a counter-hegemonic theory to the claims of the Italian state, and, as we will see, the most radical articulation of this oppositional ideal is found in the concept of *balentia*, the highly pressured male code of honour operative within the rural pastoral sector.

While the focus here is on Orgosolo, my conclusions are not unique to that village. Many ethnographic descriptions herein find their analogues elsewhere within the Mediterranean region, and, if handled comparatively, may yield theoretical insights into wider processes. Specifically, this analysis is an outgrowth of a theoretical interest in a local community's longstanding opposition to the state and a corresponding absence of a complete state monopoly over means of coercion. Therefore, the text deals at length with local responses to a historical reality in which coercive force was diffuse and decentralized. The precepts, norms, and general concern with reputation that underpin the local code of honour are regarded here as the outgrowth of a historical process that left local communities marginalized and in an embattled state. The highland Sardinian code of honour was definitively described by the jurist Antonio Pigliaru (2000 [1959]) and named by him the *codice barbaricino* (Barbagian code), after the region known as Barbagia, a folk appellation for the island's central highland district that includes the village of Orgosolo and that derives its name from the generic ancient Roman designation of *Civitates Barbariae*, barbarian peoples. Taken within a wider comparative

framework, we can see that the values of *balentia* speak to a set of social
configurations that we know to be ubiquitous throughout the Mediterranean. This is an exercise, in sum, that proceeds with a view to discern
the general in the particular.

Finally, this work is a demonstration of the links between a local
community and macro-historical trends. The following chapters are
threaded by the expression of concern over the nature of a historical
transition from a locally subdivided and self-regulating agrarian world
to one that is more effectively governed by a modern state and incorporated into an encompassing industrial or postindustrial society (Gellner
1988). Through the use of this heuristic argument – and via a presenta-
tion of the wider contexts within which the life of a community unfolds,
as well as the ideas that govern a people's understanding of its own
experiences – we may achieve a glimpse into the realities of a particular
segment of humanity at a single point in time.

I should note here that I have not used any real names, with the
exception of a few individuals whose circumstances are already widely
publicized and therefore a matter of public record, or who have already
contributed to public debates by making statements of various kinds.
Aside from this, and in the interest of protecting the identity of friends,
associates, and collaborators of this study, I have used pseudonyms for
most people and altered details where appropriate in order to protect
the identities of my interlocutors. However, I have used the real name
of the community that is the focus of this study: Orgosolo. My reasons
for this are straightforward. First, an effective pseudonym would have
required the excision of a considerable amount of ethnographic and historical detail specific to this locality, and to do so would have compromised the integrity of the account. Second, the fundamentally human-
istic tone and interpretation that I provide of the highland Sardinian
experience goes to considerable lengths to counter many of the more
simplistic understandings of social life within this district. By extension, this account of the social realities of Orgosolo dispels many of the
negative stereotypes for which it is known.

My personal and professional debts are great. The mayoral office and
town council of Orgosolo were welcoming and always willing to facilitate my residency. The staff of the local public library was of immense
help in tracking down published sources, and managed a facility to
which it was always a pleasure to escape. Above all, I thank the people
of Orgosolo who, in their unofficial roles, showed considerable forbear-
ance and patience with a bungling foreigner who arrived alone and

with intentions that may at times have appeared nebulous. Their hospitality was great and their kindness sincere, demanding nothing less than reciprocal sincerity of my own. I especially acknowledge all who adopted me into their families and friendship networks. None of this would have been possible without their collaboration, and I hope that the present work does justice to the reality they know.

Beyond Orgosolo, but still within Sardinia, my investigations benefited from discussions with faculty and graduate students at the University of Cagliari and the University of Sassari. Friendly meetings at various stages of my time in Sardinia, especially with Giulio Angioni, Felice Tiragallo, Gino Satta, and Alberto Caoci, always proved edifying. I hope that they too will find this work to be a faithful rendering and interpretation of social patterns in the central highlands. In particular I acknowledge the assistance of Franco Lai of the University of Sassari, who graciously introduced me to the world of Sardinian anthropology.

Outside of Sardinia, conversations with Tracey Heatherington of the University of Wisconsin at Milwaukee and Steffan Igor Ayora-Diaz of Autonomous University of Yucatan were always enlightening. Allan Dawson of Drew University, who kindly helped to prepare the map of Sardinia used in this book, Mauro Lo Dico of Reitaku University, and Udo Krautwurst of the University of Prince Edward Island always provided excellent and valuable insights into how the world works. Thanks also to my great intellectual ally and adversary, critic and supporter, and life partner Maggie Cummings of the University of Toronto. At the University of Calgary, input by Alan Smart, Haijo Westra, and especially Doyle Hatt, a great friend and mentor, has been indispensable. David D. Gilmore of SUNY-Stony Brook, Ørnulf Gulbrandsen of the University of Bergen, and Sabina Magliocco of California State University at Northridge have also provided helpful suggestions to improve this work, and three anonymous reviews of the manuscript likewise proved valuable. Needless to say, any shortcomings are all my own.

At the University of Toronto Press, I wish to acknowledge Douglas Hildebrand for his assistance throughout the review process and Michael Lambek for his generous encouragement to submit this work to the Anthropological Horizons series.

This book has been published with the help of a grant from the Federation for the Humanities and Social Sciences, through the Awards to Scholarly Publications Program, using funds provided by the Social Sciences and Humanities Research Council of Canada. Province of Alberta Graduate Fellowship grants, graduate assistantships within the Department of Anthropology at the University of Calgary, and the Canadian-Italian Business and Professional Association all provided funding for this research.

Academic careers take a toll on family togetherness, but luckily not, in my case, family cohesiveness. I owe a debt of gratitude to my family for their support over the years, but especially to my mother Maria and late father, Gregorio. I now have a family of my own and in 2013, with Maggie, celebrated the birth of our twins, Gregory and Lydia, who in 2015 will be joined by a new sibling. I dedicate this book to all of them, generations old and new.

Orgosolo, a partial view

Gnarled holm oak tree (*Quercus ilex*) on the Supramonte plateau

Stark landscape of the commons

Returning from the pastures

Nuraghe Ilole, with fenced-off areas for livestock, outside Orgosolo

Old friends drinking wine

Friends in a bar

Family and friends at table

The anthropologist, left, learning how to prune a grapevine

Preparing piglets for local sale

Tourists outside a souvenir shop

Rider at full gallop in the *Sa vardia* horse race

Mural commemorating the struggle for Pratobello

"Big Game Hunt at Orgosolo, Murguliai, 1899"

Painting the mural "Enjoy Orgosolo"

Bullet-riddled district map

LEGACIES OF VIOLENCE

History, Society, and the State in Sardinia

SARDINIA

N

OLBIA-
TEMPIO

Olbia ✦

✦ Sassari

SASSARI

NUORO

✦ Nuoro

Orgosolo ◉

ORISTANO

✦ Oristano

OGLIASTRA

MEDIO
CAMPIDANO

CAGLIARI

CARBONIA
IGLESIAS

Cagliari ★

30 kilometres
30 Miles

Map 1.1 Map of Sardinia

1
Introduction

Orgosolo lies 600 metres above sea level on the slopes of Monte Lisorgoni in the Gennargentu mountain range of central-eastern Sardinia. The local economy has historically depended upon the landscape of the surrounding countryside, with sheep and goat pastoralism a mainstay that has conditioned life and livelihood and provided this village of 4,300 inhabitants with its strongly identifiable cultural forms. The people of Orgosolo are not indifferent to their past, and possess an awareness of the outside world that is conditioned by their historical experience as well as by their understanding of themselves as a highland people. The wider island–region of Sardinia is marked by a juxtaposition of mountain environments and fertile valleys and lowlands, a classic highland-lowland distinction that is a common motif throughout the Mediterranean world.

Settlement on Sardinia conforms to a pattern well-known throughout the larger region: nucleated villages of tightly packed houses that dot the landscape, each a community with a profound awareness of its own history and convinced of its local distinctiveness. The peculiar lifeways of this part of the world are intimately related to geography and landscape.

Following a brief ten-day trip to Sardinia in July of 2000, I serendipitously landed in Orgosolo, where I met many Orgolesi who, without fail, showed great hospitality, always more than willing to assist my stay, share their thoughts, and indulge my curiosity. I remained for the whole week, and can still recall in great detail the excitement that comes with first getting to know a people and a place. One episode remains especially vivid, and over the coming days and weeks, then months and years, I would time and again reflect on its significance. Speaking with a group of young to middle-aged men in a local bar during one of the first days of my stay, I described my interest in collecting narrative accounts of the hardships caused by government actions on the Sardinian highlands, about which I had read before visiting. These included the antibanditry campaigns of the nineteenth and twentieth centuries, the establishment of an artillery firing range on the village commons (shared territory) in the late 1960s, and the proposed establishment of a national park (the Parco Nazionale del Golfo di Orosei e del Gennargentu) within the district that would deprive shepherds of land-use rights. I wanted to know the people's reactions to these instances of government imposition, as well as how they remembered the associated events. How did they digest this history, how did they talk about it, and how had the passage of time affected its significance? Sitting in that bar on that hot afternoon, I was struck by what one of the men said to me, seemingly a wrap-up of all that he believed necessary to say about the subject: "This is our never-ending story, but we defend ourselves. We always do, just like we did against the Romans. You know, these mountains, not even the Roman Empire reached this far."

This book is the product of this and countless other revelatory statements I encountered over fourteen months of fieldwork that unfolded in 2002 and 2003. The idea that the mountain districts of Sardinia, specifically Orgosolo and its territory, were never conquered by outside forces, but rather actively resisted them, is a widespread supposition. Why? In answering this question, a historical approach to understanding the life and times of Orgosolo – and by extension, of couse, the wider region – would in time be revealed.

Axioms and Parameters

This is a historical ethnography based in fieldwork. Its analyses and descriptions speak for themselves, and my contextualization of local lives within wider processes intends to offer meaningful insights into highland Sardinian society. All my theoretical suppositions are ethnographically grounded, with a view towards explicating the reality with which they contend.

Historically, the agrarian order of the past is seen as having generated two complementary yet opposed social-structural typologies. On the one hand were relatively autonomous tribal societies or montagnard agriculturalists that succeeded in maintaining a degree of independence from politically centralizing forces. On the other were communities assimilated into the state apparatus as peasant producers. The former escaped the effects of a concentration of power by a predatory state, and managed to maintain internal order "by preserving an intra-communal balance of power" (Gellner 1988:162). The Sardinian highlands exemplify this scenario. The rugged terrain inhibited the entrenchment of effective external control to the extent that no feudal structures were ever established. Therefore, indigenous highland communities were capable of retaining a modicum of independence until the end of the Roman period. In time, however, their autonomy too began to erode, most significantly, as we will see, following Italian national unification in 1861.

In this book, I argue that one of the most enduring features of highland culture and society is its dissident history vis-à-vis the state. Numerous features of highland culture in many parts of the world can be regarded as long-term adaptations or strategic responses to a continuous, deeply rooted struggle to keep the state at bay. I borrow this general theoretical insight from James C. Scott (2009), who takes the diversity of languages, ethnicities, and systems of socioeconomic organization on the Southeast Asian massif as evidence of a so-called shatter zone, a place of refuge for nonstate populations to take shelter from the expansionist state-making projects in the lowland valleys. Theirs are histories of struggle against the state that present parallels to dynamics found within the Mediterranean world, where highland zones served as repositories of autonomous systems, frustrating claims of state centralization that created peasant subjects on the lowlands. The social systems of highland zones were constructed on the basis of legal and economic arrangements that are not so much adaptations to montane environments, but rather to historical circumstances that had the ultimate effect of denying the entrenchment of extractive state regimes: customary forms of dispute resolution centred on blood feud, common-pool resource management, and the herding of livestock (primarily sheep and goats), an economic activity suited to the evasion of government control.[1]

The Mediterranean is famous for its historic refuge populations, many of which have taken sanctuary in the mountains as a final retreat from the kingdoms and empires that have controlled its regions. The Berbers of North Africa, the Druze of Syria and Lebanon, the Basques of Spain, the Sarakatsani of Corinth all attest to what Funnell and Parish (2001:90) call the "sanctuary theory" of mountains. The lived universe of highland peoples consequently stands opposed to the outside world, yet a symbiotic relationship exists. It is this deep association based on opposition that constitutes and defines the tone of highland life. These peoples are examples of what Pierre Clastres (1974) has called "societ- ies against the state": roughly egalitarian and autonomous groupings on the margins of powerful formations, whose mechanisms of prestige avoidance and customary forms of legal self-help have preserved their status as nonstate peoples into comparatively recent times. Despite their full incorporation into state-level societies in the eighteenth and nine- teenth centuries, such formerly independent peoples sustain a strong ethos of resistance to the outside world. In highland Sardinia, this ethos is fuelled by a clear vision of alternatives to contemporary Italian life – namely, alternatives to life within a hegemonic state, to contemporary neoliberalism, and to consumer culture. But nonetheless, local people have had to come to terms with this reality, many of them grudgingly, but others enthusiastically, as we shall see.

A number of the commonplaces that inform this work are born of eth- nographic studies that constitute the canon of Mediterraneanist anthro- pology. We are therefore prompted to ask about the attendant features of agrarian society, and how widespread they are, or were, within the Mediterranean landscape. In a classic review of ethnographic studies, David Gilmore (1982:178–9) highlights numerous characteristic pat- terns within the region, among which are included, at a macrosocietal level, a strong urban orientation and associated disdain for agricultural labour and rural way of life; sharp economic and social stratification; a history of political instability; individualist orientation in community life ("atomism"); ubiquity of both sexual segregation and the honour and shame complex; a tendency towards exclusive reliance upon the smallest feasible social unit (nuclear families or lineages) in economic production. While the rich insights into Mediterranean cultures offered by this expansive body of work are significant, they must be treated cautiously. Misreadings can lead to false assumptions of cultural uni- formity within the region, resulting in misunderstanding of cultural variations and even in a reification of local realities. As Horden and Pur- cell (2000:26) note, almost every commonplace notion about the Medi- terranean "carries its own peculiar burden of cultural history," and for this reason such notions should be treated with circumspection. Failure to do so can potentially lead to stereotyped or exoticist representations.

The modern anthropology of the Mediterranean region is a sub- specialty that was established with the publication of major theses underscoring the honour and shame values central to Mediterranean society, which were said to pervade and structure the moral universe of the region's populations to the extent that they could be conceptually bracketed off from contiguous world areas for the purpose of comparative study (see Davis 1977; Pitt-Rivers 1963; Peristiany 1966). The honour and shame construct provided a high-level principle of integration that could permit a conceptual unification of the region for heuristic purposes, comprising as it does a variable set of values that are never exactly the same from place to place and that are, even within single contexts, subject to manipulation and debate. Furthermore, the claims of centrality of honour and shame in the region were expressed in reference to the tenacity of values and world views that had become displaced in industrialized northwestern Europe. And so, any careful analyst might discern among the various regional differences a common substratum consisting of orientations that run counter to the official ideologies of the imposed nation-states of the present day (Pitt-Rivers 1963:10). In sum, we are presented with a novel concept of area study that is not bounded politically, but rather is delineated on the basis of geographical criteria and that furthermore recognizes the fallacy of such an idea as immutable tradition giving way to restless modernity.

No aspect of this perspective should be seen to constitute what Johannes Fabian (1983) calls a "denial of coevalness." Rather, this apparent imputation of continuity is inferred from the givens of physical geography and historical process. The mountains of the Mediterranean did not allow the easy integration of national populations as did the plains and woodlands of northern Europe of their inhabitants, and the communication difficulties quite simply acted as a perennial buffer, guarding local peoples from sweeping external influences. It is this cushioning effect inherent to mountainous refuge that permits continuity in local cultural forms. However, the reverse is also true, particularly on the lowland and coastal areas: long-term exchanges did lead – through cultural borrowing, intermarriage, conquest, and so forth – to considerable creolization. The inherent anthropological interest in the Mediterranean region lies in exactly this contrast, which has produced cultural convergences and a proliferation of complementary differences that resemble one another and that together constitute "a Mediterranean system" that calls out for cross-cultural comparison (Bromberger 2006).

As Horden and Purcell (2000:506) suggest, it is helpful to view the clusters of attributes associated with the pan-Mediterranean value system of honour and shame as comprising what Rodney Needham (1975) has called a "family resemblance group" or "polythetic class."

Each cluster of associated attributes recurs throughout the region with striking pattern and depth. In general, no single attribute – for example pressured masculinity, or the seclusion of women, or conspicuous hospitality – stand in isolation; rather, all reappear in unique configurations across time and space, combining and recombining in near infinite variations, thus providing the basis for a supposed Mediterranean unity. The honour beliefs of Andalusian peasants (Pitt-Rivers 1977; Lison-Tolosana 1966), Sarakatsani shepherds (Campbell 1964), Egyptian Bedouins (Abu-Lughod 1999), Algerian Kabyles (Bourdieu 1966), Sicilian peasants (Blok 1974), and, as we will see in the following chapters, Sardinian highlanders all share certain traits that indicate convergent values and world views.

I argue that the source of these convergent values can be found through an analysis of regional history. Jane Schneider (1971) provides a speculative but well-reasoned history of the origins of honour values, suggesting that their emergence owes much to the role of chronic material scarcity following the rise of states in prehistory. Marginalized pastoralists and montagnard agriculturalists were long forced to subsist on unproductive territory, leading to competition over fertile lands, grazing privileges, water-use rights, and routes of access to pasturage. This perpetuated conflict among property-holding groups that tenaciously defended their patrimony from usurpation. Based on her observations of this dynamic, Schneider (1971:2) defined honour as "the ideology of a property holding group which struggles to define, enlarge, and protect its patrimony in a competitive arena." In sum, cultural similarities among the Mediterranean populations are an outgrowth of similar ecological conditions and historical processes throughout the region, conditioning the development of societies that range along what Jane Schneider and Peter Schneider (1976) call a "pastoral-agrarian continuum." Here, the absence of state institutions to regulate access to resources, as well as the resultant conflicts, led to the proliferation of various forms of private violence in order to secure the productive means to ensure survival. Inherent to this struggle is the idea of property as an object of predation, acquirable by guile and vulnerable to theft (Schneider 1971:9). Livestock theft, therefore, condemned throughout history by all governments, is accepted by nonstate pastoral society as an activity that falls within the moral bounds of the community. Ecological pressure, coupled with a weak state presence, results in a kind of zero-sum game whereby nuclear family households or lineages must protect their interests at the expense of one another.

Pierre Clastres (2010 [1980]) theorizes this condition of latent hostility as a byproduct of non-state communities' desire to meet an autarkic ideal of self-sufficiency. The state of perpetual war that is so central to the lives of peoples extruded by processes of state-making – or "societies against the state" – is necessitated by a refusal to submit to external authority, to codified law, and generally to an imperative to claim and exclusively control their own territories (Clastres 2010 [1980]:267). In highland Sardinia, until comparatively recent times, this territorial imperative led to constant battles, as communities fought for access to resources with the goal of expanding their villages' common lands (Lai 1998). To this day, many shepherds in Orgosolo proudly proclaim their ancestors' prowess in having appropriated lands from bordering towns in order to amass what would become, at 230,000 hectares, one of the largest common territories within the central highlands. A further ingredient in this state of "perpetual war" posited by Clastres and implicit in Schneider's analysis was the centrality of systems of legal self-help premised on the threat of violence, all situated within a context characterized by a high military participation ratio (Andreski 1968), in which means of coercion were widely diffused.

Is this all ancient history? For societies that have lost their agrarian underpinnings – that have proceeded along the path of urbanization and industrialization, become dominated by the modern state, and constructed rationalized growth economies – the value orientations described above may cease to have relevance. The extrajudicial use of violence that buttresses the agrarian order and sustains the values central to it becomes an anomaly. The centralizing state that succeeds in monopolizing the means of coercion renders anachronistic much of the habitus (Bourdieu 1977) of the archetypal man of honour, whose circumspect behaviour and economical speech is superseded by the man who entrusts his protection to the state and the woman who ceases to look to male kin for her preservation. What had been ethically valued to forebears comes to be considered a curiosity, a set of values regarded as retrograde (cf. Blok 2001:202–9). But by no means have honour values and their associated characteristics become obsolete everywhere. In highland Sardinia, the *codice barbaricino* (Barbagian code) encompasses a set of norms and prescriptions that set shepherds apart from the wider society. A man who follows the Barbagian code is someone who successfully conforms to the normative local standards of masculinity, and is said to possess *balentia* (valour).[2] *Balentia* incorporates a set of prescribed behaviours that is part and parcel of the habitus of young unmarried men engaged in pastoral production. It comprises an ensemble of traits and attributes that an ideal young man should possess – masculinity, virulence, effectiveness, and vitality, as well as the maturity, restraint, and good judgment necessary to successfully assert oneself within a highly competitive social arena. In short, a *balente* is a man with honour who exhibits these traits with some success. The term has a Latin root, and is etymologically related to the Italian *valente*, and even more closely to the Spanish *valentia*, which connotes adroitness and agility, and approximates the English *valiant*. *Unu balente* is, in other words, *unu omine de gabbale* (a man of worth) or *unu omine bonu* (a good man). Not "good" in any abstract moral sense, but "good" in the Roman sense of the term – a man who fulfils social obligations and manages on a daily basis to preserve his place. The esteem associated with such a status does not diminish following retirement, and dues paid earlier in life ensure great respect in later years. I suggest that honour values such as *balentia* are a legacy of a people's violent history, amounting to an orientation toward the world born of an adaptation to difficult circumstances that perpetuates over time as social, political, and economic circumstances dictate.

In examining pastoral honour values, I have minded Eric Wolf's (2001) implied distinction between observable realities and underlying processes from which they are generated, and, needless to say, recognize that societies or cultures are not immutable or closed systems. Still, some further disclaimers are in order. Honour values and the behaviours they designate as ideal might mislead one to interpret an agonistic, if not Hobbesian, tone of life. This is a misperception that inhibits recognition of the ability of honour values to adapt to changing circumstances. Furthermore, honour is not to be viewed as exclusively dependent upon men's assertiveness and adeptness in the employment of violence. Hospitality, respect for social others, and even-handedness in everyday dealings are commensurate with wider social success, and are not in themselves extraneous to a system of honour values. Furthermore, the ideal of family unity and self-sufficiency does not operate to the exclusion of wider ties. Within highland Sardinia, dyadic ties that meet both utilitarian and emotional needs are evidenced everywhere. To be considered honourable, a man must not merely be capable of exhibiting an assertive masculinity, but must also be successful in portraying himself as respectful, magnanimous, and fair. Men and women alike should possess rounded social personas and be generally amicable and reciprocal in their obligations. Success only in the areas of assertiveness and cunning leads to social isolation. Lastly, an understanding of honour and shame that places emphasis on female seclusion is not normative everywhere, and such an assumption could blind one to distinctions among contexts.[3] Within Orgosolo and more generally throughout Sardinia, for example, the notable separation of male and female spheres has never entailed the seclusion of women.[4]

Arguably the most salient criticism of early work on honour in the Mediterranean is provided by Evthymios Papataxiarchis (2000), who notes an undue privileging of methodological individualism that emphasizes the agency of the self-interested monad. A more profitable conception of honour values is to view them as a tool for understanding local theories of gender that cast insight into competing local discourses of the self, which in turn allow for a composite view of the social uses of the rhetoric of honour and honourability. In the village of Mouria on the island of Lesbos, Papataxiarchis (2000:184) detects a cultural model of protest that highlights the centrality of an antistructural type of male identity, which is key to a counter-hegemonic theory that stands "in opposition to the socio-economic foundations of a world based on exchange." I argue that Orgosolo presents a parallel instance of such honour-as-male protest, which, as in Mouria, underscores the distinct character of the local community and upholds its traditional knowledge base, practices, and moralities as a counterpoint to those of the outside world.

Furthermore, and complementary to this view, I agree with Christian Giordano (2012a, 2012b) that any ethnography of a Mediterranean community would profit from paying close attention to the way in which local inhabitants apprehend the past. An interest in local adaptations to social, political, and economic circumstances over the long term must necessarily be concerned with "the meaning given by the actors themselves to their past in the present" (Giordano 2012a:25). Consideration of what Sharon Macdonald (2012) calls "past presencing" – how people experience, reconstruct, negotiate, and interpret the past in day-to-day life – has been central in contemporary ethnographic research in Europe, and is informed by a historical sensibility that views the past as a dimension of the present. In Orgosolo, local understanding of the past consistently underscores an apprehension of a legacy of violence at the hands of powerful outsiders, and a concomitant rejection of those hegemonic structures and institutions that would divest the community of its autonomy. Despite the fact that Orgosolo, along with the wider central highlands of which it is a part, has not been truly autonomous, by any definition of the term, for at least several centuries, a dissident

ethos vis-à-vis the outside world has long figured prominently at the
local level. The presence of the past is easily glimpsed with the oft-
repeated claim that the central highlands were never conquered by
the Roman Empire. Yet this belief is not evenly distributed, and only
half-believed by some. It is regarded as an idealization rather than an
empirical truth; in actuality most beliefs about the past are determined
by an individual's age, sex, and occupation. For example, young shepherds most wholeheartedly accept the premise of a perennial struggle
against rapacious outsiders throughout history, while everyone else is a
little more agnostic, or at least somewhat more disinterested, in this set
of representations. For shepherds, marginalized but symbolically vital
representatives of highland culture, history is a resource to be mobilized
in the creation of a charter that offers guidelines for life in the present.
Their mistrust in, and opposition to, the state and its representatives
stems from collective representations based in the historical spaces of
experience that are projected onto the horizon of expectations (Giordano 2012b:29). Their awareness of a violent history overseen by various powerful outsiders, which in the contemporary period consisted
of imperious agents of national law enforcement, as well as their recollection of misfortunes and violence suffered by their ancestors only a
generation or two removed have conditioned a general sense of vulnerability and mistrust. Therefore, local strategies of resistance to public
authority should be seen as conditioned by an awareness of the value
of autonomy, itself buttressed by recourse to historical experience that
reveals the undesirability of yielding to state coercion.

The emplacement of this dissident highland identity is noteworthy. Orgosolo is a toponym that marks the identity of its inhabitants,
a place that has gathered unto itself countless memories and imaginings made up of collective representations and practices heavily sedi-
mented through time (see Escobar 2001). This is a locality conditioned
by its particular geography and its historical experience, and animated
by a rich social life. Like any locality, though, Orgosolo is not a static,
secure, inert place. Rather, locality is always in process of becoming,
forever defined in dialectic relation with the nonlocal. To follow Arjun
Appadurai (1996:189), locality – which he defines handily as "a structure of feeling, a property of social life, and an ideology of situated
community" – struggles against centrifugal forces that would minimize
its salience, challenge its ontology, or even vanquish it altogether. The
three factors responsible for this, according to Appadurai's formulation,
are the nation-state, diasporic flows, and the proliferation of electronic

and virtual communities (1996:198). In Orgosolo, these are manifested in a number of ways, from the integration of pastoral production with the global economy and the imposition of a exogenous judicial system – both central to Sardinia's integration into the modern era – to the contemporary processes necessary to urbanize and tertiarize the Sardinian economy and herald its integration into the postmodern era. The cultural particularisms of the locality do not accord with the nation-state's desire for homogeneous national space, just as it rejects the emergent transnational order and its constitutive global flows.

There is no consensus as to what vision Orgolesi should embrace for the future. On the one hand, localists champion the cultural vernacular of the central highlands, defined by images of dissidence and resistance to the outside world, and understand Orgosolo to be an exemplary space, ethnolinguistically distinct certainly from Italy and even from the rest of Sardinia. To traditionalists, Orgosolo should strive to maintain its local character just as they, as individuals, gain their personal definitions from association with surrounding communities. In contrast to these "contextualized persons" (Geertz 1983:66), we have cosmopolitans, who herald a more polished and standardized interpretation of personhood, one that is defined by individualism and whose styles are more urbane and reflect a bourgeois sensibility. These two ideal-typical personas coexist within Orgosolo, each one expressing considerable ambivalence towards the other. The efforts of the former to "produce and reproduce locality under conditions of anxiety and entropy" (Appadurai 1996:181) are a central theme in my analysis. Localists look askance at their counterparts who have forsaken the local in their pursuit of urbanity and cosmopolitanism. Localism is the metaculture of difference; it presents the principal challenge to the "neoliberal cultural complex" that constitutes cosmopolitan thought and feeling (Hannerz 2010:7). The story presented here is long in the making, and is based on an examination of the long-term processes involved in the integration of local spheres into progressively larger political, economic, and social formations.[5]

The Community

Orgosolo is located within the Barbagia zone of the central highlands. This is not an official designation coinciding with any administrative unit, but refers instead to an area with a folk designation that has roots in Roman antiquity. As a historically dissident territory, the central highlands were never effectively penetrated by Rome, and so designated with the epithet *barbaria* (land of barbarians), an appellation counterpoised to *romania* (land of Roman rule) (see Mastino 2006:39ff.). The term *Barbagia* is today locally embraced by *sos barbaricinos*, the Barbagians themselves, and evokes the image, one that is in wide circulation throughout all of Sardinia, of highlands that house "real" Sardinians – the ones who are free, who breathe mountain air, who were, and still are, shepherds. And so, in popular imagination Barbagia appears to be isolated, and not just from the outside world. Every village in this land-of-villages is deemed its own small universe, as even the Sardinian novelist Salvatore Satta (1987:10) suggested when he wrote of "minuscule settlements as remote from one another as are the stars." Anyone who stands on a high place and surveys the horizon cannot fail to notice how the landscape is dotted with nucleated settlements that appear as densely packed clusters. Each of these villages has clearly defined criteria of belonging, with residents whose ancestors go back multiple generations. Roots run deep, and Orgosolo, like other highland villages of Sardinia, retains elements of what Eric Wolf describes as the "closed corporate community" (Wolf 1957, 1986). People share a broad interest in policing the boundaries between insiders and outsiders, and the question of belonging is central to much public discourse. Membership within the community delimits legitimate rights to communal resources (forest, fields, pasture); an egalitarian ideology underpins social relations that have an omnipresent, agonistic edge; local jural norms contrast with those of the state; and outsiders are viewed with characterisitic suspicion. Of course, diagnosis of such a social formation should not come at the expense of some recognition of the fluidity of the boundaries between the local community and the outside world. At no time has Orgosolo, or other villages in the district, ever been isolated, bounded, or sealed from the outside world. Rather, Orgosolo has long been incorporated into a social order structured by a strong urban-rural dichotomy (Redfield 1955), and today is enmeshed within the highly mobile world of the early twenty-first century. This adaptation to the realities of modern times is strikingly apparent, putting a further shine on those aspects of local life that appear to present continuities with the past.

A casual *passeggiata* (promenade) through Orgosolo during the early evenings provides a first impression of these realities, and brings to light the ways in which this contrast plays out. While first impressions are necessarily superficial, here is one related to contrasts too stark to leave unconsidered.

A paced walk starting from the north end of the village heading east, then south, then eventually redirecting in a westerly direction, covering the whole length of the village on the main avenue – a walk of thirty minutes or so – will reveal different facets of Orgosolo. What do we see? We begin with the town hall, a modern two-storey red-brick building that is the focus of all local administrative processes, originally situated on the outskirts but now enveloped by modern building developments. The parking lot reveals a handful of newer commuter vehicles, mostly clean and well-maintained compact cars, easily distinguishable as belonging to middle-class functionaries rather than shepherds. We must qualify this statement by noting that the markers of a shepherd's vehicle are numerous, and because few Orgolesi own more than one car, their vehicles, which are used extensively in the countryside, are immediately apparent. Shepherds' vehicles first and foremost are versatile. Compact Toyota pickup trucks, as well the ubiquitous small Fiat Panda 4×4 hatchback, are both popular choices. These vehicles stand out because of the stainless steel milk containers they sometimes carry; they are often splashed with mud and are in various stages of wear and tear. Marked by nicks, scratches, and dents, they are obviously used extensively outside of built-up areas. These cars are not usually found in the parking lot of the town hall. Rather, town hall functionaries, as salaried workers, are more engaged with an economy of taste that aligns them with Italian mainstream society. Not having fully rejected the highland Sardinian identity – they are among its official representatives, after all – they nonetheless have little in common with the life they would willingly proclaim as authentic, namely, the life of the shepherd.

Southeast of the town hall stands the detachment and barracks of the Polizia Nazionale, on the Via Rinascita byway. Guarded by a locked gate, 2 metres tall, it is effectively segregated from the rest of the community. Almost directly across the road from the police detachment is a tended public garden, Piazza Don Muntoni, which gives way to a small bar, frequented primarily by shepherds and blue-collar workers, as well as occasional small groups of off-duty police officers. Aside from transactions related to official business, there is infrequent interaction between police and locals in the public spaces of Orgosolo. Further east on this road, two bars, on opposite sides of the street, almost face each other. One is a sports bar that caters to a younger, more urbane clientele; it is one of only two such establishments in town where women are occasionally seen. The other caters to an older clientele of shepherds and skilled tradesmen employed in small shops nearby.

The Via Rinascita winds south at its easternmost end and continues beyond the village limits; at the break in the road, however, we turn westward onto the Corso Repubblica. Proceeding about 100 metres on this main avenue we encounter the public library and middle school on the left, and the Piazza Caduti in Guerra (unofficially known as Piazza Su Muntilhu) on the right, with twin bocce lanes, usually surrounded by elderly men. This piazza is an exclusively male space; women are only seen there during the Feast of Saints Peter and Paul (the town's patron saints) at the end of June, as well as throughout mid-August during the festivities surrounding the Assumption of the Virgin Mary. Proceeding further west, we enter the most intensely lived-in part of Orgosolo, at the centre of which is located the Chiesa Parrocchiale Santissimo Salvatore (Parish Church of the Holy Saviour). A focal point of community life, it is a site where the women of the community gather on a regular basis, especially during Sunday services; yet it is a location that most men in the community tend to avoid. A gender-specific anti-clerical sentiment renders the church a predominantly female space, an observation I once shared with parish priest Don Michele Casula, which prompted an outburst: "The men of Orgosolo never come to church! They're embarrassed to be seen here!" The evident disregard that local men, especially shepherds, have for organized religion indicates a strongly materialistic orientation that embraces a nonmystical view of the world and of human fate. This disposition has been noted elsewhere in Sardinia (Magliocco 2006:66), as well as within other Mediterranean locales on the Iberian Peninsula, where lay anticlericalism is longstanding (see Brandes 1981; Gilmore 1984; Riegelhaupt 1984).

Any mention of anticlericalism in Orgosolo brings forth the memory of the tragic death of Don Graziano Muntoni, a parish priest shot to death under mysterious circumstances on Christmas Eve of 1998. No suspects have ever been arrested in connection with this murder, and the crime remains unsolved. My cautious inquiries regarding this event elicited two local theories. According to some interlocutors, Don Graziano frowned upon the heavy drinking and lack of discipline among young men who frequented local bars at all hours of the day and night, and was exuberant in his chastisement. In this version of events, he was the target of *balordi* (hooligans), primarily young shepherds (or, as we shall see later, *pastori finti* [pseudo-shepherds], in the estimates of many local people). These men brook no reproach; they lord over the central sites of village space and are not above the use of intimidation and violence in their demands for respect. Some interlocutors offered other interpretations, often in a tone of terse indifference: Don Graziano – a charismatic figure – overstepped the bounds of his welcome in Orgosolo, and behaved inappropriately. This interpretation reflects an understanding of violent action as an inevitable consequence of *il mal comportarsi* (bad behaviour); as one young man told me, *avrà fatto qualcosa* – he must have done something.[6]

The length of the Corso Repubblica, upon which the parish church is located, is also lined with shops and numerous bars, or *tzilleros* (sing., *tzilleri*). Incidentally, the bars in this area are frequented almost exclusively by shepherds and are known for having confrontational atmospheres, unlike bars elsewhere in the village. Along the following 75 metres a dozen or so bars are clustered, sometimes only a few doors apart. This short stretch of avenue is physically and symbolically the heart of Orgosolo. It is here that one finds the largest concentration of shepherd-owned off-road vehicles, with their owners either inside the bars or lingering at the entrances and scrutinizing passers-by.

The shepherd's dress visibly marks him as belonging to a distinct category. While most Orgolesi dress in restrained urban middle-class Italian fashions, the shepherd remains a holdout, clothed in black or dark brown velvet trousers and light wool sweaters, plain white cotton or dark polo shirts, dark jackets, and heavy black boots. Jackets and trousers, the most important elements of the shepherd's sombre habit, are not mass-produced, but are made locally by tailors skilled in the manufacture of classic Sardinian attire. Within Orgosolo, two artisans provide their sartorial services, creating made-to-measure outfits for paying clients. This style of dress, stereotypically Mediterranean in appearance, has its roots in the period following World War I. While most younger shepherds no longer wear the black or brown wool *bonnette* (country cap), often of English origin and manufacture, in winter they frequently don black knit nightwatchmen's or fishermen's caps, with closely cropped hair and a short beard or unshaved stubble. This traditional shepherd's outfit is understood to be a conservative style, appropriate for older men, although it is by no means receding in popularity among the younger demographic. Although older generations adopted these items unself-consciously and as a matter of course – they were, after all, comfortable, practical, sturdy, and the standard country fashion throughout Europe for the better part of the early- to mid-twentieth century – contemporary young shepherds adopt them self-consciously.[7] With the habit comes the mannerisms and gestures appropriate to the shepherd; the bar provides the context within which they are displayed (Sorge 2009).

The male-dominated public sphere is not the whole picture, and there is a striking diversity of lifestyles. This becomes apparent if we look beneath the surface: processes of broader adaptation to present-day national and global realities become apparent. This diversity is itself a byproduct of the porousness of village boundaries, which would in itself constitute a fieldwork scenario with almost limitless avenues of exploration. I therefore needed to impose limitations in terms of the topics and questions I could address, in the end producing a view of life within Orgosolo that aims above all to provide a window into complexity. Following Clifford Geertz's (1973:22) dictum that anthropologists do not study villages, but rather study *in* villages, I perceive Orgosolo to be an ethnographic site marked by a convergence of people, processes, and associated social artifacts that cast a light upon realities that far transcend the locality. Not inconsequentially, however, Orgosolo is also a classic village community whose inhabitants view themselves as distinct from other such places, and are aware to varying degrees of the historical depth of their collective experience. In this regard, Orgosolo as a fieldsite corresponds in actuality to a unit that is profoundly meaningful to actors on the ground.

The chapters presented here harness the elements of the larger narrative of life in the central Sardinian highlands, past and present. This is not possible without a survey of the double helix of the Sardinian experience: landscape and history. One of the patterns that emerge in my discussion relates to the role of geography in conditioning life on the central highlands across time. I suggest that highland Sardinia was, and in some ways continues to be, a dissident zone, and that history – from antiquity through to the early modern period – reveals a marked incapacity of outside political forces to effectively penetrate its society. The formative effects of this on highland culture are intimately related to the role of landscape, and parallels can be found elsewhere within the Mediterranean.

But the emergence of the modern nation-state with the unification of Italy in 1861 would inaugurate a period of gradual transformation. The late nineteenth-century military "pacification" of the central highlands of Sardinia appears to have required the dissemination of a peculiar discursive formation, arising out of the national imperative to render the dissident highlands legible to the modern state. Unruly mountain folk had to be reined in, by force, consequently entailing the elimination of bandits – those classic blood-vengeance fugitives of the Mediterranean mountains – by *carabinieri* (paramilitary police) and army soldiers. Criminologists trained in the pseudoscience of craniometric measurement appeared on the scene during this period, and furnished the Italian government with interpretations of social conditions that would prompt illiberal approaches to newly framed problems of rural "criminality." Local people denounced the acts of violence committed by the Italian state during this period, which continued well into the mid-twentieth century.

The present book focuses on this history; furthermore, it situates its analysis with reference to the worlds inhabited by men, and, to an important extent, shepherds. Pastoralism has long been, within local as well as outside imaginings, metonymic with highland Sardinian culture and society. I employ a style of analysis that begins with a focus on the particular then zooms out to achieve a wider angle. The intention is to understand local forms as embedded within succeeding layers of historical, political, and economic frames, to contextualize the classic images and representations of highland Sardinia and question the widespread view that this area is beholden to an antiquated style of life – that it is, somehow, frozen in time. This is what highland Sardinia is in the minds of many Italians, including many urban Sardinians. Certainly, it is not a vision that speaks to the complexity of life in the twenty-first century, but nonetheless it persists because it has a historical foundation, reflecting the very real experience of marginalization born of the violence meted out by a succession of powerful outsiders. This experience has been formative, etched on the social memory, and lends a distinctly dissident ethos to these mountain districts, a byproduct of their violent encapsulation by political formations imposed from without. Today, this same dissident ethos, embodied in the figure and symbol of the shepherd, faces numerous challenges. The reason is straightforward: The model of the shepherd provides one among many options for young men, and relies on a singular way of being, and no longer a dominant one at that. Regardless, he remains a symbol of "authenticity" to many. To non-shepherds, to non-Sardinians, and even to himself, he is a holdout against modernity, urban life, and the outside world. I am referring here to stark, forthright, emic categories that are salient at the local level. These are collective representations that stem from local re-elaborations of history, based on a vision of the persistence of the past in the present. I begin with an overview of the pertinent elements of history that are responsible for these outcomes, and from there examine the long-term political significance of a pastoral adaptation to a montane environment. Indeed, recognizing the role of landscape in conditioning local forms allows me to throw some of the more roughly textured aspects of life in the Sardinian interior into sharper relief.

A significant part of the ethnographic analysis in this book borrows James C. Scott's (2009) felicitous concept of "barbarism-by-design," used by him in reference to the development of social forms among dissident nonstate peoples of the Southeast Asian plateau that militated against the establishment of government authority. Barbarians, according to this definition, are generally peoples whose histories of resistance to powerful political formations allowed them to maintain their relative autonomy until the modern era. I argue that in Sardinian history, the use of a mountain landscape as a strategic resource for the maintenance of local autonomy, the institution of a customary legal system premised on the threat and use of violence, as well as a clearly-defined code of honour, *balentia*, are byproducts of circumstances encountered by local people throughout their history. The apparent remnants of this historical experience are seen in the day-to-day lives of shepherds, whose economic activities render them marginal figures within the community, but whose symbolic weight as heirs to a proud pastoral tradition makes them objects of ambivalence among non-shepherds. Shepherds are widely viewed as anachronistic figures. Their tendency to remain closed off from the outside world is a source of consternation, and their own sense of themselves as inhabiting a world distinct from that of the non-shepherd, present an image of subcultural involution fuelled by a form of male revanchism that resists the destabilization of the old order. At the same time, the wider community does not hold its value orientation of *balentia* to reflect the original meaning of the ideal, but rather views it as a corruption of the standards of generations of shepherds who lived in a bygone, possibly more heroic, era of pastoralism. However, for all their marginality, shepherds defiantly monopolize some of the most central public spaces in Orgosolo, giving this village its traditionalist appearance, while their public performance of masculinity, at once exuberant, gregarious, taciturn, and agonistic, determines much of the tenor of social life within the community.

My examination of Sardinian men's lives hinges upon recognition of four interrelated themes that condition local assumptions and understandings. First, there is a widespread ideology of local opposition to the state, especially on the part of the more traditionalist sector of pastoralists who are the principal focus of the book. Second, over the past 150 years, political forces have played an important role in disrupting the integrity of the locality vis-à-vis the outside world. The outside world is threatening to varying degrees: it is a source of danger to local interests, but it is also a source of yearning for younger people who envision possibilities of self-realization that transcend a local existence. Third, there has been a definite marginalization of the pastoral sector, a metamorphosis of the shepherd from a cultural standard–bearer to a tragic figure, and a decline in the prestige of pastoral life. Lastly, the transformation of the pastoral economy in the contemporary period has resulted in an underclass of disenfranchised rural men mired in a style of life that is at odds with what the majority of young people desire. This is especially true of younger women, who more enthusiastically embrace the ideals of a cosmopolitan orientation than do their male counterparts. The story is one of social transition, and contains undertones of cultural decline, loss, and the inability of young men to adapt to the ethos of late modernity. As for the concept of modernity, it is used throughout this work to refer to a set of cultural, economic, and political transformations that coincide with the emergence of a new ontology following a rupture from an earlier order characterized by technologically simple, locally subdivided agrarian communities built on stagnant economies and structured by intimate face-to-face relations. The process was a gradual one that bore witness to several interrelated developments, including the rationalization of the economy, the bureaucratization of the state, the technologization of society, the rise of individualism, and the development of a linear conception of time.

In the latter half of this book, I provide a synthesis of the contrasts that mark social life in Orgosolo today. We see that this community is, as ever, a place where recognizably Mediterranean ways of being are manifested in social interaction, bearing out the suggestion that the realities encountered here comprise an iteration of wider truths that have been reproduced throughout the region as a byproduct of underlying processes. I present the wide scope of diversity in Orgosolo by zooming out to reveal a larger picture that includes the full range of social life within the community. The disparity among social types in Orgosolo speaks to the coexistence of two systems of orientation, one localist and inward-looking and the other cosmopolitan and outward-looking, each premised upon contrasting views and definitions of what Orgosolo is and should become. For localists, day-to-day life entails a series of engagements with place-based practices – notably work routines and patterns of sociality – that firmly root people within their communities. Conversely, cosmopolitanism is marked by a projection

of desires and aspirations onto the global plane, and its central personas are locals whose styles have become "inflected – even afflicted – by
cosmopolitan scripts" (Appadurai 1996:63). Unlike localists, cosmopolitans are defined by a life-world that excludes the materiality of physical grounding in a rural locality, and appear to eschew everyday life
within the community. I note a synthesis between these two ontologies,
and present the suggestion that, despite a divergence in vision of what
the good life entails, there exists a shared commitment to Orgosolo and
its fortunes.

   I conclude this study by examining the ties that bind and shield people from the insecurities of existence and cohere and unite the community in opposition to the outside world, but that also serve as a
mechanism of social control. In Orgosolo discretion in the management
one's personal affairs is a concern of the highest order, resulting in a
stifling atmosphere. Within the public realm, the potential for gossip
and slander is present on every plane of interaction. The nuclear family remains the most immediately relevant and credible unit to most
people; beyond it lies an uncertain world where nothing is quite as it
seems. A careful examination of local sentiments yields a complex pattern that sheds light on a particular dynamic of social cohesion and
fragmentation associated with a historical experience of marginalization and scarcity. In the end, Orgosolo lives up to its reputation as a
dissident community.

2

Landscape and History

The setting is a private cantina, or a *chisina rustica* (rustic kitchen). I am conversing with a new friend, Angelo, a *servo-pastore* (servant shepherd, a hired herdsman akin to a sharecropper) in his early forties with whom I had been drinking in a local bar for several hours that night. Now that we are alone, my steady consumption of *acquavite* has emboldened me to introduce a topic about which I had been curious for some time, but had hitherto been too cautious to broach. Throwing caution to the wind, I finally asked, "Is there much theft of livestock in these parts?" Angelo furled his eyebrow, thrust out his chin with his mouth open, and said, "Ehhhhhh ... no! No, Antò! That's all in the past now." A pause as he went about his task – frying potatoes and reheating some boiled mutton for a late night snack – then a summary dismissal of the question: "No one steals anymore. When we had this problem, a long time ago, it was because people were poor. Now we buy food at the *supermercato*."

Several months later, towards the end of my fieldwork, Angelo and his *cricca* (friendship group) graciously organized a going-away lunch for me, an *ispuntinu*, at a *cuile*, a sheep-herding station in the countryside. Angelo, ebullient when tipsy, placed his arm on my shoulder. "So, Antò! I hope you found what you wanted here! Now you can go home now and tell everyone how good stolen meat tastes!" Laughter all around.

The prevalence of livestock rustling in the Sardinian interior is not a new phenomenon, and Angelo's reticence on the subject is typical. His joking tone and the knowing laughs of the company present revealed the subversive truth of his remark, lightened by the festive atmosphere. The topic did not come up again, which was just as well. I learned over the course of more than a year in Orgosolo that candid discussion of livestock rustling was off-limits, although there is wide-spread awareness that it is endemic to the pastoral economy. It was common knowledge that certain members of the community were especially successful *ladri di bestiame* (animal thieves) and were there-fore able to acquire wealth that they then reinvested elsewhere (most notably in coastal real estate or in their main houses in the village). A shepherd's success, however, should never be predicated on animal theft, and certainly the law-abiding shepherd should be considered the norm rather than the exception. Despite this, a shepherd's ability to protect his flock on the open pastures is imperative. He must be expert at managing his material resources (herding station and sheep dogs), effectively master the techniques of herd identification through the use of bells and markings, and be capable of mobilizing social resources that will help him to retrieve his herd if it disappears.[1] Notwithstand-ing the most law-abiding shepherd's best intentions, the exigencies of the pastoral life frequently lead to actions that hover on the margins of legality.

Although increased mobility and technologies of instant communica-tion and rapid travel have challenged the distinctions that have arisen out of long-term ecological adaptations, we should not suppose that such distinctions have altogether vanished. In Sardinia, mountains and lowlands have long been home to starkly different lifestyles and their respective sociocultural correlates remain evident today. The discussion to follow will outline broad historical trends in Sardinia in order to pro-vide the context necessary for an examination of how circumstances might condition the emergence of customary legal norms and systems of orientation that encapsulate the code of honour, *balentia*. In address-ing this theme, I follow James Scott (2009) in arguing for the primacy of mountains as a political category, suggesting that many features of highland culture are to be regarded as long-term adaptations, or stra-tegic positionings, which emerged over time and that were intended to keep the state at bay. I conclude with an examination of the acts of violence that accompanied the emergent Italian nation-state's "pacifica-tion" of the central highlands in the nineteenth and twentieth centuries.

Landscape

Sardinia's fragmented geomorphology is dramatic, with mountains, deeply incised valleys, rolling hills, few agriculturally important plains, and plateaus and escarpments characteristic of much of the landscape in the northern interior. Today travel throughout the island is relatively easy. However, well into the twentieth century, winding dirt trails and mule tracks, which in the highlands were frequently washed out by seasonal storms and surface runoff, provided the only means of travel (Le Lannou 1941:14ff). Many modern provincial and secondary roads were originally constructed on pre-existing tracks and remain tortuous, especially in the most mountainous and hilly terrains. The most impressive peaks on the island are found within the Gennargentu mountain range, with its tallest summit, Punta La Marmora, rising to a height of 1,834 metres above sea level, at a distance of 30 kilometres from the Tyrrhenian waters to the east. Approaching its eastern shore by sea, the island presents itself with its back resolutely turned to the Italian mainland. When not rising directly out of the sea, numerous impressive ridges line much of the eastern coast at a short distance from the beach sands. As one would expect, no natural ports are found along this eastern coast.[2] The northern and western coasts are more hospitable, but not significantly so. No important maritime traffic has ever been sustained by the landings at Santa Teresa di Gallura, or the ports of Porto Torres, Alghero, and Oristano. Finally, the island's principal seaport, Cagliari, derives its importance not from the ideal morphology of the Gulf of Cagliari, which is characterized by an arc of sand with a low shelf, but instead from its proximity to the island's most fertile and accessible land: the Campidano plain (Le Lannou 1941:24).

Patterns of settlement reflect a preference for life away from the coast. A cursory glance at detailed maps of Sardinian coastal areas reveals a concentration of settlement at safe distances from the sea. The island possesses no great seafaring tradition, and life in coastal settlements was historically precarious owing to incursions from Barbary Coast pirates. By the early nineteenth century, the practice of slave-raiding declined, but settlements along the Sardinian coast remained few and sparse. Since the end of World War II, small coastal towns and villages have expanded and become important resort centres in a thriving tourist industry. The 10-kilometre coastline of the Costa Smeralda (Emerald Coast), extending from Golfo Aranci in the south to the Gulf of Arzachena in the north, is today an exclusive luxury resort destination catering to the world's most privileged vacationers.

Just as Sardinia is bisected by the 40th parallel, so too is the island conceptually divided, by Sardinians, into two parts, corresponding roughly to this parallel – the north and the south (or, in Italian, *capo di su* and *capo di giu* [head of the top and head of the bottom, respectively]).

The reasons for this division, albeit crude, lie in the island's topography, as the northern half is generally characterized by taller hills and mountains, whereas the south has rolling hills, flat plains, and a more hospitable environment. The north-south distinction perhaps takes on greater meaning when we consider that the island's principal massif, the Gennargentu range, is located in the northern "half," while the island's largest and most fertile plain, the Campidano, is in the south. These two formations, by their sheer dimensions, constitute the principal topographic features of the island, and are also exemplary of the two contrasting (geographical as well as conceptual) categories of highlands and lowlands.

Highlands and Lowlands

Much can be ascribed to physical environment in the conditioning of social forms in Sardinia, and a close look at social structures and economic regimes reveals a notable contrast between the mountainous interior and the rolling hills and plains of the lowlands. On one side is a pastoral society, historically adapted to difficult-to-access high places; on the other, an agricultural society, incorporated into wider agrarian regimes and moulded by all the social and cultural influences that these entail. This duality within rural society in Sardinia persists, albeit in attenuated form. In much public discourse at the local level, highland villages are construed as having been, until recent times, isolated, remote, and untouched by history. Local self-images are informed by an island-within-an-island thesis of central Sardinia, ultimately built upon a stereotype that is perpetuated locally and that resonates throughout the island. Shepherds and non-shepherds, urban and rural folk alike believe the highland interior to be a repository of "archaic" ontologies. This view accords with longstanding stereotypes of central Sardinia that emanate from the hegemonic centre, and stems from a discourse premised on the notion of primitivism in turn born of the alleged isolation of highland folk from wider historical currents. This erroneous conception of mountain folk has tended to thwart any appreciation of the extent of their interrelations with regional and national contexts and unduly emphasized, as I discuss below, apparent cultural archaisms (see Loi 2001:41–60). Sardinian inland districts were never isolated from external social, economic, and political influences. This is especially true today. While the use of local dialects prevails, standard Italian is now universally spoken, the mass media are widespread and their images ubiquitous, and all amenities, lifestyle choices, and career opportunities that are open to Italians are also available to Sardinians. It may seem then that anyone who adheres to an image of highland seclusion and solitude is longing for simpler times and more "authentic" values. But there is more to this notion than mere romanticism. The stereotype of the independent montagnard living among the mountain fastness and guarding against lowland encroachment is an image produced by an understanding of regional history that is informed by discourses of primitivism and that reflects urban biases. Locally, this stereotype has been adopted and given a positive spin.

Many forces have conditioned highland Sardinian culture and society, primarily the mountainous landscape. Mountains provided friction; they were a barrier to communication and sheltered their inhabitants from outside forces. Although mountains cannot directly isolate populations from one another, they do hinder internal communication and mobility. This was exacerbated by the longstanding paucity of effective external governance. One might ask, therefore, what are the long-term sociocultural correlates of a lack of effective government and how is order maintained in the absence of established state structures? I argue that from antiquity until contemporary times, the highlands constituted a "political landscape" (Olwig 2002:18ff.) – a polity endowed with legal institutions and mechanisms connected to a system of social and economic organization conditioned by the givens of the natural environment – which effectively demarcated it from the surrounding region. As non-legible spaces, such landscapes impede efforts to consolidate political authority, and as such are sought to be diverted to purposes that suit the interests of the state rather than its recalcitrant inhabitants. But in central Sardinia no state could effectively realize the transformation of this political landscape by the imposition of a new relationship between law, land, and justice until much later in history. As Le Lannou (1941:22ff.) notes, no significant external authority has made its presence felt within the Sardinian highlands since the fall of Rome. Before Italian unification, external laws were not systematically enforceable. This should not be attributed solely to the dissident stance of local people, but to the nature of the landscape, which constituted a "region of refuge" (Beltrán 1979). To put it bluntly, mountains yield little of value to predatory states. The Roman period saw the comprehensive transformation of the Sardinian plains into latifundia, producing grains for export to cities on the Italian mainland; on the highlands, however, Rome's legacy did not extend beyond the creation of a military perimeter.[3]

Throughout the Mediterranean, blood feud as a mechanism of legal self-help was most persistent throughout the more mountainous regions (Braudel 1972:38ff.). In his candid style, Gellner (1988:163) writes of "feud-addicted mountain tribesmen who managed to survive late in European history," noting that vendetta is peculiar to societies not definitively subjugated before the modern era and only recently subjected to enforceable laws. Again, landscape features prominently in this reckoning, as poor infrastructure and difficult communications hindered movement of state resources into inaccessible areas. As James Scott notes (2009:54), the premodern state ran out of political breath as it encountered rugged terrain and dispersed populations. Mountains are therefore seen in this context as a refuge for state-evading peoples who could there regulate their affairs according to indigenous mechanisms. Here, the "friction of terrain" (Scott 2009) is a geographical resource to be harnessed during evasion of the state, even if the resulting autonomy came at a price, with regions of refuge necessarily located within ecological margins. In such "societies against the state" (Clastres 1974), conventions of blood feud, premised on ideals of collective responsibility and balanced opposition, serve as the mechanism by which internal order is maintained, and are emblematic of a conscious rejection of political centralization and its consequences.[4]

A review of Sardinian history will further clarify the axes upon which the highland-lowland dichotomy presents itself, and sets the stage for the introduction of themes to be elaborated throughout this book.

History

The Nuragic Bronze Age (1800–238 BCE) witnessed the flourishing of an indigenous Sardinian civilization (Floris 2002:48). By the Roman period, Sardinia had already been colonized by Phoenician settlers and would later fall under Carthaginian (Punic) control. However, it was after the Roman conquest that external control of Sardinia intensified significantly, and with it increased dispersal of its indigenous population away from the coastal areas and fertile agricultural lowlands. This demographic shift was already well underway – Carthage controlled much of the southern lowlands, and instituted a system of intensive agriculture through the employment of slave labour on latifundia. In the previous Phoenician period (ninth century to early fifth century BCE), indigenous populations inhabited the island at a short distance from the coast, and enjoyed a degree of peaceful coexistence for approximately two centuries (van Dommelen 2001:130). This would come to an end with Phoenician military expansion in the seventh century BCE, led by the now allied city-states of Karalis, Sulci, and Tharros. Expeditions to displace the Nuragic population to the southern limits of the central highlands were meant to secure access to fertile lowlands. The ensuing Nuragic revolts compelled the confederated city-states to appeal to Carthage for military assistance in the sixth century BCE (Casula 1994:31–32), which led to the eventual clearance of indigenous inhabitants from the agricultural lowlands.

Evidence of a Nuragic past in the lowlands has since been found mainly in the form of *nuraghi* – megalithic Bronze Age conical towers constructed of irregular blocks of local stone, usually basalt or granite, and often several storeys tall with an external diameter of 10 metres or more. The dimensions of these structures suggest a defensive role, and a cluster of two or more intercommunicating towers points to broader local networks of military defence (cf. Blake 1998:61). An estimated seven or eight thousand such towers, in varying states of disrepair but some remarkably intact, are a conspicuous part of the Sardinian landscape.

The Carthaginians did not succeed in completely pacifying the northern portion of the island, and the central highlands were not subject to any effective external rule. In his *Description of Greece*, Pausanias (X.17.9) attributes the failure of Carthage to subdue the Sardinian highlands to the "strength of the mountains," which cushioned its inhabitants from external threat. With the exception of the port city of Olbia on the northeastern coast, which consisted of a small Punic enclave, foreign culture did not spill into the north (van Dommelen 2001:139), while the tribal populations of the central highlands maintained de facto autonomy the longest and steadfastly resisted the eventual Roman expeditionary campaigns (Meloni 1990:71–83).

The Roman history of the island is marked by the creation of the Provincia Sardiniae et Corsicae in 227 BCE. Most of the great transformations subsumed under the name of Romanization occurred during the Imperial period, with the reorganization of major cities, the creation of an island-wide infrastructure, and expansion of latifundia into the agricultural lowlands (Meloni 1990:97–138). The Roman arrival did not augur well for the restive mountain districts. In an attempt to pacify the highlands, the consul Tiberius Sempronius Gracchus led a protracted campaign beginning in 181 BCE and lasting until 174 BCE, with disastrous consequences for the vanquished. As reported by Livy in his

History of Rome (XLI.28.8), Gracchus would dedicate to the Roman god Jupiter a plaque, held in the Roman temple of the Mater Matuta, upon which was engraved the following inscription:

> Under the command and auspices of Tiberius Sempronius Gracchus the legion and army of the Roman people conquered Sardinia. In this province more than eighty thousand of the enemy were slain or captured. The state having been most successfully administered and the allies set free, the revenues restored, he brought back home the army safe and secure and enriched with booty; for the second time he entered the city of Rome in triumph. In commemoration of this event he set up this tablet to Jupiter.[5]

Evidently, in addition to required state building, Roman expansion brought with it institutionalized mass slavery and the deployment of the category of barbarism for peoples who escaped imperial reach (Fiskesjö 2012:168). These marginal refuge populations exemplifed the most common form of resistance in the ancient world, which was, as David Graeber (2011:183) explains with reference to the Middle East, "always less a politics of rebellion than a politics of exodus, of melting away with one's flocks and families – often before both were taken away." In Sardinia, such dissident highlanders engaged in skirmishes with Roman legions until the fall of Rome, and incursions on the agricultural lowlands would persist until modern times. Diodorus of Sicily (*Library of History*, V.15.4), writing at the beginning of the first century CE, informs us that in the face of Punic aggression, the lowland Nuragic Sards "fled for safety to the mountainous part of the island and built underground dwellings, and here they raised many flocks and herds which supplied them with food in abundance." The use of dugouts, in addition to the rugged nature of the landscape, allowed these highlanders to retain their freedom. As Strabo (*Geography*, V.2.7) also noted in the early years of the first century CE, Sardinia remained relatively unpacified, and valuable resources had to be expended to guard against highland incursions. Although the lowlands were suitable for agriculture, any advantage to settling on territories neighbouring the highlands was counterbalanced by considerable danger. Namely, in addition to being malarial in the summer months, the lowlands were continually laid waste by marauding montagnards. Strabo (V.2.7) provides a description:

> There is however an evil, which must be set against the fertility of these places; for during the summer the island is unhealthy, more particularly

so in the most fertile districts; in addition to this, it is often ravaged by the mountaineers, whom they call Diagesbes, who formerly were named Iolaënses ... There are four nations of mountaineers, the Parati, Sossinati, Balari, and the Aconites. These people dwell in caverns. Although they have some arable land, they neglect its cultivation, preferring rather to plunder what they find cultivated by others, whether on the island or on the continent, where they make descents, especially upon the Pisatæ. The prefects sent sometimes resist them, but at other times leave them alone, since it would cost too dear to maintain an army always on foot in an unhealthy place. They have, however, recourse to the arts of stratagem, and taking advantage of the custom of the barbarians, who always hold a great festival for several days after returning from a plundering expedition, they then fall upon them, and capture many.

The Tavola di Esterzili, an inscribed bronze tablet discovered in the village of Esterzili in the Ogliastra region of the southern highlands, testifies to the establishment of this *limes* (ancient Roman fortifications of a frontier). The inscription warns the highland Gallilensi of dire consequences should they encroach upon the lands of the Patulcensi Campani, lowland peasants under direct Roman control.

Faced with such a predicament, Rome could only contain the highland populations with the establishment of a guarded perimeter, outside of which agricultural production could be sustained. The term *barbaria* would be applied to this highland region, the exact boundaries of which were fluid. Further, although the collective populations of the highlands, the so-called Civitates Barbariae, "are recorded as paying homage on an inscription of either Augustan or Tiberian date, a military garrison of auxiliary units was needed to keep a watchful eye on the interior for much of the first century" (Wilson 1996:443). To confer the term *Civitates Barbariae* onto these populations was to effectively invent barbarians, to recognize the highlanders as the antithesis of state-endowed, governable subjects. The luminous centre was defined against its barbarian frontier (Scott 2009:116ff).

While settlement in the highlands helped ensure a degree of security against periodic incursions into the coastal areas, and in turn saw the development of an economy based largely on transhumant animal husbandry suited to a mountainous landscape, Fernand Braudel (1972:150–1) notes that by the sixteenth century Sardinian production was closely tied to the regional Mediterranean economy. However, such incorporation was by no means as recent as that. The Romans had exploited the Sardinian plains, a reliable and secure source of grain, by the period of the late Republic, and had extracted lead, copper, and iron from the southwestern Iglesiente district (Wilson 1996:442, 447). Yet Roman cultural influence in the central highlands remained marginal. While little is known about the features of highland social organization during the Roman period, religious practices remained local in origin and village settlements maintained their original patterns (Wilson 1996:447–8; cf. Sotgiu 1980). The short-lived Vandal presence in Sardinia, following the end of Roman rule, was usurped by Byzantine Greeks in 534 CE. The Byzantine period is one of relative calm in Sardinia, disturbed only by intermittent attacks by North African corsairs that would last until the eighteenth century. The period of later Byzantine rule, during which the island was left to all but its own devices,[6] saw the emergence of the Giudicati di Arborea. The island was divided into four indigenously administrated regions – Arborea, Cagliari, Torres, and Gallura – each ruled over by a set of *prinzipales,* justices who were selected by, and often linked to, influential families within the regions (Schweizer 1988:9). Marc Bloch (1961:247) refers to these *prinzipales* as rural chiefdoms. They ruled through laws enshrined in the Carta de Logu, a constitution that delineated commoners' legal rights and obligations, outlined administrative processes on the island, and defined the role of local potentates in the administration of justice. Law enforcement was draconian, and included bimonthly rounds of inspections to tally heads of livestock as a preventive measure against theft, with corporal punishments meted out to individuals convicted of misdemeanors. Less serious offenses occasioned the levying of stiff fines.[7] Internal repression, however, is not always discordant with economc success; this period saw strong commercial links with Barcelona, Marseilles, Pisa, and Genoa, although trade would dwindle once Sardinia came under Aragonese rule in 1324.

The unification of the kingdoms of Aragon and Castile in 1469 resulted in a united Spain whose rule was primarily interested in the exploitation of the countryside. The mines were eventually closed as mineral needs were met by South American sources, and the agricultural plains were divided into large feudal estates, with absentee landlords living in the coastal cities or the Spanish mainland. The legal and political structures of the Giudicati era were weakened by the imposition of feudal governance (Day 1968:144). The most successful absentee landlords enjoyed affinal and blood ties to the regional *prinzipales,* the potentates of the Giudicati, and oversaw a latifundist agricultural regime managed by a pliable peasantry. Rapacious overseers policed peasant villages and imposed exacting rents that deprived their charges of sustenance, precipitating famine and population decline (Boscolo 1967). As a result, the fourteenth to eighteenth centuries witnessed the abandonment of innumerable villages as peasants aggregated in larger centres (Day 1968). The legacy of this subjection lasted into the modern era. Giovanni Lei-Spano (2000 [1922]:101) notes the persistence of latifundism in the early years of the twentieth century in the western part of the island, where tenancy contracts left peasants in a state of perpetual debt, presenting a state of affairs analogous to Anton Blok's (1974) description of "rent capitalism" in western Sicily. It is noteworthy that the period preceding Spanish rule did not witness the rise of feudatories; rather, tenure was based on a communal model in which villagers possessed usufruct rights on lands adjacent to the settlement and beyond (Cagnetta 1975:128; Masia 1992:71).

The Kingdom of Sardinia and Piedmont was inaugurated in 1720 on the basis of the 1718 Treaty of London. The island-wide abolition of feudal structures and the eventual emergence of new forms of land tenure would come much later. The 1820 *Editto delle Chiudende* (General Enclosures Act) gave private citizens the right to claim and enclose common land. This law, which was intended to stimulate agriculture and make land taxable, sought to put an end to customary practices of land use. The greatest benefits were accrued by large and wealthy families who were capable of organizing the labour necessary to enclose land with dry stone walls, often built with granite blocks extracted from Nuragic structures (Pungetti 1995:51–2). Furthermore, those successful in enclosing land did not necessarily cultivate it, but rather extracted a fee from herders who had never paid to graze their livestock on these previously communal lands. The emergence of this parasitic rural bourgeoisie occasioned wide discontent. Following numerous revolts, the Savoy administration, as part of its 1835 legislation abolishing feudal holdings, forbade the further construction of fences on pastures and permitted the demolition of those that cut across transhumant routes (Pungetti 1995:53; Le Lannou 1941:160–6). From this period we have a fair number of accounts describing differences in land use and household structures between shepherds and farmers, as well as the relations between the two.

As in the highlands, the structure of social and economic life in lowland Sardinia during the mid-nineteenth century was provided by the *bidda,* or nucleated agro-town (Oppo 1990; Angioni 1989:181–3).

For their livelihood, settlements depended on expansive agricultural lands for the production of specialized crops (Oppo 1990:484). Through a system of crop rotation and fallowing known as *vidazzone*, the *komunella* (village councils of elders) oversaw the hiring of local guards to protect farmland from grazing flocks, thus ensuring that no conflicts would occur between shepherds and farmers (Mientjes 1998:137). In more exclusively agricultural towns, the *scolca*, a locally organized detail of field guards, was overseen by the *maiore de iscolca* (major of the scolca) to protect sown land from predation. These *maiores*, who were linked to the state and who would come to enjoy ownership of common lands once they handily enclosed and appropriated them, were frequent targets of bandit predation (Rosetti 1982:158–9).

Le Lannou (1941:124–7) affirms the role of ecology in compelling lowland farmers and highland shepherds to coexist in a state of perpetual unease, if not outright conflict.[8] Sardinian anthropologist Franco Lai (1998:77–8) writes of border wars throughout the eighteenth century between farmers and highland shepherds. Initiated by the latter for the purpose of claiming territorial rights and access to resources, these frequently escalated into bloody battles.

Orgosolo's reputation had already been set by the end of the Savoy period. In an account provided by the geographers Vittorio Angius and Goffredo Casalis in their encyclopaedic 1833 survey of the island of Sardinia, we are told that

> Orgolesi are a people known for their spirit of vendetta, for raids, and for the animosity that their bandits unleash against the forces of order ... Full of spirit, they do not fear danger and do not withdraw at the sound of fire if they are carried away by rage, or if they need to venge an injustice, or must respond to the cries of help of other outlaws imploring them for assistance against the attacks of troops ... Among the many hirelings acting as guides and spies to facilitate arrests, I do not believe we could find a single Orgolese. To study them well is to notice in them a great moral depth, and when they shall become better cultivated they will be one of the most generous peoples. (Angius and Casalis 1992[1833]:658)

In this description, Orgosolo, a single nucleated settlement, seems the perfect archetype for the entire highland region of Sardinia. Less than thirty years later, on the eve of Italian unification another state-sponsored geographer, Alberto Della Marmora, provided us with an analogous description of Orgosolo in his French-language *Itinéraire de l'Ile de Sardaigne* (1860). Della Marmora's description seems comparatively unkind:

> On Monte Novo we find the chapel of San Giovanni, and not far from the foot of this hill we find a locality called Fontanabona surrounded by the huts of shepherds, all bandits from the village of Orgosolo. To arrive there, some precautions must be taken, and above all one must have guides who know those people. That is what I did, but notwithstanding such I was received with more than twelve rifles pointed toward my person, with the injunction to take no further steps toward those men, who had an attitude of scarce hospitality and even less benevolence. Finally, after considerable negotiations and an infinity of questions pertaining to the real objectives of my visit – which consisted of a desire to mount the summit of Monte Novo with my geodetic instruments – I was received in a somewhat more courteous manner, which means that the barrels of the rifles pointed directly upon me were lowered. This courtesy however was not without a certain suspicion as to the actual reasons for my presence. It must be said that the bandits of Orgosolo are in general of the worst kind. They are perpetually in a state of alert against the forces of order who would like to surprise them in their almost inaccessible refuges, where they hide after raids, which almost always consist of the rustling of livestock. Sometimes they subtract from the landowners of nearby settlements, of which they are the terror, entire flocks of sheep and sometimes draught animals. (Della Marmora 1997 [1860]:53–4)

The discernible change in tone from 1833 to 1860 might not be incidental. The more pejorative stance of the emergent Italian nation-state towards the Sardinian highlands reflects a determination to rein in elements of culture and society perceived as archaic, corrupted, or barbaric. However, the desire to rationalize or render legible (i.e., knowable and therefore governable) the highlands of Sardinia and its institutions in order to incorporate them into the political structures of national modernity predates these writings. We find the first concrete example of such intent in the 1820 General Enclosures Act, and again in the post-unification period, when the 1865 Legge sugli Ademprivi (Law on the Commons) saw the abolition of all Church-held lands and common-pool resources. This entailed a wholesale usurpation of large tracts of communal land – the *ademprivi*, on which commoners previously had usufruct rights – by the same emergent rural bourgeoisie (Pira 1978:147). The 1868 Rivolta di Su Connottu saw a near civil insurrection in the provincial capital of Nuoro, as disenfranchised shepherds from the region descended upon the town to protest for several days and nights, laid siege to the regional legislative offices, and destroyed records of the transfer of *ademprivi* to private ownership. Their battle cry, *torramos a su connottu!* (let us return to custom!), expressed a desire to revert to the previous resource regime, to resurrect the customary, known system of common-land use (Pinna 1992:33). From these protests, lands that had become privatized but left fallow by their owners were reverted back to common use and the stone walls that cut through pastoral migration routes were dismantled. However, some damage had been done. Woodland was purchased and felled by speculators who in turn sold timber to railway and mining companies; the loss of forest cover exacerbated soil erosion and led to an accumulation of malarial waters in valley bottoms.

The ideology behind the General Enclosures Act speaks to a modernizing state's ultimate goal of controlling the national territory and its inhabitants. Whereas in antiquity, interest lay in the containment of nonstate peoples, attitudes within the modern period were explicitly informed by pseudoscientific theories that justified more heavy-handed measures of repression. A national strategy of violent "pacification," discordant with the avowed liberal-democratic ideals of the emergent national elite, sought to eliminate any elements of rural tradition thought to be a liability to national interests. Although an overview of the modern history of highland Sardinia aims to provide a picture of the patterns of sociohistorical development of this area, we must note that old stereotypes and images persist. Statist perceptions can be directly traced to the beginning of the nineteenth century, and would later also come to be expressed through environmentalists' claims as to the inability of local people to capably manage forest ecosystems (see Heatherington 2010:131ff.).

In a Modern State

We have made Italy, now we must make Italians. (attributed to Massimo D'Azeglio, 1861)

Here modern Italy has a lofty mission to accomplish, and a great colony to civilize. (Niceforo 1898:6)

Under Savoy control, the Sardinian interior remained intractable. Highland communities maintained a degree of autonomy, but were situated on the social, political, and economic margins of an overarcharching order of great wealth and prestige, and had no direct access to sources of power and authority. As such, they may have appeared as self-contained communities with long-standing local peculiarities. Nuances of dialect between villages were – and still are – noteworthy, with inhabitants of neighbouring settlements distinguishable by their speech.[9] Throughout Italy, personal identity was strongly tied to traceable bloodlines. Outsiders were (and in many places still are) viewed with apprehension. The various cultural influences on the numerous regions of the Italian peninsula, along with their longstanding encystment from one another, worked against the emergence of a shared consciousness that could transcend region and locality. Divergent economic and land tenure regimes also complicated things. How might model citizens be made of such a collection of peoples?

The criminologists had an answer. The last decades of the nineteenth century saw the flourishing of the school of positivist criminology and its erstwhile practitioners' increasing influence on national policy. The work of Cesare Lombroso and Alfredo Niceforo, among others, solidified the image of a national dualism that pitted the "Nordic" northern half of Italy against the (negatively connoted) "Semitic" and "African" southern half and island regions. Largely of northern, often Piedmontese, origin, the emergent post-unification elite were earnestly concerned with the problem of how to unify the diverse regions of Italy into a coherent national whole, including the more "corrupted" specimens of Italic stock. Some Italians, offspring of miscegenation (which in this context included procreation between Italian and non-Italian "races") were viewed as racially inferior, requiring stricter control, containment, and guided stewardship. The most severe cases were found in regions with populations allegedly descended from non-Italian populations altogether, such as Phoenicians and Arabs. Highland Sardinia comprised one such population. The northern elite, as well as some intellectually co-opted southerners (such as Niceforo, a Sicilian), devised the methods and procedures for the control and containment of their racially corrupted countrymen. As noted by Mary Gibson (1998:101), an inherent contradiction or tension is to be noted between "the biological determinism of racial analysis and a naive but often sincere desire for social reform and progress."

Criminological investigations were concerned with the physical and mental characteristics of individual malefactors. Punishments were to suit the character and personality of the malfeasants, who were sorted into prefigured sets of categories according to their degree of *pericolosità* (dangerousness) (Gibson 1998:102ff). A nebulously defined concept of "race" determined not only how punishments were to be meted out, but also how regional cultural differences were understood and explained. Catalogued lists of "atavistic stigmata" – pronounced phenotypic traits determined by genetic inheritance and apparently found with greater frequency within given regional populations – signalled evolutionary failure, and provided some of the bases for corrective procedures. Skin colour, cranial size and shape, facial structure, stature, thickness and colour of hair, and dentition were among the physical characteristics that determined whether one was a *delinquente nato* (born criminal), or *delinquente occasionale* (occasional criminal) (Lombroso 1876:3–15). Atavistic stigmata, furthermore, found their greatest distribution among the non-Nordic peoples. Within Sardinia, Sicily, and Calabria, higher-than-average homicide rates were seen to be "fundamentally due to African and Oriental elements" (Lombroso 1876:140).

In *La Delinquenza in Sardegna*, Alfredo Niceforo (1977 [1897]:29ff.) modified Lombroso's formulations, claiming that atavisms that made up "born criminals" occasionally combined so infelicitously as to render entire subregions *zone delinquenti* (criminal zones). The Barbagia district was named the principal criminal zone in Sardinia, and here, Niceforo, to his infamy, individuated Orgosolo as apex and epicentre. "Among the delinquents native to Orgozolo [*sic*] ... we have discovered the imprint of atavistic stigmata to quite a surprising degree, more than among any other Sardinian delinquents. Orgozolo [*sic*] is the village that imparts vitality to the fine fleure of the delinquents of this area; it is the criminal node of a criminal zone" (Niceforo 1977 [1897]:21).

For its countless misdiagnoses and ill-conceived explanations of observed and recorded phenomena, Niceforo's *Delinquenza* remains of interest for some descriptions that appear indicative of a Hobbesian view of life:

> As within primitive clan organization, where thefts were considered glorious and honourable, so today those shepherds still possess – because of an arrested mental development – the sentiments of those early times, and even have the proverb: Chie no furat no est homine (he who does not steal is not a man). Until recently, a shepherd of those areas would not have given his daughter to a man who was not valorous and courageous and an old hand at life in the forest and in raids. Some Sardinians have told us that to have among their relations a famous brigand was 'for us like having a relative who is a government minister, or an ambassador.' (Niceforo 1977 [1897]:44–5)

Setting aside the singularly opprobrious tone of the passage, the value orientations described are those most often associated with honour systems of agrarian societies. These are predicated on the ability to establish and maintain social precedence, usually through cunning yet circumspect action, and sometimes physical force. The collected maxims and aphorisms of highland Sardinia by the noted novelist and folklorist (and Nobel laureate) Grazia Deledda (1995:84ff.) reveal no paucity of such proverbs.[10]

With regard to violence, Pitt-Rivers (1977:4) observes that "[t]he reputation of a dangerous man is liable to assure him precedence over a virtuous man; he may not be thought privately to be honourable, but while no one is prepared to question the matter, he is treated as though he were and granted the precedence which he claims. On the field of honour, might is right." Values of honour are central to an orientation that is markedly at odds with the normative standards of bourgeois urban society, in which violent action is generally disruptive to social life (Blok 2001:103ff). In sum, Niceforo's account captures what can only be called the social tragedy of a forced transition from a locally subdivided world caught within an agrarian predicament to a culturally standardized and economically diversified social formation. It is, in other words, a work that could only have arisen with the emergence of a system in which authority was legitimated by a set of abstract ideals enshrined within the institutional complex of the hegemonic state. Within this emergent system, furthermore, Niceforo and other criminologists were not the only, or even the first, advocates of the thesis that highland Sardinia was plagued by a dangerous class of born criminals, of a defective category of persons who should be brought to heel. Nineteenth-century urban elite in Sardinia saw the pastoral communities of the central interior as culturally and economically backward, regardless of the fact that the pastoral economy was, by that time, already well integrated into larger regional and world markets (Loi 2001:146). As Vargas-Cetina notes (2000:231), little has changed over the last century; island authorities today continue to view pastoralism as a problem and pastoral communities as culturally stagnant, despite the fact that the central highlands were "once the locus of Sardinia's participation in the world market."

What then were the existing political and economic conditions in Sardinia during the era of national integration? The first statistics on crime in Sardinia had already been compiled by the mid-nineteenth century, and consistently revealed higher rates of theft, arson, and homicide in the highlands compared with the rest of the island (Lei-Spano 2000 [1922]:171). Consideration of how disruptions to rural life contributed to a rise in unrest can help explain why. At the end of the nineteenth century, the Sardinian rural economy was in a phase of considerable growth. The high demand for pecorino (sheep's milk cheese) among Italian emigrants to the Americas prompted a doubling in the number of sheep on the island, from 845,000 in 1876, to 1,877,000 by 1907 (Clark 1989:270). As the region opened up to larger markets for milk and cheese, the growth of the pastoral economy led to the development of a monoculture in the highlands that came at the expense of small-scale gardening. The increase in head of sheep in Sardinia, almost all of it in Barbagia, was accompanied by an expansion in livestock rustling, the brunt of which was borne by villages in the surrounding districts (Moss 1979). This relationship, based on negative reciprocity, solidified long-standing distinctions between the mountainous interior and the surrounding districts, with the balance of exchange favouring the former. Within the context of a modernizing nation-state, this development evidently confirmed ideological categories that classified highlanders as a subversive population of bandits and malefactors.

Despite considerable exports to North America, the French market remained important; however, the 1887 tariff war with France saw the adoption of protectionist measures by the Italian government, prompting French economic retaliation. Before 1887, an average of five vessels a week sailed from Porto Torres to Marseilles alone, loaded with wine, olive oil, and livestock. After the implementation of trade restrictions, the decline in export volume was drastic and severely affected the northern, more pastoral part of the island.[11] Mining too was in a slump; the manufacturing centres in the distant south were incapable of absorbing the newly unemployed, leading to inevitable social repercussions. Rates of homicide and attempted homicide increased by approximately 40 per cent in the closing decade of the nineteenth century, as did rates of kidnapping, although less markedly (Clark 1989:272; cf. Floris 2002:547ff.). The dismal reality of economic climate in the central highlands was clearly illustrated in November 1894 when the coastal town of Tortoli-Arbatax was attacked and looted by an organized group of outlaws. This large-scale *bardana* (raiding expedition) – among the very last raiding expeditions in Sardinia – would strengthen the Italian government's resolve to extinguish banditry, rife during this period, with a fervour not observed since Roman antiquity.

The ecclesiastic authorities also viewed banditry as a scourge to be eliminated by force. In a circular to local parishes dated 22 July 1899, an entry titled "The Spirit of Obedience and Zeal in Duty," by Salvatore Demartis, Archbiship of Nuoro, notes the following:

> Sardinian banditry, increasing day-by-day in frequency and in audacity, without many theories of communism or socialism, rejects any form of government, [and] desires to rebel against whatever authority and establish in the forests an empire of terror and a system of true anarchy. Assassinations, thefts, vendettas, open revolt against public authority, decrees – [these are the] laws of the new kings of the forest ... they instill fear into the souls of the good, that almost all of them remain passive and muted, suffering grave harm and dishonour. A state of affairs that is truly unacceptable. (1899:140)

This entry was recorded on the heels of the Conflitto di Morgogliai (a firefight between bandits and forces of order in the district), during which the Nuoro detachment of the *carabinieri* and two Italian infantry units, totalling 210 men, hunted down five outlaws operating on the Orgosolo commons (*La Nuova Sardegna*, 12 July 1899:2; Brigaglia 1971:123). The event was recorded for posterity in a series of photographs, the most infamous depicting members of the *carabinieri* posing, in the style of a big game hunt, with the corpse of Elias Serra-Sanna. The aforemenioned ecclesiastic circular did not record any of these details, nor does it contain reference to the ongoing exercise of which this episode was part. Public security and military forces had, in the two months preceding the Morgogliai incidents, succeeded in killing sixty-four outlaws in similar fashion (*La Nuova Sardegna*, 11 July 1899:1). La Notte di San Bartolomeo (the Night of Saint Bartholomew), the most comprehensive dragnet operation in Sardinian history, took place on the night of 14 May 1899, and led to the arrest and detention of more than three hundred men throughout Nuoro province on suspicion of criminal association with the fugitives (*La Nuova Sardegna*, 17 May 1899:2; cf. Bechi 1914).

Church attitudes towards the social ills of highland Sardinia would retain a similar tone in much more recent times as well. In a 26 November 1954 entry in Orgosolo's *Liber Chronicon* (parish records), we find the following:

> In locality "Sas Molas," between Orgosolo and Locoe, the famous bandit, Pasquale Tandeddu, has ended his days. The forces of Order have made themselves proud for having succeeded to eliminate he who for many years has been the number one danger and the terror of the neighbourhoods of

Orgosolo and all of [the province of] Nuoro. The glad populace quickly realized that Tandeddu was done down by his own old companions who have killed him by betrayal. It seems that the village has been liberated of a weight that afflicted it tremendously. But ... in Orgosolo, has peace finally arrived, or will it all start up again?

Tandeddu's death is recorded on the same day as this entry, and several Orgolesi recall the bells of the local Church of Santa Croce ringing in celebration upon receipt of the news.

Throughout the central Sardinian highlands, until a generation or two ago, bandits were generally viewed benevolently by the locals, and often admired for their prowess and intractability (see Schweizer 1988:106). However, Orgolesi and other Sardinians of my acquaintance never viewed banditry as necessarily heroic, and the concept of a laudable "social banditry" is absent on the island. Today, it is well accepted that bandits were people to be acclaimed, feared, or possibly pitied, compelled as they were by circumstance to forego a peaceful existence.[12] It is widely recognized that a man generally became a bandit as a result of ill fortune. The greatest objection expressed by the locals, which today forms an important element of their appreciation of surrounding historical events, is not against the capture and prosecution of bandits who arose from within their own ranks, but rather to the procedures used to combat banditry. These procedures were rooted in an official ideology that reduced all highlanders to the status of criminals; guilt was assumed over innocence, and a heavy-handed justice system decided upon the fate of men on the basis of suspicion. The public security operations carried out during the final years of the nineteenth and first years of the twentieth centuries are euphemistically referred to by local people as the period of *caccia grossa*, a big game hunt (see Bechi 1997 [1914]). A mural found off the main road running through Orgosolo, the Corso Repubblica, depicts the notorious image of the six *carabinieri* posing with the body of Elias Serra-Sanna. Its caption reads "Caccia grossa a Orgosolo." Such a reminder speaks to local beliefs that state authorities have always considered rural Sardinia a place to be administered by force. This sentiment persisted in the two and a half decades following the Second World War, in which the Italian government, with an elevated sense of urgency, took to patrolling the Barbagian countryside and arresting suspected malefactors using heavy-handed measures. The extensive abuses of this period are well-documented, and interviews carried out by Franco Cagnetta describe the humiliating interrogations – and beatings – of men, young and old, suspected of misdemeanours or of collaboration with wanted outlaws (Cagnetta 1975:253–87). Cagnetta's historical survey, *Banditi a Orgosolo*, later inspired filmmaker Vittorio De Seta (1961) to direct an award-winning drama of the same name that presented a fictionalized account of outlawry in Sardinia. Perhaps more than any local event or episode, this film succeeded in diffusing an inescapable association between Orgosolo and banditry.

A comparatively progressive attempt to understand banditry and rural crime in Sardinia was permitted by the Commissione Parlamentare d'inchiesta sui fenomeni di criminalità in Sardegna in 1969. The resultant 1972 report sought to provide remedies to the economic conditions faced by rural highlanders and, more importantly, uncover the root sociological and economic causes of banditry and rural crime. In the four years before the establishment of this parliamentary commission (1966–9), 120 homicides and 34 kidnappings were registered in the province of Nuoro, and 130 suspects were actively sought for connections to these and various other crimes (Fadda 2002). Evidently, the problems blighting highland Sardinia had never been resolved, and new remedies were required. The results of this report seem striking for their condemnation of the pastoral economy, key to life in the central highlands yet continually held responsible for cultivating a closed world mired in lawlessness. The authors isolate two variables – pastoral production and the physical barriers between pastures and human settlement – which, when combined, provide the conditions necessary for the kinds of criminal activity characteristic of the highlands. The report notes that crime in Sardinia should be traced to "historical, geographic, and cultural factors which limit social exchanges and external solicitations, and have contributed to the persistent socio-economic and cultural underdevelopment of the island" (*Commissione parlamentare d'inchiesta* 1972:121). The rates of violent and other crimes decrease with lower elevation and greater population density, leading to the inference that indices of criminality decrease in frequency as you move away from the highlands toward the foothill and lowland communities north and south of Nuoro. Pastoralism, in sum, is never absolved from its longstanding association with criminality. The inaccessibility of high pastures, lack of permanent employment and steady wages, and a general exclusion from larger social, political, and economic processes are cited as endemic problems. Outside intervention this time takes on a decidedly more modern edge. Efforts to introduce industrial enterprise into these so-called economically stagnant communities include the establishment of an Enichem oil refinery at Porto Torres in the north of the island, a plastics factory near the village of Ottana in the province of Nuoro, and a paper mill in the eastern coastal town of Arbatax. There is also the proposed national park. A renewed push for the establishment of the Parco Nazionale del Golfo di Orosei e del Gennargentu in the central highlands allegedly aims to protect the environment while providing local people with an alternative source of income. Such a park, however, would also severely restrict shepherds from herding their livestock on customary pasture lands. Such (yet-to-be fulfilled) efforts to disenfranchise highland shepherds have always been predicated on the basis of expert knowledges that assumed an inability of local people to manage their common-pool resources responsibly. As Tracey Heatherington (2010:130–2) has shown, the cultural essentialisms that inform environmentalist discourses constitute a form of ecological alterity that envisions a triumph of rational resource management regimes over customary land-use practices that allegedly harm the environment. At stake is the vision of an idealized pastoral landscape—a site of space and leisure meant for tourist consumption—which is decisively rejected by shepherds, who will not accept the appropriation of their cultural and economic inheritance. Similarly, the proposed establishment of a military base within the Pratobello district on the Orgosolo commons was justified on the grounds of purported benefits to the local economy. In central Sardinia, as in many other European regions, we see a ubiquitous process in which peripheral areas are redefined according to essentialist definitions imposed by the centre. Corsica in France (Ravis-Giordani 2001 [1983]), Crete in Greece (Herzfeld 1988), and Sardinia (or more generally *il meridione* [the south] in Italy) have all been regarded by their respective national political elites as flawed, backward, and deficient societies.[13]

The 1972 report provides no sustained consideration of the historical and geographical challenges characteristic of pastoral production. Likewise, no attention was devoted to emic principles of social control, and how conflict might be regulated according to customary norms. The Sardinian case, therefore, requires somewhat more than an appreciation of proximate factors, but also an understanding of historical processes, which was evidently not deemed relevant by the commission. I suggest that a more ample view of the complexity of customary law is to consider its manifestations in reference to a sliding scale. On one extreme, where there is no overarching state presence, we should expect local communities to freely engage in legal self-help when necessary, such that disputes and conflicts and their related details become public knowledge. However, where communities are subject to an overarching political structure whose legal system has not supplanted local systems of customary law, the violence exercised by non-state actors is concealed, and processes of dispute settlement must operate covertly, with their proceedings hidden from public scrutiny. The stance of the wider community will tend towards circumspect non-involvement and *omertà* (deliberate silence) or, to use George Ravis-Giordani's handy phrasing, such a rupture in social relations *ne laisse aucun place à la parole* (leaves no place to the spoken word) (Ravis-Giordani 1990:42). This latter stance of deliberate extrication is also due to a desire to avoid possible consequences of cooperating in official investigations of acts of unlicensed violence. At the furthest end of the spectrum, where the state has managed to fully legitimate itself to the populace, and the presence of its agents is conspicuous and generally welcome, then we might plausibly declare the passing of a localized, particularistic, customary legal system, for it will have been supplanted in its entirety by a universalistic one imposed from without.

Evidence of some attitudes within Orgosolo regarding legal self-help in the face of a conspicuous police presence is to be found in the single moniker, often employed emphatically, if not derisively, within the context of conversation involving these latter: *sa mala iustitia*, the evil justice. Agents of the state are often, but not necessarily uniformly, regarded as representatives of an illegitimate authority imposed from without, there to adjudicate disputes that they are incapable of understanding and ill prepared to handle. Further and more concrete evidence of local attitudes towards practices of legal self-help may be discerned from reactions to violent acts committed within the region over the period in which the research for this study was conducted. Acts of violence and intimidation within Orgosolo and neighbouring villages – such as the bombing attempt on the doorstep of a private citizen in the summer of 2002, the shooting death of a young man visiting Orgosolo from neighbouring Mamoiada a few months earlier, a string of violent murders in Oliena that same year, the guerilla-style attack by unknown gunmen on a nighttime *carabienieri* patrol in the nearby village of Orune, the arson of a bartender's car in early 2003, and the shooting through the shuttered front windows of a different bar in Orgosolo a few weeks before – were all regarded as unfortunate if not extraordinary events.

When carried to their logical conclusion, self-help practices can escalate to tragic levels. Arson, vandalism, and even murder are the evident outcome of disputes that cannot be resolved more peacefully. When acts of violence do occur, they are not widely discussed or even acknowledged publicly. But in private, people do talk, and their talk reflects an ongoing concern with unlicenced use of violence. That said, there is no consensus on the matter. The existence of *disamistades* (states of enmity) between two or more individuals is a given, an inescapable element of existence within society and a product of conflicting interests or of real or imagined slights to personal integrity. The means by which such states of enmity are managed, and interactions between opposing parties structured – be they patterns of avoidance or violent confrontation – are contingent upon factors that at best enter the public domain as scattered fragments of information via networks of gossip.

Orgosolo Today

None of the foregoing aims to perpetuate a reified view of highland society as captive to static values, agonistic and oppositional in nature, violent and inward-oriented. Such a view is consistent with a failure to recognize that not only do local structures of violence parallel those found elsewhere in the Mediterranean, but that such structures are the product of intelligible political, historical, and economic forces. Nor does the preceding seek to ignore the many aspects of life in Orgosolo, and the central highlands in general, that are little different from those of similar-sized towns and villages throughout Sardinia. At the time of writing, there is an administration in the town hall led by a mayor who is not affiliated with an official party, and numerous town councillors who are *sardisti* (soft nationalists), reservedly partial to the regional autonomist movement. However, aware that support for the autonomist movement in Sardinia is moribund, the latter are generally noted for their political moderation. Sympathy for the outright separation of Sardinia from Italy is absent outside of the small nationalist class, and, interestingly, in view of the history outlined above, the movement toward regional autonomy has little to no support among the electorate. The results of the Italian national elections of 2013 reveal that the Sardinian autonomist Party, Partito Sardo d'Azione (Sardinian Action Party), and the separatist party, Indipendenza per la Sardegna (Independence for Sardinia), received 2.94 per cent and 1.14 per cent, respectively, of the popular vote in the province of Nuoro (Ministero dell'Interno 2013a). In the 2009 regional election in

Sardinia, the Partito Sardo d'Azione won four of seventy seats in the regional legislature, while the hardline separatist parties, the Indipendentzia Repubrica de Sardigna (Independent Republic of Sardinia) and Unidade Independentista (Independentist Unity) won no seats at all, and the Movimento per le Autonomie (Movement for Autonomies), a pan-regional movement advocating for greater autonomy and legislative powers for the southern Italian regions, won one seat.[14]

The Partito Sardo d'Azione is the oldest and most stable nationalist party on Sardinia. It was formed at the end of World War I, thanks to the efforts of some ex-combatants of the famous Brigata Sassari – a decorated Sardinian regiment noted for its effectiveness in key WWI battles, especially in northern Italy – in mobilizing grassroots demands for greater political rights on the island. Its leadership demanded a degree of political and administrative self-determination, and received early popular support. Despite some early successes, support for the Partito Sardo d'Azione would collapse and remain in the single digits for most of the remaining century. This evident failure is due to a few factors, according to Eve Hepburn (2009), most notably the party's reluctance to choose a spot on the left-right continuum, its penchant for deemphasizing class or social-economic policy issues, and its general ideological incoherence. My own inquiries at the local level reveal a widespread doubt about the merits of substituting one set of political masters for another and a general distrust of the would-be leaders of an incipient national entity that has limited viability considering the small size of its population and economy, which together have contributed to the meagre support for nationalist politics in Orgosolo and indeed throughout Sardinia.

Outside of nationalist politics, the population of Orgosolo is moderately politically engaged, and, in the 2009 regional elections, boasted a 69 per cent voter turnout rate (which, albeit, declined to 59 per cent for the 2013 national elections).[15] As for local political allegiances, these are as fragmented as they are elsewhere in Italy. Electoral choices made by Orgolesi do not differ greatly from other centres in the province of Nuoro, and fall on the centre-left of the political spectrum. Growing frustration in the early years of the second decade of the twenty-first century with European Union–mandated austerity measures in response to the 2008 recession and its aftermath has seen the rise of the Movimento Cinque Stelle (the Five Star Movement) led by comedian Beppe Grillo. In Nuoro, this party gained 25.4 per cent of the popular vote in the 2013 national elections, which placed them on a par with the Italian average; in Orgosolo, it earned the support of 30.8 per cent of voters.[16] Persistently high unemployment rates, especially among youth, a general trend towards neoliberalization, and stagnant wages have exacerbated already-high levels of cynicism and discontent throughout Italy towards the established political parties at the national and regional levels. Highland Sardinia is not unique in this regard, but the forms of marginalization and expressions of alienation seen there are, to a degree, *sui generis*. As Tracey Heatherington (2001) points out, from the 1970s onward, increasing apathy towards organized politics and distrust of bureaucrats has been countered in Orgosolo by an enthusiastic valorization of local standards of sociality based on norms of hospitable exchange and discourses of moral authenticity that stand in contrast to political artifice. Cultural realities in central Sardinia are themselves the products of historical processes that have shaped the parameters of people's visions and expectations; local people have recourse to a body of symbols and values, manipulation of which allows them to subvert the status quo. As for the widespread discontent among young men – the principal focus of many of my observations – it too resonates with the symbolic elements of the rural highland culture, and specifically presents a refraction of the norms and standards of the old order through a moment of economic crisis and rapid change.

In this vein, I suggest that the values that animate social action at the local level should be historicized and understood as long-term responses to extant circumstances. This will be the focus of the next chapter, which on the one hand historicizes the marginalization that led to the emergence of local value orientations that centre on concepts of honour and, on the other hand, asks what happens to these orientations under vastly changed circumstances. As we will see, the realities of the twenty-first century complicate the image presented above. In Orgosolo, the various definitions of *balentia* are strongly contested and incorporate much more than outward appearance and comportment. The *balente* inhabits a moral universe distinct from others, with exigencies of its own. The following, therefore, moves beyond the description of the performative aspects of *balentia* and instead considers those less visible elements that are central to the value system and that share many similarities with honour complexes elsewhere.

3

On Barbarism

The situation of populations that have deliberately placed themselves at the state's periphery has occasionally been termed, infelicitously, secondary primitivism. Their subsistence routines, their social organization, their physical dispersal, and many elements of their culture, far from being the archaic traits of a people left behind, are purposefully crafted both to thwart incorporation into nearby states and to minimize the likelihood that statelike concentrations of power will arise among them. State evasion and state prevention permeate their practices and, often, their ideology as well. They are, in other words, a 'state effect.' They are 'barbarians by design.' (Scott 2009:8)

This chapter examines the code of *balentia,* which is expressive of the ethos of a historically dissident nonstate people, or, as the classic state-centric vision would have it, "barbarians." If the people of Barbargia were hostile to the state, and therefore conceptually barbarians, they were so by design and not simply because they were remnants of an earlier era, somehow bypassed by time or incapable of more "civilized" states of being. Their marginality was a direct result of a conscious decision to resist incorporation into a state, and their establishment of alternative social, economic, and political forms rendered them less amenable to external control, regulation, and legibility (Scott 2009:76). A customary legal system that included practices of violent self-help, indigenous regimes of common-property resource management, along with an ideology of individual autonomy that is central to the code of *balentia,* have all helped to sustain a powerful symbolic boundary around the community that persists to this day.

I argue that the values of honour and patterns of violence that conditioned the highland experience constituted long-term responses to geographical, ecological, and political marginalization. A key axiom of the present approach is that marginally autonomous peoples maintained their state-repellent, non-legible, spaces through indigenous mechanisms that operated on the basis of well-defined norms of social action. These constitute "state effects," to use to James Scott's term; in Sardinia, these have historically included the code of *balentia*, as well as its associated practices of vendetta (which resulted in the second-order effects of banditry and outlawry), and, as we see later, practices of hospitality that maintained a village cohesiveness to the exclusion of outsiders (Sorge 2009). These processes, in their entirety, are set against a widespread awareness of the past in the present, and carry a historical burden that strongly conditions local conceptions of the nature of political authority. I begin with a discussion of violence, in which I question persistent stereotypes of highland Sardinia by outlining the historical bases for the emergence of honour values. I then examine more closely, in later sections, how *balentia* structures social action, specifically in relation to an ethos of resistance to state authority. This will set the stage for an examination, in the next chapter, of how the concept of *balentia* has changed through time, and how it is contested today at the local level with the emergence of alternative social ontologies and the gradual but steady transformations in cultural values.

Myths and Realities of Violence

The exigencies of pastoral production required – and continue to require – shepherds to judiciously exercise force (Angioni 1998:1132; Meloni 1984:253). Antonio Pigliaru (2000 [1959]) defines what he calls the *codice barbaricino* (Barbagian code) as a form of customary law buttressed by the threat of violent action, which regulates behaviour through a set of coercive norms that are expressed most vividly through their enactment in blood feud. As a set of legal injunctions, this *codice* sets the parameters for the use of violence in response to offences of various kinds: from theft, to insults, to the bearing false witness, and (most seriously) to offences committed against the family and household. Notably, the *codice barbaricino* contains no mechanisms for the peaceful resolution of violent conflict, only prescriptions for the regulation of violent action. As Pigliaru writes, "offensive action committed for the fulfilment of the requirements of vendetta constitutes in turn a new motive for revenge" (Pigliaru 2000 [1959]:152–3). Thus, we are presented with what he calls *un codice di guerra* (a code of war), which, as with Clastres' concept of "perpetual war," reflects a reality of latent hostility pervaded by agonistic relations and suspicion of social others, both within and among communities. With the entrenchment of state authority, these same centrifugal forces arising out of the use of unlicensed forms of violence account for the phenomenon of banditry and outlawry, which has strongly characterized the early modern and contemporary history of central Sardinia. For Pigliaru the *codice barbaricino* encompasses the whole community, which in turn embraces it in opposition to the official legal system and for whom the blood feud is not simply "an individual practice, but a social one; not a practice of a select number within the community, but of the whole community" (Pigliaru 2000:61).[1] Blood feud, therefore, sits at the core of what Jacob Black-Michaud (1975:128) elsewhere calls "a social system in its own right," a state of affairs that not only conditions social life, but, within pastoral societies of the Mediterranean and Middle East, constitutes it.

Violence here appears normative and integral to the social order, but is it correct to label all societies with prominent honour systems as inherently violent? Although this belief is widespread in Italian popular thought, there is little ethnographic evidence to support it. Many of my exchanges with interlocutors outside the central highlands were about how dangerous it is to live in the Sardinian highlands, how circumspectly one should behave when visiting the area, and how tortured social relations among villagers surely must be. Of all the beautiful places in Sardinia, why would a foreigner ever choose to live in those mountains? There are not enough anecdotes to fully express the awe that non-Barbagians expressed when I informed them of my decision to live and study in Orgosolo. Stereotypes abound regarding the ease with which highland Sardinians are moved to passion by the slightest personal offence. Newspaper and television reports of violent crime in the Sardinian interior provide an image of a restless and violent folk, a culture that is set apart from that of the wider society (see Loi 2001). Addressing these stereotypes requires consideration of the conditioning effects of the agrarian historical experience, without succumbing to the temptation of imputing straightforward historical continuity to value systems.

The descendents of Scott's "barbarians by design" are heirs to a spirit of dissidence integral to their historical refusal of state authority. The customary legal forms that were (and in many cases continue to be) premised on the threat of violent action fundamentally circumvent the legal norms of the hegemonic state. The code of *balentia* is one example of a long-term adjustment to historical circumstances within an agrarian social order.

Here, three key axioms should be highlighted for their centrality to the present argument. First, as Gellner (1988) so aptly showed, the widespread use of coercive force by private individuals was normative within agrarian society, but disruptive to the fabric of modern industrial society. Second, in areas where official legal systems were imposed upon pre-existing systems of unofficial customary law, the unlicensed use of violence that fell within the local community's moral bounds were codified as criminal. Third, the widespread legitimation of a state's claim to monopoly over the use of coercive force corresponded with a decrease in the frequency of its use in the private settlement of disputes and attainment of personal ends – indeed, the two are inversely related (Elias 1982). These points require closer examination.

In an agrarian society characterized by labour-intensive food production and storage, the use of coercion was normative; within an agonistically competitive arena, it best assured access to scarce resources and maintained control over storable wealth. In such a context, as Anton Blok (1974) suggests in his study on Sicilian mafia, the ability to "make oneself respected" was central to an individual's self-preservation. In these kinds of scenarios, the premium commonly placed on male offspring ensured that households or lineages continued to expand and protect their collective patrimony.[2] A surplus of resources required their defence, and the heavy dependence upon agricultural resources that this required periodically pushed agrarian societies to the limits of their ecological capacity. This predicament occasioned conflict over access to resources; as such, surpluses had to be defended from predators. According to this cyclical logic, periods of particular scarcity (and it was not a question of whether scarcity in agrarian society was endemic or not; rather, it was the degree of scarcity that mattered) intensified competition and conflict. Within these historically autonomous local communities that escaped external control, violent honour codes were the outward embodiment of the norms and values of a society marked by a high degree of internal competition over access to scarce resources (Meloni 1996:119–20).[3] Within the wider, stratified society, the extent of the famine experienced in especially lean periods depended on one's place in a rigid hierarchy, as entrenched inequalities determined entitlement to resources (Gellner 1997:18).

The state, for its part, was held back in its drive for conquest by the logistics of military campaigning; there were limits to the amount of territory and resources any political formation could claim and control. As capstone entities brought to power through the displacement of weaker groupings, the authority of agrarian states was based on an incomplete infrastructural penetration of society (Hall 1994:21). Their institutional frameworks were not elaborate, and they usually could not succeed in imposing a normative order upon the entirety of the realm they sought to control. As James Scott (1998:2) puts it, "[t]he pre-modern state was, in many crucial respects, particularly blind; it knew precious little about its subjects, their wealth, their landholdings and yields, their location, their very identity. It lacked anything like a detailed 'map' of its terrain and its people." These states were agglomerations of despotic interests and had limited reach beyond the urban centres and agricultural hinterlands. As a further corollary of this, mountainous and inaccessible regions did not warrant the expenditure of resources necessary to effectively subdue and control their populations. I have already suggested that this is, in large measure, a result of the fact that the mountains yielded little that could be of use to expansionary, resource-seeking predatory states. Beyond the effective reach of these states, then, were those autonomous communities that maintained an effective intracommunal balance of power, with unwritten customary laws that were enforced according to locally determined moral-legal principles. Within such small self-governing local groupings, inequality is minimal and a high political-military participation ratio is maintained (Andreski 1968). Among the political units of the agrarian period in general, these local self-governing communities of independent producers belong at one end of the spectrum of political authority. That is, they are free agriculturalists and montagnards neither subject to external authority nor possessing any capacity to exercise control over others (Gellner 1983:13).

Of course, the foregoing scenario is generic in its scope, and relies upon an ideal-typical representation of agrarian society. Broadly, though, it does provide a background for the current case. Not only did central highland Sardinia hold out against the politically centralizing tendencies of predatory states, but it also maintained this status until the modern era. The discernable remnants of a longstanding tendency to reject externally imposed structures of authority are evidence of a local society that maintained a high degree of de facto autonomy from overarching forces, beginning in antiquity and continuing through to the recent Savoyard period.

Modern states, for their part, presuppose as well as perpetuate the unique social preconditions required for their emergence and continued existence, and are therefore qualitatively and structurally different from the capstone entities that were their forerunners. Political sociologist

Michael Mann's (1993:55) Weberian formulation of the modern state as an institutionally differentiated and centralized entity that exercises control over a demarcated territory through force-backed authority provides us with a suitable operationalization of the concept. Working alongside these key elements of the modern state are the four "institutional clusterings" of modernity: heightened surveillance, centralized control over the means of violence, capitalistic enterprise, and industrial production (Giddens 1987:5ff.). In addition, consensual recognition of the state's claim to a monopoly over the legitimate use of violence is essential to the success of the democratic modern state (Elias 1982). The generation of such widespread consent is symptomatic of a decline in tolerance on the part of the body politic towards forms of unlicensed violence. The effective "pacification" of a citizenry is necessary wherever the economic foundations of a national polity are provided by industrial production. Where the overt threat of coercion was once normative to social relations, under changed conditions it becomes disruptive. A stagnant economy, characterized by endemic scarcity, underwrote the necessity of violence for the preservation of livelihoods, but such violence is an aberration within an economy based on industrial production and unlimited growth. To phrase it differently, the normative orientations of mechanical solidarity are not those of organic solidarity. Rather, the normative orientations of modern industrial society, or organic solidarity, or *Gesellschaft*, or whatever, are structured in accordance with the broader sociological correlates of modernity: the conceptual separation of spheres, single-strandedness of social relationships, social atomism, fluidity of occupational roles, increased social mobility, open markets, state education, as well as linguistic and cultural unity achieved through shared participation in a script-based Great Tradition (Gellner 1983; cf. Deutsch 1966). In other words, the emergence of social openness and the normalization of those scientific, liberal, or libertarian values and beliefs that ensure success within industrial society come to replace "non-rational," "traditional" beliefs and values now regarded as reflective of what Hayek (1978) referred to as "atavistic communalism." The agrarian society, as such, is bypassed in size, wealth, and power by the modern industrial state society.

    The success of the increasingly wealthy and powerful modern state relies on a high degree of individual self-discipline on the part of the citizenry. The pacified subject must maintain an aloofness of sorts as he executes his daily rounds. Work is valued for its own sake; should the bourgeois ideal of peaceful and pleasant toil be hindered by a necessity for alertness against sundry forms of violent harassment, productivity will decline. An alternative set of values emerges and becomes entrenched. As Norbert Elias points out, the practice of physical violence becomes proscribed and removed from the experience of day-to-day life:

> That the taboo against acts of violence is so deeply impressed upon adolescents in developed state-societies, is in good part connected with the growing effectiveness of the state monopoly of power. In the course of time the personality structures of individuals adjust to this. They develop a certain reluctance or even deep revulsion – a kind of disgust for the use of physical violence. (1982:136; cf. Blok 2001:208)

In not all cases, however, will modern states succeed in generating the total consent of its governed populations. The difficulty faced by the modern state to secure its claims to legitimacy – either in its avowed right to adjudicate disputes, the extraction of resources through taxation, or generally in the enforcement of its laws – will depend upon the extent to which a resistant population was already effectively subjugated and controlled from without before its encapsulation by the modern state. It is relevant to the present case that effective state formation, as well as the expurgation of violent action from the day-to-day experience of a citizenry, should be considered in tandem with the persistence of honour values. Where "the sublimation of violent impulses" (Elias 1982) is fairly advanced, we discover an accompanying set of values signalling a transformation in habitus from something appropriate to a rural, localized setting and its Little Tradition, to one more typical of an urban setting and its Great Tradition. We may well point out that urban and rural dwellers have their own respective habitus, defined by characteristic forms of comportment and modes of thought. There is therefore a further dimension to Elias' (2000) concept of the "civilizing process" and it has to do with the dichotomy between Great and Little Traditions, as well as the perceptible shift towards an urbanization of preferences and orientations. Urban centres in stratified agrarian state societies radiated power to their hinterlands. They featured entrenched social classes as well as a complex division of labour, with inhabitants long subjected to control by government. On the other hand, the more inaccessible rural areas could retain some autonomy from the social and political influences of the metropole, and this is especially true the further removed they were from centres of power.

Where state authority was limited or distant, and where endemic scarcity prevailed, a premium was placed on the ability to claim precedence over competitors. An ethos that would appear anachronistic if transposed to the highly altered circumstances of urban society is apparent. The sublimation of violent impulses, or at least their restraint by external authority, defines the urban life (Osborne and Rose 1999), and Elias' civilizing process entails precisely the imposition, and subsequent normalization, of the values of the urban elite class onto the entire realm governed from the core. But before the emergence of industrial society and modern forms of statehood, the civilizing process could not effectively extend beyond urban confines. As Julio Caro Baroja (1963) notes, no shortage of contrasts has been recorded between town and country from antiquity to the present, indicating an entrenched dichotomy that persists throughout the history of Mediterranean thought. This dichotomy is accreted to ambivalent judgments regarding the backwardness of the countryside and the refinement of the city, as well as the moral purity of the former and the corruption of the latter. Such a view of course elides the history of relations and continuities that throughout the Mediterranean have long bound together the city and the countryside through perennially uneven relations of power (Caro Baroja 1963:40).

As in history, so in the present day. There is an urban ambivalence towards people among whom the internalization of bourgeois values has not proceeded apace. They are easy to perceive as proud bearers of an intangible genuineness, for they are the carriers of an authentic "primitiveness" that one cannot help but romanticize. Their values and behaviours were not rendered innocuous or overlain with urbane affectation. Concurrently, they may be perceived as backward figures for their apparent inability to adapt to contemporary conditions. Due to urban conceit, they are viewed as living exemplars of premodernity, clinging steadfastly to their anachronistic existence with taciturn determination.

It is such caricatures that inform urban perceptions of highland Sardinian culture and society. In popular discourse – on the island and beyond – "traditional" honour values seem to constitute the crux of the problem of violence in the rural highlands, and lie at the root of the widespread urban tendency towards both the romanticization and the condemnation, of Barbagian culture and society.

At this juncture, I will document the emic perspectives on the cultural categories of *balentia* and *balente*. I suggest that the *balente*'s modus operandi is upheld by a set of value orientations associated with a pastoral habitus that explicitly rejects urban values. It is also defined by its adherence to customary legal norms that run counter to the laws of the state. These latter are regarded as a "state effect," a byproduct of a marginal peoples' rejection of external constraints based on a reflexive drive to maintain local autonomy. As we will see, the resultant reality was – and in many ways, is – no panacea. Throughout modern history, the institutions designed to evade state authority came to entail the proliferation of outlawry, of *omertà* (the code of silence or non-cooperation with police authority), and, by extension, social fragmentation at the community level. The remainder of this chapter is therefore concerned with the sociocultural precipitates of the highland experience, with specific reference to the state-evading practices associated with *balentia*.

Balentia and the *Balente*

The *balente* is a subject of ambivalence in Orgosolo. On the one hand, he exemplifies a style of manhood closely associated with conservative traditionalism, and as such provides a living link to an imagined agrarian past. On the other hand, he can be regarded merely as a local tough, a rudderless young man who has yet to find his place and who gleans his identity through an unconvincing performance of an antiquated model of masculinity. This divergent conception of *balentia* speaks to the entrenchment of divergent modalities, exemplary of a tension between localist- and cosmopolitan-oriented townspeople. My present aim is to examine *balentia* as an ethos and code of conduct dependent upon a recognizable set of values that reappear in myriad ways throughout the wider Mediterranean.[4]

First, *balentia* has a well-defined place within the life-course of an individual. An elderly man cannot be a *balente* – he may have been when he was young, but the strict adherence to a code of honour and the relentless performance of this role is superseded by his adoption of a wholly different status upon retirement. The elderly need not claim precedence, for they are people to whom respect and consideration are eminently due. Likewise, children cannot be *balentes*, for they have responsibilities appropriate to the young and, furthermore, their security and esteem are the concern of their parents and guardians. Women cannot be *balentes*, for *balentia* refers to a strictly male code of honour. This does not mean that women have no role in maximizing the reputation of the household, but rather they do not do so by overtly asserting

their precedence. Because *balentia* is confined to the world of pastoralism, its unique exigencies should be considered foremost, with specific
reference to aspects of shepherds' archetype and performance.

The habitus of shepherds involves particular ways of moving, dress-
ing, and acting, which distinguishes them from non-shepherds. The
ethos of the *balente* – equally a matter of practice as of discourse – is
central to lives of young men engaged in this occupation. The *balente*
possesses the ability to succeed in the world of pastoral production,
and his technical know-how and mode of being mark him as a member of a distinct social category.[5] Similarly, the *balente* exemplifies a
socially conservative ethic that represents a kind of continuity with the
standards of the preceding generation. Aggressive masculinity, heavy
drinking, and the maintainance of social networks that demand great
expenditure of time defines their universe, especially if they are young
and unmarried. Likewise, shepherds' schedules and daily routines further set them apart from the rest of the community. On a typical day,
a shepherd may take an early morning coffee in a neighbourhood bar,
and return there in the early afternoon while breaking from tasks in
the countryside. From noon to two o'clock, the consumption of alcohol
commonly begins in all of Orgosolo's twenty-seven drinking establishments. A shepherd will return to the pastures at about four o'clock in
order to complete his day's work and head back to the village between
six and seven o'clock in the evening to deposit the sheep's milk in
refrigerated stainless steel containers for processing. By nine o'clock,
he will have eaten dinner at home, and will return to the bars until closing (midnight). The ability to travel back and forth between village and
pasture is due to the adoption of motorized transport, now deemed
essential to the shepherd's work, as well as the availability of subsidized feed for purchase. Every active shepherd I knew in Orgosolo
made use of available resources to facilitate his enterprise, as opposed
to older shepherds who lived on the pastures for months on end, isolated from family and community. In Orgosolo, these older shepherds
are now retired, and pastoralism is widely recognized as not being
what it once was. Shepherds today, especially younger men, patronize
the bars and taverns with greater frequency than their forebears. Furthermore, they successfully monopolize the most prestigious public
space of the village – the central portion of Corso Repubblica, the main
avenue, where a dozen or so bars patronized exclusively by shepherds
are clustered. This is especially evident in the evenings, by which time
most people have gone home to wind down for rest of the day.

As in innumerable other Mediterranean rural contexts, loud talking, assertive posturing, and competitive drinking, all set within exclusively male centres of convivial sociability, are markers that identify the socially successful man. The taciturn, quick-witted individual who jokes sardonically, exercises an earthy machismo, and establishes his social preeminence in the company of his peers, displays all the marks of a *balente*. Until a generation or two ago such behaviour was expected of the majority of men in the community, as most were engaged in pastoral production. Changing norms have affected the pastoral sector, which now employs fewer men than ever. As a result, shepherds today stand as carriers of a proud cultural heritage that is on the wane. They have continued to engage in an occupation emblematic of highland culture – the tending of livestock on pastures. Although they are easy to romanticize, if they are to acquire social success in spheres beyond their own they must know how to shed the habitus that marks them as rural countrymen. As we will see below, this is a tall order. Therefore, although sharing the same dialects, numerous cultural presuppositions and ideals, raised in the same village, subject to a standardized system of state education, and bound by the same legal system, men engaged in the world of pastoralism are part of a distinct category separated by a clear social boundary. Surface appearances suggest a dynamic of subcultural isolation, with insiders inhabiting a distinct universe. While this does not speak to the reality of shared family and associational ties that integrate shepherds into the wider community, a very important distinction remains: the potential for violent action and its centrality within pastoral life.

As a code of honour, *balentia* emerges from a world view characterized by competition for social advantage, endemic scarcity and insecurity, and suspicion of the intentions of social others. Furthermore, the *balente* does not follow the code of *balentia* unreflexively, but rather acts in accordance with a system of incentives and constraints, knowing that his actions will determine his quota of recognition and esteem within the community.[6] Much of the foregoing has suggested that the practice of livestock herding is enmeshed in structures of violence in that the threat of violent action is never wholly remote from the individual's experience. Insecurity in the countryside is common throughout the Mediterranean, at least wherever nucleated settlements are the norm.[7] The villages and towns of highland Sardinia are all of this type, leaving the space outside of the community scarcely populated and therefore free of social controls. Livestock herding is carried out in this socially

hollowed-out space, where animal rustling, arson, and general conditions of distrust are burdens about which the people of Orgosolo lament
but in the end accept as inevitable.

Within this space, a shepherd knows that he may need to make up
his losses by taking from someone else what had previously been
taken from him. This poses a moral quandary, for the need to ensure
the success of the pastoral pursuit operates alongside the more universal injunction to do no harm to social others. The Cretan shepherds examined by Juliet du Boulay (1991:46) face the same dilemma
precisely because of this contradiction inherent to the success of
their herding activities.[8] Shepherds must have the ability to negotiate a contradictory set of values with circumspection in order to
acquire an honourable reputation. Among pastoralists in Sardinia,
any anxiety over doing the right thing is offset by an outward pattern of livestock rustling that prohibits theft from a co-villager, sparing the community from a major source of discord. In sum, society
encourages the *balente* "to commit acts that are, at the same time,
esteemed and condemned" (Paine 1989:658), a contradiction that
imparts a sense of moral ambivalence to social action that needs not
be urgently resolved. This is rendered all the more poignant by the
fact that in fulfilling the requirements of successful herding, *balentes*
do not reproduce values that are normative across all sectors of the
local community. Rather, they operate within alternative systems.
As Benedetto Caltagirone (1989a:87–8) has demonstrated, livestock
rustling was institutionalized in Sardinian history, and was usually
conducted via a preferential relationship of negative reciprocity that
every pastoral community had with at least one other neighbouring
village. Orgosolo and Fonni were traditional competitors, as were
Arzana and Desulo, and Orune and Bitti were always in each other's
sights (although, among well-known traditional village enmities,
Bitti is famous for being Orune's perennial victim). These compromised relationships between villages were offset by the creation of a
wide network of alliances across entire districts that could be called
upon for assistance in recovering missing livestock. Such alliances
can have numerous latent functions, and bear witness to the embeddedness of pastoral production within social relations layered with
reciprocal obligations. The successful shepherd has allies throughout the highland districts and beyond, and can mobilize support
whenever he needs it.[9] Therefore, with respect to the institutions and
relationships of the wider society, the exigencies of the shepherd's

life marginalize individuals by requiring them to operate in a parallel system of exchange, which further integrates members of the pastoral sector with one another as it distances them from the wider community. Of course, a rejection of external authority here is not incidental.

External Authority

In his *Prison Notebooks*, Antonio Gramsci (1975) argued that the Italian peasant – a category that included pastoralists as part of the larger rural proletariat – does not understand the state. According to him, peasant society is internally fragmented as a result of its grinding poverty, and peasants are incapable of expressing their discontent in a focused, articulate fashion as a result of their lack of political consciousness. Furthermore, they have neither national consciousness nor class consciousness. Banditry, kidnapping, arson, and other sundry forms of violence directed against agents of authority should not be confused with class struggle, but rather are products of desperation driven by what he called a "generic hatred" that is fundamentally feudal in its sensibility (see Mattone 1976). Peasants are incapable of thinking of themselves as a collective with shared interests, and do not apprehend the complex structures of inequality within which they are enmeshed. This renders them incapable of effectively organizing any systematic opposition that might succeed in altering the macropolitical and economic arrangements of the wider social order. Consequently, their individual acts of violent resistance can only be futile.

Eric Hobsbawm (1969) took his lead from Gramsci and declared that all varieties of peasant revolt – a category in which he includes banditry – constitute a form of primitive rebellion that is fundamentally apolitical and reformist rather than revolutionary in scope. Hobsbawm's figure of the "social bandit" is a hero to the local society, which provides him with moral and economic support. His exploits are celebrated, and his renown held up as an example of local resistance against the state, the overlord, the oppressor. The social bandit is an avenger of injustices who holds out a glimmer of hope for the development of a proletarian consciousness among the rural poor.

In a famous response to this idealized conception of social banditry, Anton Blok (1972) provides a wholly different viewpoint. Far from accounting for the full expression of banditry through space and time, he says, Hobsbawm's focus is too narrow to adequately explicate reality. It presses into service a revised image of outlaws whose careers and trajectories, when examined carefully, are revealed to have done nothing to further the interests of the peasantry. On the contrary, bandits acted to further their own individual interests As specialists in the unlicensed use of violence, their single measure of success was how effectively they managed to generate fear and respect. Furthermore, the conditions of outlawry required protection by powerful patrons, which yields Blok's key hypothesis on the question: "The more successful a man is as a bandit, the more extensive the protection granted him" (Blok 1972:498). As seen in the previous chapter, Sardinian bandits' violent demise at the hands of Italian police forces following unification leads to an appreciation of the vulnerability of a marginal category of outlaws who generally enjoyed limited protection. In the modern era, the Sardinian bandit is an unprotected fugitive whose routes to outlawry characteristically involved the commission of a misdemeanour followed by an evasion of government authority by absconding from the local community. Much like what Stephen Wilson (1988) writes about Corsica, banditry in Sardinia too was commonly a byproduct of episodes of feuding or other acts that conform to local customary legal norms, following which men took to the maquis to flee their enemies as much as the agents of the state. In Orgosolo, the esteem that such blood feud bandits could garner was always tempered by a sense of pity for their unfortunate plight (although they could inspire respect for their boldness).[10]

Even if not locally regarded as a hero, one such figure in Orgosolo, the former bandit Graziano Mesina, is today accorded considerable honour for his many feats of daring and his general prowess when he was a young man. As one of the more colourful examples of *balentia* in contemporary local history, Mesina, nicknamed *La primula rossa* (The Scarlet Pimpernel), would begin his career in the 1950s as a charismatic trouble-seeking youngster. In 1956, at the age of 14, he would encounter the first of many run-ins with the law, on that occasion arrested for illegal possession of a firearm. In 1960, as a result of a longstanding conflict with a local family (specifically, shepherds who herded on adjacent pastures), his brothers would be framed for the kidnap and murder of a local merchant, Pietrinu Crasta. Graziano's retaliation – the murder of a member of the opposing Mereu clan – would force him to flee and live as a fugitive, until he was eventually apprehended and condemned to life in prison for this and subsequent crimes, including more murder and kidnap. In his early years, as a blood feud bandit, Mesina earned a special renown as an escape artist, having freed himself from police shackles nine times out of an alleged total of twenty escape attempts. The head of a loose band of associates, he kidnapped men – never women or children, adhering to apparent standards of gallantry – for purposes of extorting ransom. Ranked among Italy's most wanted fugitives, he remained at large until 1968, by which time he had gained recognition for his bravura, his adroitness, and his heroism. But Mesina's purported heroism was an external construct, and not a product of local discourses. Throughout the 1960s, he received regular fan mail from throughout Europe, and enjoyed the company of a young Swedish admirer, in addition to a long string of lovers who allegedly met with him secretly during his years as a fugitive. His renown inspired the Italian communist and publisher Giangiacomo Feltrinelli to travel to Sardinia to recruit the outlaw – whom he evidently regarded as a Che Guevara–like figure – into a revolutionary plan that would transform Sardinia into "the Cuba of the Mediterranean" (Pisano 2005:45ff.). Mesina did not accept the commission, which would have been bankrolled by the wealthy Feltrinelli, ultimately rejecting the politicization of his outlawry. As ever, banditry remained a resolutely apolitical phenomenon, just as bandits remained resolutely free of ideological entanglements.

The ethos of *balentia* is underpinned by an ideal of autonomy and self-sufficiency that ill-tolerates any political encumbrances or infringements of freedom. The outlaw's rejection of the state and his total avoidance of its official agents provide an extreme example of anti-statism, but within Orgosolo and throughout Sardinia's mountainous districts, the *balente*'s relationship to *polizia* and *carabinieri* is limited to conventional cordiality. Little attempt is made to incorporate the lone off-duty police officer into the circle of sociability. However, any officer who enters a bar should recognize he will likely need to subjugate himself to the will of local actors, who will insist on paying for his drinks and, by extension, create a sense of reciprocal obligation. What does this obligation consist of? A young acquaintance of mine, Bustianu, an underemployed shepherd and barfly, had some very clear ideas about this, especially on one particular occasion in which he was left particularly chagrined after an incident that highlighted the police's impersonal law enforcement practices:

The police are *bastardi e ipocriti* [bastards and hypocrites]. Or maybe they don't understand us. Imagine that you were an off-duty cop, and you come into a bar, we start chatting, we create a rapport, and you drink something and I pay for it, you say thank you and even shake my hand when you leave. Good, now, tell me: would you permit yourself to pull me over one day and ask for my papers, and give me a ticket because I did not have insurance? No, you would not, instead you would give me a warning, let it pass, and I, out of respect for you, would not do it again. But *uno stronzo* [a piece of shit] does not see it like this, instead he has to be a *rompipalle* [ball-breaker], all impetuous, and give me a ticket that I don't have the money to pay! I was not doing anything bad, you understand, just running an errand and I was driving only a few metres.

The setting for this animated rant was outside one of the shepherd's bars in the centre of Orgosolo one late July night. Drinking and carousing in the local bars into the wee hours is *de rigueur* for many young men, especially in the summer, and loud and even unruly behaviour is not rare. Who should happen to drive by on this particular occasion but two police officers in a patrol car. Noting the general commotion, they decided to idle their vehicle for several seconds in front of the bar where we were standing in an apparent attempt to stare down noisy revellers, whom they probably hoped would pipe down and bring their drinks back inside. This amateurish intimidation tactic backfired: "*Che cazzo guardi!* [What the fuck are you looking at!]," yelled Bustianu at the top of his lungs. The patrol car remained still, the young men inside – no older than their mid-twenties and probably lacking the poise that older officers would have – clenched their teeth, turned red in the face, and drove off slowly to loud jeers and insults. Such tense moments involving police officers leave no doubt as to the ease with which already tenuous relations between local men and law enforcement officials can turn unpleasant. In this case, the situation was fuelled by alcohol consumption and aggravated by a reminder that the functions and roles of law enforcement are not compatible with local standards and expectations. It does not help that a majority of *polizia* and *carabinieri* who patrol Orgosolo are young officers involuntarily posted to these distant rural towns, only getting to choose more desirable assignments in larger towns and cities later in their careers. Exacerbated by the fact that most officers are around the same age as the young shepherds, the relationship between the two is characterized by a tone of agonistic contest. Young men adopt a generally snarly disposition towards the police, marked by posturing, hostile glares, and in some cases outright challenges intended to test the young officers' mettle, including the discharge of firearms against police property, an act that is intended less to harm than to rattle wits. This is a near-constant feature of local life, and seems to serve as a reminder of how fraught the question of legitimacy is regarding external authority as far as shepherds are concerned.

Overall, the general consensus on the subject of police agents is that they should be treated with a modicum of respect, but only insofar as they do not intrude into regular routines. Everyone recognizes that there are good and bad police officers, more or less helpful or imperious; however, with rare exceptions, they are not befriended, and only structurally incorporated according to their status as representatives of the state. As such, police officers rarely establish ties to the highland communities to which they are posted. On two separate occasions I was informed that the presence of young police officers is deleterious to local girls' maintenance of their virtue, and that there was no shortage of young women who had allegedly dashed all hopes of finding acceptable marriage prospects because of previous intimate relationships with police officers.

The injunction to avoid extensive affiliation with the police was extremely serious, a fact that was made apparent during the early stages of my fieldwork. I had informed a small group of young shepherds with whom I was sitting in a private cantina – in the interest of testing limits as much as to set the stage for what I thought would be a funny anecdote – that I had that very morning walked into the *carabinieri* detachment and spoken to the *maresciallo* (captain). The conviviality of a moment before came to a sudden halt. "So, you talk with *carabinieri*?" said a new acquaintance, raising his eyebrows and offering a sardonic half-smile. I informed the men present that I did not regularly do so as a matter of course, but that I had to on this particular occasion because I had misplaced my international driver's permit. In Italy, lost official documents require by law, a visit to the nearest prefecture or detachment to fill out official forms. My explanation was accepted, and the anecdote, centred on the *maresciallo*'s poor knowledge of geography – he had asked me whether I had come to Italy from Canada by rail or by air – produced the expected mirth. The uneasy moment following the group's initial silence spoke to these men's vigilance towards potential sources of outside danger. The anecdote that I related, fortunately accepted as humourous, confirmed what most local people already think of agents of the state arriving from distant parts of Italy. They are viewed, in a general and all-compassing sense, as not only incompetent but notoriously

unversed in local norms. Most of the young officers on duty at Orgosolo, both *polizia* and *carabinieri,* were not born and raised in the central highlands of Sardinia. Most are not Sardinian at all. The practice
of posting agents of state police to areas to which they have no ties
is unexceptional, and is in fact the norm among most national police
forces in modern states. But in Orgosolo, this fact only exacerbates
the hostility toward these officers' authority. People of Barbagia cannot expect that officers born and raised in mainland Italian or Sicilian
towns and cities would be capable of understanding the lives and
circumstances of local people. As the chief inspector of the Polizia
Nazionale in Orgosolo, Stefano Camastra, himself a Sicilian, casually
lamented during a brief conversation,

> too many people here are suspicious of us. They think we want to harm
> them. Therefore, whenever there is a dispute, or whenever something
> happens, they sort it out among themselves. And if we come to know,
> we inquire, then they stay quiet. Of course, some things they can sort out
> for themselves. Like small accidents or quarrels, right? But the problems
> begin when people break the law or some violent act is committed, and
> nobody says anything.

He is correct, and the ideal-embodying refrain, *torrare a su connottu*
(to return to [known] custom) here takes on a central importance to
the value system of the *balente. Su connottu,* "the known," encompasses all the practices that make up the unofficial legal code of highland Sardinia. This, the customary law, is counter to "the unknown,"
those laws imposed from without that comprise the virtual antithesis
of local conventions and practices in all areas of justice. Therefore,
legal self-help remains the norm in many respects, and calling upon
external authorities for help runs counter to the code of *balentia.* Stolen
livestock is dealt with through an appeal to the assistance of trusted
affiliates and intermediaries, and not by contacting the state authorities (Ruffini 1978). Once more, the exigencies of animal raising on
far-flung commons, where the presence of state authority is slight at
best, conspires to make the shepherd someone who potentially, even
in spite of his law-abiding intentions, engages in illegal activities. The
evasion, or at least avoidance, of state authority is itself necessary
for reasons of individual honour as well as for the purposes of livelihood. An example of this may be found in a story recounted to me

by an elderly interlocutor, Tzia Grazia, shortly following our formal introduction. The story is as compelling for its emphatic (but friendly) candidness as it is for its subtext:

> You come from far away, just like my father! My father came to Orgosolo as a young man. He married my mother, who is from here, and so he moved and lived in Orgosolo too. He was a shepherd, and he started shepherding. It was not easy in the beginning, because people are suspicious of anyone who comes from afar. And it was not easy for my father to fit in, but he proved himself, and he came to be well-loved by all. He proved himself when the police arrested him. As a shepherd he had to live in the countryside, and at his *ovile* [sheepfold], the police one day came to ask if he had seen any bandits. There were some suspects in that area, they said. He replied no, that he didn't see anything, and he insisted that he knew nothing about anyone's whereabouts. Oh, *la giustizia* [the justice], what they did to him! They beat him so badly, almost to kill him! But he never said a thing! He showed to all how he was able to respect and not hurt those who welcomed him. And he became so well-loved and respected!

First-hand accounts of such heavy-handedness by the police in the 1950s have been extensively reported by Franco Cagnetta (1975), and in many instances relate to local people's unwillingness to cooperate with state authorities. Individual self-help in the form of blood feud, livestock rustling, arson, and other misdemeanours are in innumerable ways tied to the practice of animal husbandry in remote territories.[11] From this follows the evasion of state authority; as a result, secrecy and discretion are necessary to protect oneself against real or perceived dangers. The ability to dissimulate, to tell a convincing lie, is an important skill, one that is to be used judiciously when dealing with structures of authority and, more broadly, with one's fellows. An anecdote neatly illustrates the need for discretion in mundane interactions. After a pleasant hour spent speaking with Giuseppe in a shepherd's bar, he, along with a small entourage of friends, decided to leave. "Leaving already? Where are you going?" I asked. With bellicose humour, Giuseppe replied, "Now you're being indiscreet!" "How?" I said. "You never ask anyone where they are going," he replied. "For instance now I might be going to women,[12] and if I told you the truth it would be embarrassing. So instead, I would lie." With a laugh, he continued, "but then I would lie anyway, even if I were going home to dine!" After a jovial pat on the shoulder, he saluted me and assured me he would return later to continue our conversation.

This observation is supported by those of ethnographer Gino Satta (2001). The preoccupation with discretion in social interactions was expressed to him in a similar fashion, albeit with an apparently more serious tone:

> You must never tell anyone where you are going.
>
>   Why?
>
>   Because it's not done. One can never know ... If someone asks you where you're going tell him that you're just going [without saying where], or tell him a place and then go in the other direction. (Satta 2001:93)

Lower on the same page, Satta writes the following:

> It being tacitly recognized that one has the right to not say too much about oneself, it is considered good manners not to ask. Direct questions are almost always avoided, and responses, even to the most innocuous ones, are often extraordinarily elusive. Questions themselves are often formulated in such a way that they require responses all but void of informative content, conferring upon many formal interactions an almost surreal character. To someone encountered in the street, for example, one asks "[you're] going?" or even "strolling [around]?" to which the interlocutor responds by simply repeating the same word in the affirmative.[13]

Towards the final weeks of my stay in Orgosolo, over another conversation with Giuseppe, I was provided with what seemed a curiously anthropological excursus on the nature of local human relations, namely that if Orgolesi are suspicious of outsiders, it is a result of past history:

> We aren't like people in Canada. You have in your country a mix of populations. English, Irish, French, Italians, and so on. They all came together to build a country. We never had that. The only outsiders we ever knew were the Carthaginians, Romans, Spaniards, et cetera, and then the Italians who started off badly but now thank God they're a bit better. But still, even if we're modern and everything, we associate outsiders with danger. We're closed, but only because we have had to be, and we have had to defend ourselves with our silence.

The strongly felt need for discretion is likely a byproduct of numerous factors, most conspicuous of which deal with the uncertainty of outsiders' intentions, particularly toward to the nuclear family or close-knit friendships. Here, as evidenced by Giuseppe's observations, the past gives rise to a social legacy in which a salient kind of public mistrust has arisen from a history of negative experiences (Giordano 2012b:28). Disparate historical eras are collapsed and treated as an undifferentiated past awash with intrusions and oppressions. If that is what the past was like, why should the present to be any different? In the local imagination, the integrity of the locality has always been under threat from forces that present an alternative to the cohesiveness of village life. Such a vision of the past conditions local expectations in the present, and serves as a charter for the kind of disposition it is most prudent to adopt vis-à-vis the outside world. In sum, we are here presented with a legacy born of long-term adaptation to a violent past that, in turn, also gives forth a local code, *balentia,* which self-consciously maintains a safe distance from the mechanisms of official authority.

With specific reference to today's shepherds, it is incorrect to claim that their values of *balentia* are reliant upon the construction and performance of a deviant identity. Nonetheless, pastoral production may bear witness to social action taking place on the margins of legality. The individual agency of the shepherd is constrained by the structures through which he operates, and he understands that illegal activity remains a necessary element of the world he inhabits. Where a state monopoly over means of coercion is well entrenched and widely accepted, the *balente* may stand apart from the rest of society but must safeguard his world from prying eyes. In an altogether different context – western Sicily – it is widely accepted that the ideal person is one who "minds his own business" (Blok 2000:xxviii). As with western Sicily, so with central Sardinia. The inwardness of groups regarded by the state as potential malefactors is well-known and provides considerable obstacle to any form of outside investigation; for example, that secretive associations established on a basis of mutual trust between individuals and groups must exclude outsiders, thus yielding the characteristic guardedness central to the world of the *balente.*

Yet, in the early twenty-first century, *balentia* represents something more than all of the foregoing. It is a highly contested category, and symbolizes a young man's yearning for a way of life that is under threat. In addition, the performace of *balentia* is tinged with a profound nostalgia that arises out of a sense of dislocation resulting from the passing of a specific style of masculinity and its associated ethos. This code of honour once provided the element of resistance against the state and defined local society as "barbarian" to the outside world; now it is something that renders the holdouts – young shepherds – a kind of living anachronism. The following chapter examines this question with special reference to local understandings of manhood and masculinity today.

4

Anachronistic Men

An incessant pounding on my front door at six o'clock in the morning makes for a rude awakening, especially after a long night. Then there is hollering through my open window: "Antò! Tony! We're going, or we're not going? You decide!" It was Angelo. I was several months into my fieldwork in the spring of 2002, and making rapid progress in meeting people and gaining access to their lives. The previous night's revelry with Angelo, a *servo-pastore* paid to herd and manage livestock that belonged, in this case, to his second cousin Giovanni, whom we shall presently meet, would be the first of many nights out with him and his hospitable clique. This was the first time I experienced Angelo's candid willingness to include me in his daily rounds. On this occasion, I would accompany him to his cousin's sheepfold to participate in a sheep shearing in a nearby town. It would be very interesting for me, he said, to partake of this singular event within the pastoral production cycle, and I agreed. But it would be even more interesting, he added, to meet his cousin Giovanni.

Giovanni, I am told, is *un vero uomo*, a real man. Fifteen years earlier, he had been released from prison, having served a lengthy sentence for murder. His deed, in this context and in the circumscribed world of Sardinian shepherds, was an especially courageous one for which he had earned a reputation as *unu omine balente*, a serious, honourable man. His was not an act of random violence or a consequence of a hot temper, but rather premeditated murder in the first degree. His victim was a man forty-five years of age who in the previous decade had killed Giovanni's older brother, apparently as a result of a long-running dispute over rights of access to certain pasturelands. Following his release from prison, Giovanni was welcomed back to the community by his extensive network of kin and allies, each of whom provided him with several heads of sheep and all the tools necessary to begin life anew, as a shepherd, in his late thirties. Giovanni is a real man, alright. He is a successful shepherd, now married and a proud father. His broad smile, quick wit, hospitality, firm handshake, loud voice, solid forearms, and burly beard show that he has mastered the game of performative excellence as someone adept at "being good at being a man" (Herzfeld 1988:16).

However, I would later discover that Angelo's praise of Giovanni was tempered by one reservation. As soon as he committed his deed (in Angelo's words, *dopo aver fatto ciò che doveva fare* [after he did what he had to do]), he turned himself in to the local police authorities, likely sparing his own life, and pre-empting a cycle of revenge killings. Instances of such direct appeal to external authority among perpetrators of vendetta are relatively uncommon, and indicate a degree of acceptance of official justice as instrumental in forestalling greater bloodshed. For this reason, Angelo says, Giovanni did the right thing. "*Eppure* ... And yet ..." With what I would later come to appreciate as his usual forthrightness, Angelo spoke his mind on the matter: "Here it's *nostra consuetudine* [our custom] to manage things our own way, and we prefer not to have *la giustizia tra i coglioni* [the justice system up in our business]."

I will return to Giovanni later, but the purpose of this vignette is to provide a glimpse into a very real corner of life in Sardinia that is under pressure in the twenty-first century. The *balente*, beholden to protecting his livelihood, well-being, social integrity, and kinfolk within a highly competitive and agonistic social arena – who is required to claim respect through the threat or use of violence, and who resorts to practices of legal self-help that stand opposed to the judicial norms of the state – is locally viewed as a figure of romantic exaltation as well as a target of condemnation. He is an anachronism, and regardless of the moral criticism or approbation that he may receive, he is to every non-shepherd a figure destined to be replaced, for better or for worse, by a different kind of man, a more polished product of modernity or postmodernity. What, then, are the *balente*'s prospects for survival? This question can only be answered by examining the transactions and performances that speak to the contested nature of values within the local social field. The values in question here are those that underpin the code of *balentia*, which are profitably regarded as a byproduct of historical experience rather than as the reflection of some cultural essence. Since the post-war period, a range of social and economic changes have occasioned a rupture in traditional patterns of life by providing younger generations with alternatives to the lifestyles of their forebears. Despite this, it would be incorrect to infer the absence of a continuity of cultural forms and symbols, even if they are subject to profound shifts in meaning. I begin with a discussion of the impact of transformations in the pastoral economy that followed the introduction of new techniques of livestock herding, as well as the rise and eventual decline of industrial manufacturing and the corresponding emergence, in the late twentieth and early twenty-first first centuries, of a thriving tertiary sector. All of these factors have been central to rapid changes in value orientations and world views locally, and have contributed to the marginalization of a distinct social category of shepherds that appears as a highly pressured holdout against neoliberal modernity.

Shepherds' Lives

In Sardinia, as throughout Italy, standards of masculine identity are in rapid flux. The classic, normative models of virility have undergone radical transformation, leaving men everywhere with no straightforward sets of expectations to follow in their construction of a male identity (Ciccone 2009). Contemporary public discourse in Italy suggests that the Italian man is not what he used to be, or that maybe he has completely disappeared. The broad parameters of this public mourning are familiar: boys are failing, girls are succeeding; men are checking out of the workforce as women are entering it in larger numbers than ever before; women are earning a greater proportion of university degrees, as men's enrolments are in decline; an increasing number of women are raising children alone as men evidently shirk their parental responsibilities; and so forth. Locally, the more socioeconomically mobile individuals whose lives are significantly removed from the pastoral sector speak frequently in explicit judgment of the young, unmarried men active in that domain.

Men's occupational categories in Sardinia coincide locally with definite social types. The shepherd, a conservative countryman par excellence, is counterpoised to the urban individual, who is deemed a model of success by the standards of late modernity, but who is alternatively seen as having forsaken the older standards of rural manhood. From the vantage point of locally contradictory perspectives, men who identify clearly with one of these two social types can be regarded as either

successes or failures. As I elaborate below, this is one of the many sociological side effects involved in Orgosolo's adaptation to the neoliberal
realities of the early twenty-first century. But first, back to Giovanni.

   My friend Silvana tells me that Giovanni is a brute.[1] Not only that,
he is also a psychopath, and I should not spend any time with him. It
could be dangerous for me to associate with him, she says. She does
not elaborate, but offers up platitudes about the cold-bloodedness of
first-degree murder and condemns his seamless reintegration into the
community following his release from prison: "I can't accept that somebody like him should live freely here, and that children should think
that he is some kind of example to follow. This is one of the less pleasant
aspects of our *paesi montani* [mountain villages]." Silvana is a person
of note. In her early forties, university-educated, a successful engineer,
unmarried, and childless, she is a role model for younger local women
who aspire to a modern career and to the many personal freedoms that
this would entail. For Silvana, Giovanni is a symbol of utter failure, the
worst of what Sardinian culture has to offer. He drives a small truck
to and from his pastures, wears muddy boots and smells of livestock,
carries a pocket knife, which he uses for various work tasks but also to
eat and sometimes to clean his teeth, and his Italian is inflected with a
heavy rural accent. Moreover, he is capable of homicide. For Silvana,
Giovanni represents a way of life that most people have left behind. To
her relief, people like him are not in the majority: "Thankfully, we're not
all so backward here!" Along with other cosmopolitan-minded locals,
she espouses a rather different interpretation of the honour of the classic shepherd and his *balentia* that emphasizes only its positive, idealized, aspects: sobriety, self-restraint, discipline, hard work, as well as
hospitality and generosity – a set of standards informed by a spirit of
open-handedness and nonconfrontation. That is what shepherds ought
to be like, or anyway once were. To Silvana, *balentia* is, or should be, a
cultural ideal of personal decorum, not encumbered by considerations
of precedence, confrontation, or violence, and not in conflict with any
aspects of the law. In sum, Silvana's notion of *balentia* appears as a
highly sanitized conception of a code of honour that certainly does not
include vendetta. She is forthright in her condemnation of violence, violent action, and violent masculinity, which she believes are the bane of
highland Sardinian life but which too many people deny:

   I know that people here, shepherds especially, are sensitive to hearing it
   said that the feud thrives here, but it does. Just do an Internet search and

type in the words *faida* [feud] or *disamistade* [Sardinian word for compromised friendship, lit., "disamity"], and you will see all the many latest victims of *faida*. Of course, we should not generalize, but what, are we pleased only when people say how gracious and hospitable we are? It's true, but … *but* … we are not only angels, and not everyone loves peace here. So let us just accept ourselves for what we are, and know that things must change.

Now, what would Giovanni, or a man whose experiences and styles of life are not too dissimilar from his, say of a person such as Silvana? I do not know because I never asked him, but my friend Gonario – a shepherd in his mid-thirties – did have an opinion or two. For all his *braggadocio*, Gonario is the archetypally introspective shepherd; on one occasion, despite being a man of thrifty vocabulary, he did not mince words when telling me what he thought of career-oriented local women, especially one person whom he refused to name, but hinted I might already know:

> There is this woman in town – you even know her too – this woman is always travelling … This woman, is *sempre in giro* [she always travels around], here, there, everywhere! She says she travels for work, always in Milan and Rome and who knows where else. If you want to know what I think, I think she knows men in all these places. She visits them for a few days, and then when she's satisfied she comes back. And of course, she's not married! I don't know anyone who would ever marry her!

As Tracey Heatherington shows, such disapprobation of feminist womanhood is sometimes extended to unmarried women who circulate in the domain of electoral politics and who, at the very least, are regarded as untrustworthy, liminal, out-of-place figures (2010:198).

For the town of Baunei, 50 kilometres southeast of Orgosolo, Laura Assmuth (1998:162ff.) has shown that transformations in definitions of desirable womanhood are long in the making, and generations of girls and women born in the 1960s onward have lives that are permeated by consumerism, driven by ambition, and resolutely opposed to the standards and way of life of the older generation of middle-aged and elderly women. The ideal of *realizzarsi* – of self-actualization in the sense of achieving wealth and status beyond that of a traditional rural householder – is central to young women's aspirations, and, according to Assmuth, such women have been at the vanguard of a rapid process of social transformation in rural Sardinia. The skilful management of a household and a central role in the reproduction of local culture through childrearing – the marks of a *casalinga* (housewife) – provide no satisfaction to young women whose personal visions are informed by images of urban lifestyles and ideals of obtaining rewarding and remunerative work outside the home. Having earning and purchasing power is central to the well-being of any married couple as well, according to these younger women, as one salary is not enough to fulfil ideals of modern consumption (Assmuth 1997:165). According to Assmuth, while patterns of increasing consumerism were already widespread on the island by the 1970s, the chief bearers of a culture of affluence and consumerism are the generations born in the 1960s and after. But whereas the increasing affluence of the 1970s inaugurated an increase in consumerism and the emergent urbanization of young women's style, young men in the pastoral sector would opt to spend increasing sums on food and drink, which would give rise, throughout central Sardinia, to the construction of rustic kitchens, now *de rigueur* in many homes, and a concomitant preoccupation with feasting, especially within the context of that local institution, the *ispuntinu* (a sumptuous picnic). This masculine-inflected traditionalism stands in stark opposition to the urbane orientations of many young women, which are synonymous with a trangression of moral boundaries and an indulgence in moral degeneracy, according to local traditionalists. As Gonario told me over the course of the same conversation related above, "they always go out, go to discotheques, drug themselves, eat in fancy restaurants, and *fanno la bella vita* [live the good life] while we are here with nothing." The perceived decadence of life in the city is noteworthy. But such tirades should not be taken at face value. Rather, on the countless occasions in which pastoralist men adamantly proclaimed their views on anything (not just on local women), what I witnessed were performances intended for consumption among insiders within an insecure traditionalist male-dominated pastoral sector felt to be under siege. The outside world, with its aesthetics and values, provides alternatives to a traditional, "authentic" style of life that is firmly rooted, emplaced in the locality, and regarded as unique and irreproducible. Images of cosmopolitanism that circulate across all media are in evidence everywhere in Italian popular culture, their exaltation of urbanity, consumerism, and individualism both a source of consternation to localists and at the core of widespread feelings of cultural anxiety that affect local life.

The archetype of the ideal man espoused by such traditionalists – confident, tough, and unflinching – is anachronistic, and no longer constitutes the dominant persona of the twenty-first century. The changes that these localist men are experiencing today reflect the total transformation of a social order, and yet its denizens are not about to go quietly. Changing men's lives in Sardinia in particular, and Italy in general, may be considered from within a wider historical perspective – namely, one that adopts a frame of reference that sees men as targets of a conceptual domestication. The idea of the "domestication of men" is of course not new (see Ortner 1978; Wiener 1998). It is strongly suggested in the work of Antonio Gramsci (1975), who understood changes in Italian family life over the first two decades of the twentieth century to be a direct result of the emergent Fordist economic order, a system in which economic production and consumption were to be based upon the stability of the nuclear family, itself to become a site of consumption and of social reproduction.[2] This new institutional nexus required the disciplining of masculine as well as of feminine labour; the man who worked to exhaustion in a regimented factory environment would find a few hours' respite in the evening in his home, which was presided over by his wife. In Sardinia, this evident structural requirement of industrial production, and consequently of modernity, motivated post-unification Italian governments to curb, or at the very least regulate, pastoral production – an enterprise that sees an investment of masculine labour in the propagation of herds of livestock far into the countryside, spaces effectively beyond state control, and generating proceeds that are not easily taxable. Rendering the countryside legible has everywhere "simplified the classic state functions of taxation, conscription, and prevention of rebellion" (Scott 1998:2).

In this context of siege, what Michael Herzfeld (1988) calls "performative excellence" began to appear in social transactions on the Greek island of Crete. As holdouts to modernity in a now thoroughly interconnected world, pastoralists cannot be unselfconscious actors within their encapsulated universe. Theirs is a traditionalism that undermines the dominant order. Herzfeld's performative excellence refers of course to Cretan men's concern with effectively adhering to the exacting standards of masculinity to which men are constantly upheld: how well they are able to appear "good at being a man," how much *braggadocio* and virile posturing they are capable of performing convincingly. To paraphrase Ernest Gellner (1983), the impact of industrial modernity on the agrarian universe of formerly autonomous, laterally insulated communities rendered the economic foundations of local existence out of date, and – as in the current case – effectively isolated the traditionalists who persisted in the herding of livestock on open pastures. Therefore, highland shepherds in Crete, Sardinia, and elsewhere have come to comprise a distinct social category, a minority widely regarded as having somehow been left behind and said to be, to use that peculiarly modern epithet, *arretrati* – backward. The changed affective structure of the modern national citizen displaces Antonio Pigliaru's claim of blood feud as a social practice that involves the consent of all members of a community. Likewise, Alberto Ledda's (1971:145) suggestion that blood feud and livestock rustling and their corresponding rules are practices that conform to highland patterns of life is no longer appropriate to the changed circumstances of the twenty-first century, and the wide condemnation of these practices points to a change in values and orientations. Simple livestock rustling, within the old order, was a method by which one might make up for losses occasioned by the uncertainties of herding in harsh environments. Such a practice was not considered equivalent to stealing; rather, it was the clandestine appropriation of livestock, "wealth on the hoof," from unknown others who did the same in turn when the need or opportunity would arise. Protecting one's herd, increasing it through capable herd management, and, when necessary, taking livestock from competitors (who may have been in a similarly precarious position) were some of the elementary expectations that governed life on the pastures. The final aim to which all of the shepherd's energies were directed was the ability to meet the collective needs of the nuclear family. As Michelangelo Pira (1978:315) notes, young men in the Barbagia district who could not provide sufficiently for their family, with or without livestock rustling, could only find a wife with difficulty. To such a figure, only condemnation and slander could be proferred. Pira (1978:315) recorded the feminizing insult that such a man *es unu chi si morit in sa chisina* (is one who would let himself expire before the ashes of the kitchen fire), reluctant to venture away from the warmth and comfort of the hearth, and deprived of the fortune that could only favour the brave.[3]

With the advent of the twenty-first century, the era of late modernity, deindustrialization, labour mobility, the de-skilling of the labour force, and the triumph of the service economy, the stable nuclear family has ceased to be a structural prerequisite of the macroeconomic order and the role of men as providers has become far from obvious. The current crisis of male identity, in Italy and elsewhere, is fundamentally tied to this transformation, and it is a crisis that also affects rural shepherds on the outer edges of Europe, a social category that has long been marginalized. Economic insecurity, poor marriage prospects, and an inability to take advantage of opportunities for social mobility within the white-collar sector have all taken a toll on highland men's esteem, and have led, furthermore, to the emergence of a male revanchism expressed through an opposition to elements of the emergent neoliberal order – specifically, to consumerism, urbanism, cosmopolitanism, and mass-mediated popular culture.[4] In Orgosolo, the evident end result has been an involution of the shepherd's world that now more than ever stands opposed to the world of non-shepherds. This can be observed at even a superficial level, specifically in the conservative form of dress donned self-consciously by shepherds, who present a striking similarity in substance and style to the similarly marginalized and unmarried peasant men of Béarn described by Pierre Bourdieu (2002). These forlorn men have recourse to little else besides their condemnation. One other interlocutor, this time a local bar owner, related another story of the pretentiousness and opportunism deemed characteristic of women who have turned away from traditional values and obligations. His tone is especially judgmental, in large part because his target of opprobrium is a woman: "The daughter of one of our neighbours left and never came back. She was an only child and her parents sacrificed everything for her, and then she abandoned them. Now she lives in Genoa, married to a doctor, and she only comes to visit on holidays. If only you could see her, what a spectacle! She is now *una grande signora*! [a grand lady] "[5]

Among men, the distinctions between shepherds and non-shepherds are more than stylistic. The performative criteria of *balentia* and its associated masculine bravura are central to the maintenance of pastoral men's social distinctiveness. Furthermore, the world of the shepherd is associated with a range of exigencies that integrate the pastoral sector and distinguish it from the rest of the community. Violent interventions, the rectification of wrongs, and the avenging of slights real or perceived are commonplace. While the pastoral milieu should not be regarded as inherently violent, the possibility of violence is everywhere and implicit within *balentia*. This does not mean that acts of physical violence are ubiquitous. To the contrary, the appearance of social harmony is highly valued. But acts of violence that do occur are often devastating, usually carefully planned and executed, and never random or senseless. Often they are presaged by acts that serve as a warning to the intended victim, the victim's familiars, or to the community at large. Threats spray-painted on walls, handwritten lists of targeted individuals nailed onto the gates of a village cemetery, and the delivery of a funereal wreath to a man who was eventually killed all occurred in Orgosolo and the neighbouring village of Oliena in the period from 2002 to 2003. Also within Oliena, a mid-morning gangland slaying in a busy piazza by masked gunmen (*La Nuova Sardegna*, 11 December 2002:1); in Lula, the ambush of a police cruiser late at night by another team of gunmen with high-powered automatic weapons (*La Nuova Sardegna*, 28 January 2003:1). Both events bore witness to the dramatic outbursts to which expressions of violence can be given. In addition, livestock mutilation, bombings, and destruction of property, among other forms of intimidation, all frequently occur, to the displeasure of local people and to the consternation of police authorities. Despite this, the everyday image of social life in Orgosolo is one of neighbourly coexistence, of general conviviality beset by no rivalry or malaise. This is obviously not the whole story.

Two possibly related events punctuated the end of 2007 and start of 2008 in a style that seemed to underscore an evident turning inward of the pastoral sector from the wider society, or that accepted standards of honour and honourable action were being distorted. The first event was a murder that occurred in broad daylight on 29 December 2007; the victim was an elderly retiree, the renowned local Sardinian language poet and former political activist, Peppino Marotto (*La Nuova Sardegna*, 30 December 2007:1). Several days later, on 4 January 2008, a double murder took place, just outside the village limits; the victims were brothers, Egidio and Salvatore Mattana (*La Nuova Sardegna*, 5 January 2008:1). This bloodletting was a shock to Orgosolo, not only because of the age and status of the first victim but also for the auspicious dates on which the homicides were committed. These crimes remain unsolved, but, as with the murder of Don Graziano Muntoni on Christmas Eve of 1998, local opinion speaks to one of two possible explanations. First, Marotto may have been a victim of his alleged habit of reprimanding young troublemakers on the streets for their hooliganism, who, evidently, would no longer continue to suffer his reproach. Alternatively, his murder might have been a settling of accounts dating back several decades to his earlier years as a young shepherd, pointing to the enduring salience of vendetta and its absence of time limits. The murder of the Mattana brothers also has two local interpretations: either it was an immediate revenge killing for the murder of Marotto or it was intended to confound police authorities.

On a return visit to Orgosolo in July 2008, Lena, Marotto's daughter and one of my key interlocutors in 2002–2003, did not speak to me of her father's murder. However, as a bar owner, she had in previous years shared with me the frustrations associated with managing her business. Most of the challenges pertain to fear of certain patrons. Fieldnotes dating to March 2003 contain snippets of a short conversation I had with her at her home, sitting by the hearth with her husband, Mauro.

> Sometimes, a bar owner will get a certain type of customer, a little *balenteddu* [diminutive of *balente;* a wannabe], and, if lucky, he'll have some of his friends there, and they will start showing off their handguns, in plain sight! Now, a bar owner is not entitled in Orgosolo to enforce house rules, and if someone does kick out one of these hooligans, then they better be careful or they'll end up with a bomb at their bar. And so, if they stay and no one tells them to leave, and the police come? Then what? A bar owner is caught in the middle of things, and could lose his license! You go and speak to bar owners in Orgosolo, and they will all tell you this. People are worried for their safety because of how firm they must be with people like this, people who act like *i padroni* [the bosses] of this town.

Lena's position on the murder of her father is, at any rate, clearly laid out in a press release published on 7 January 2008 in the pages of *La Nuova Sardegna*, one of two regional newspapers and the most widely circulated daily in the province of Nuoro. This release is striking for its complete denial of allegations widely circulated in print and televised media of any connection between the murder of Peppino Marotto and the Mattana brothers, followed by a total renunciation of vendetta and a nod to values of pacifism, for which I have always known to be central to Lena's own values and world view:

> Zia Michela [Peppino's wife], Lena, and the entire Marotto family, grief-stricken by the tragic end of the Mattana brothers, neighbours with whom there has never been a dispute, reject in the strongest terms any association of these deaths with that of our beloved Peppino ... The Marotto family has full confidence in the justice system and rejects vendetta, and above all desires to reconfirm the values that Peppino Marotto believed in, which are those of solidarity, justice, and brotherhood.

The rejection of vendetta and adherence to pacifist values remain options to members of the community, and there is no reason to suppose that customary principles should be coercive. Matteo, a young man in his late twenties, born in Orgosolo, but a resident of the city of Nuoro by choice for most of the past decade and an occasional bartender on coastal resorts during the summer months, provides an example of possibilities open to youth. Matteo's rejection of dominant masculinity complexes is total, and his tolerance of local standards of male sociality is low. As the eldest child of a local shepherd killed under mysterious circumstances twenty years earlier, local expectations pointed to an eventual revenge killing. But Matteo had other ideas, hoping to leave Orgosolo and obtain training in the culinary arts, and maybe open a restaurant some day. By any measure, Matteo was a hard worker on his way to eventual success, even if his chosen path was punctuated by shaky fits and starts. Not able to live and work further afield, he was fond of visiting friends and family in Orgosolo in his free time. One of his friends in Orgosolo – unusual for this community – was a young police officer who worked in the local precinct. This fact was a source of local consternation, and his awareness of this sometimes made him wary visiting his hometown. As Matteo told me,

> I have always been a pacifist, and have always been glad for everyone to know this about me. And therefore, just for this reason, I'm afraid I might one day come to suffer consequences, strangely. For example, I was at the tobacconist's a few weeks ago, with my friend Agostino, who happens to be a *poliziotto*, and we were about to get in the car to drive to Nuoro to meet other friends for the evening, when a couple of guys walked by, and one of them said to me, loud enough for everyone to hear, "Instead of making friends with cops, you should find the man who killed your father." But *che cavolo* [what the hell]! What is that! Here's this ruffian trying to shame me! Why? For what? How am I supposed to find this man who killed my father? Should maybe I just find someone convenient and then get a gun and shoot him? It's ridiculous! If I even knew who did it, then I would report him so he would face justice, and I wouldn't kill him like an animal. But there, see, here is the issue, in Orgosolo, you can enjoy no freedom when you're different from everyone else. This is why I want to leave. Orgosolo is never a place where I could live, it's only a place that I could inhabit, and I don't want to.

Evidently, Matteo has come to accept, although deeply resent, his inevitable loss of status and reputation within one sector of the community for his failure to execute the customary practices central to *balentia*. His decision to opt out of local life obviates any concern for the consequences of his renunciation of blood feud, be they social or economic, for the simple reason that an outright rejection of honour values denies its centrality as a social standard. Because he is a man, his own rejection of vendetta entails a different range of consequences than it does for Silvana or Lena.

The murders of Peppino Marotto and the Mattana brothers, and of Matteo's father too, for that matter, remain unsolved. In cases of homicide or other violent crimes, local people rarely cooperate with authorities for fear of endangering their own well-being. Yet, public secrets and local gossip reveal one striking piece of information: young, disenfranchised shepherds with nothing to lose – unmarried men between twenty and forty years of age, subsisting on the margins, characteristically pitted against their similarly marginalized equals – are the normal perpetrators as well as targets of these acts of violence. They present a troubling mutation of the pastoral world, a sector where agonism, suspicion, despair, and violence are pervasive. As Gonario tells me, "Shepherds don't have a happy life. If only you knew how many take antidepressants. We're like wild animals, always in the countryside, no one will marry us, stuck in these mountains like so many prisoners." This feeling of despair and alienation is very real, and appears to be a result of structural changes within the pastoral economy that have occurred since the post-war period, yielding the current situation of cultural precarity. Even more than this, we are faced with a situation best defined in the forceful terms used by Karl Polanyi (2001 [1944]), namely, of a "social calamity," a condition of cultural dislocation borne by subjects extruded by the entrenchment of an economic order that displaces the denizens of the outgoing system. While social calamities are primarily cultural phenomena that are not easily measured by income figures or population statistics, the economic system may provide the vehicle of destruction, causing "lethal injury to the institutions" that formerly governed social life (Polanyi 2001 [1944]:164). The forces that prompted this transformation – specifically, *the* Great Transformation, to use Polanyi's famous term – are fundamentally exogenous, and imposed structures of modernity (and eventually postmodernity) from without. Local peoples everywhere were left in a situation of having to manage circumstances that would dominate their lives and structure their experiences in the new order. The full incorporation of the central highlands into the modern nation-state has had lingering effects upon the most marginal of communities, and their self-definitions vacillate by necessity between two modalities: either accepting or rejecting the cosmopolitan, urbane values of the new order. The salience of locality is maintained via an awareness of what history has had to offer. Chanelling Appadurai (1996:181), it seems that the centrifugal forces of modernity that are the source of social wear and flux, uncertainty and volatility, in local life are the goliath against which self-definitions compete.

My friend Angelo the *servo-pastore* provides a further example of the despair, the wounded pride, of so many local men. His younger sister, Luigina, is employed in an electronics store in Sassari that specializes in cellular communications, and represents a further instance of the ability of local women to adapt to opportunities in the new economy, at least compared with men. Although I had never met Luigina, I knew that she was held in high esteem by her big brother, who never tired of praising her intelligence and accomplishments. Her graduation with a *laurea* (the main post-secondary degree in Italy) from the University of Sassari a few years earlier was a momentous occasion for her and her entire family, and was celebrated with great pride; she was the first of her family to receive a university degree. While her success is relative – after all, she has been facing a precarious job market, as are countless other young people in Italy today – she, according to Angelo, escaped the plight of a life in Orgosolo. "But I still wish she was here more often. It's a pity, but she is happier not being here, of this I'm certain." In an introspective moment, having a slow smoke while slouched in an old chair inside his *cuile*, sheep-herding station, Angelo shares a thing or two about his own perceived sense of failure and, between puffs, reflects on the alternatives to what his forty years of life have offered him, if only he had been born under different circumstances – namely, mine.

> You are very lucky, Tò. You came here, lived for a year, met so many different people, and soon you will go back and teach at a university. And they paid you to do this! I too would have liked to have done what you do. To travel, see the world, to study, meet people. But I'm here, and I'll be here forever, with the sheep. You are lucky to have been born in a civilized country. Here, we're animals. You, [laughs heartily] you will leave us here and go back home and bed all the women you want with the stories you will tell them about your adventures in the *montagne selvagge* [wild mountains] of Sardinia!

Angelo's own success with women is limited. On the table beside him, a copy of *La Nuova Sardegna* is still open on the last page, where a small personals section advertises escort services; earlier, he had been making phone calls to arrange an appointment for the following day. Poor Angelo's luck has been scarce, and his experiences are indelibly inscribed on his not-so-old body – a defective back, strained by the regular milking of livestock, crooked and missing teeth, and a slight physical disability, the result of a wound suffered years earlier from an act of violence. His own past enmeshment in a world of extralegality – like many shepherds, Angelo has had numerous brushes with the law, but never served hard time – represents a microcosm of the tragedy that is so often the shepherd's life.

Transformation of the Pastoral Economy

In Sardinia, a reconfiguration of gender expectations has followed an inexorable tertiarization of the regional economy.[6] The rise of the service economy requires skills and aptitudes that favour a feminine workforce, therefore excluding young men from a wide range of emerging opportunities. The angst felt and expressed by local men engaged in the pastoral economy revolves around the precariousness that characterizes their lives. Excluded from the new economy, there are only so many cooperatives and *caseifici* (cheesemaking facilities) to purchase their raw milk, and only so many local and regional family-owned butchers and restaurants to purchase mutton, goat, pork, and, to a lesser extent, beef. As a result, innumerable men supplement their enterprises with additional work, mostly odd jobs, or make do with a bare-minimum level of economic activity, relying on family networks and often on financial assistance from aging parents, to get by.[7]

In addition, the herding of livestock and the upkeep of flocks are tasks that are today less arduous than they were in the past, as transhumant migration has all but ceased to be vital to highland shepherding. Likewise, the use of commercially available feed, purchased at subsidized prices, has meant that great portions of common lands, especially the vast Supramonte plateau, today remain unused for herding. According to Orgosolo's *assessore alla pastorizia* (town councillor for pastoralism), about 75 per cent of existing animals in the village are kept ("pastured" would be an inaccurate term) on about 10 or 15 per cent of all the commons year-round. Motorized transportation has made this possible, and has also altered the pastoral economy by rendering residence away from the village during the winter months unnecessary. A shepherd can now can drive out to his sheepfold twice daily, carry out all necessary tasks, and return to the village where he spends the rest of his time. An excursion to commons contiguous to the village reveals a striking abundance of small herds of sheep, cattle, and pigs left to graze untended. Animal husbandry of all forms thrives in Orgosolo, with a proliferation of variably sized registered *allevamenti* (stockraising units): 114 registered sheep and goat-raising units, 103 registered cattle operations, and 42 registered swineherds (ISTAT 2010). Registered enterprises are individually owned, and a herder may diversify his holdings by registering two operations (for example, be simultaneously a cattleman as well as a shepherd). In instances in which holdings exceed one man's ability to work independently, a *servo-pastore* may be hired, and these may as often be registered as unregistered employees. In sum, stockraising's contribution to the local economy is noteworthy in Sardinia, even if official data indicate that agriculture, forestry, and fisheries together contributed 3 per cent of the region's gross domestic product in 2011, while the service sector contributed 81.8 per cent (Banca d'Italia 2013:55).[8] Furthermore, shepherds, already enduring low profit margins, saw a precipitous decline of 27 per cent in cheese prices from 2008 to 2010 as a result of a drop in US demand for Pecorino Romano cheese during that period (Furesi, Madau, and Pulina 2013). From a financial standpoint, the pastoral sector is ailing.

In terms of productive practices, highland pastures lying fallow during the winter months (a seasonal practice called *su vardau*) are a thing of the past. As a result, shepherds now reside in the village year-round, which, according to many of my interlocutors, has led to a greater masculine presence within the village. Many non-shepherds, in their wistful imaginings of the past, were fond of saying "we don't have real shepherds here anymore, but we have plenty of *pastori finti* [pretend shepherds]," men who apparently only look and play the part, but are not subjected to the harshness of the transhumant shepherd's life. Among some interlocutors, these *pastori finti* cannot be *balentes,* for they have never had to test their mettle living in the remote pastures nor have they been subjected to the harsh elements for months on end, struggling for their bread. Daniele, a married, middle-aged, shop owner was fond of the term *balenteddus* (little balentes),which he used in derogatory reference to young umarried men who dressed and played the part of shepherds, but were little more than *balordi* or *teppisti* (yobs or hooligans) who know only how to posture and strut, carry firearms, and shoot streetlamps and road signs for amusement – a common occurrence and the bane of the local administration. What this jibe makes reference to is nothing less than the contemporary manifestation of a profound shift in masculine subjectivity within the highly altered circumstances of late modernity. Not wishing to work in the highly profitable tourism sector on the coastal resorts where expensive hotels do brisk business in the summer months, or in office service jobs in the cities of mainland Italy (which, as noted, offers few opportunities for them), many young men opt to stay in Orgosolo year-round, working part-time in the local forestry department as handymen doing odd jobs, or even as facilitators in small local ecotourism outfits.[9] These activities, at least, allow them to work outdoors, where their subservience to employers is kept at a minimum and where a tone of egalitarian respect is the norm. In sum, shepherds' awareness of their own marginality is concealed by their masculine persona that underscores ideals of autonomy and toughness, traits that are emphasized where the indices of success have come to constitute a moving target as far as young men are concerned.[10]

The moniker of *pastore finto* applies to young men who do not engage fully, but rather seasonally, in pastoral production, the rest of the time working at various odd jobs as opportunities arise. An important source of steady but seasonal income is afforded by employment in the Foresta Demaniale Montes, a protected territory under the jurisdiction of the regional forestry department, the Azienda Foreste Demaniali, encompassing 4,635 hectares of common lands. Orgolesi avail themselves of two hundred seasonal positions on a six-month rotating basis – one hundred positions in the winter and spring months, and another hundred in the summer and autumn. The presence of this protected district, and the employment it offers (reforestation, manning fire lookout points, maintaining dirt roads, collecting fallen timber for distribution as firewood, etc.) has been a mixed blessing for the community. As numerous seasonal forestry workers suggested, it keeps many young men from leaving Orgosolo permanently, which has been good for the maintenance of a steady local population. However, seasonal employment on this site also makes workers unemployable elsewhere; the six-month commitments are full time, but what to do during the other six months? Many young men do not want to be seasonal employees forever, and resent the predicament such work places them in. For the remaining six months, most only manage to work occasional stints in construction or as *servo-pastori*. Such circumstances are not enviable, but the positions are nonetheless highly prized.

These underemployed shepherds are heirs to a much longer historical and economic development associated with the emergence of an
international market in Pecorino Romano cheese at the end of the nineteenth century. Primarily meeting demand among Italian immigrants
to the Americas, the increased production of Pecorino Romano from
the 1950s through to the 1980s saw an expansion of the pastoral sector
in central Sardinia along with the dwindling of small-scale agriculture,
which could not be effectively modernized because of the high degree
of fragmentation of land ownership (Mientjes 2004:174). Two generations in, however, the emergence of pastoral monocropping would lead
to the eventual saturation of demand for pecorino in global markets,
which would have serious consequences for the sustainability of local
pastoral economies (Vargas-Cetina 2000). The collapse of milk prices –
in the first decade of the twenty-first century, prices fluctuated between
€0.65 and €0.75 per litre, less than the cost of production – has rendered
pastoral pursuits barely remunerative without subsidies provided
under the European Union Common Agricultural Policy. However,
since 2000, these subsidies have been phasing out owing to pressure
from the United States and the General Agreement on Tariffs and Trade
(GATT) (Vargas-Cetina 2011). The Movimento dei Pastori Sardi (Sardinian Shepherds Movement), a small but militant shepherd's union, has
called attention to the plight of the Sardinian shepherd in the twenty-
first century through street protests and occasional campaigning, but
to seemingly limited avail. Fortunately, rural highland Sardinians,
especially shepherds, have always been flexible and dynamic in their
socioeconomic activities, ably responding to difficult economic circumstances by engaging in pursuits – labour migration, tourism, handyman
and construction work – that buffer against the uncertainty of pastoral
production (see Mientjes 2004:185–6). In Orgosolo, many small, unregistered shepherds to whom herding is a part-time endeavour do not
draw from EU subsidies, but rather supplement their income through
other forms of irregular employment, exemplifying the composite economic strategies widely adopted locally.

It is worth nothing that although the increased male presence in the
village year round has not entailed an increased masculinization of the
domestic sphere, it has led to an increased ruralization of village space.
The presence of shepherds within the centre of Orgosolo, drinking and
whiling away the hours in the many bars that cater to their tastes, and
the proliferation of old, beat-up work vehicles on village streets that are
used primarily for completing tasks related to livestock raising, present

a mutation of an older pattern that saw men out in the distant pastures for months at a time only to return for holidays and festivities. Perhaps even more noticeable than this is the ubiquity of horses raised and kept in stalls maintained on small holdings just outside the village. The popularity of raising horses in central Sardinia is tremendous, and the favoured breed, the Anglo-Arabo Sardo (Sardinian Anglo-Arabian crossbreed), is a source of great regional pride. However, the modern pastoral economy does not require the use of horses, and the equestrian pastimes of my friends and acquaintances are a matter of aesthetic pleasure and, it hardly needs to be said, a definitive marker of rural, pastoral identity. One can see horses on the streets of Orgosolo any time of day, any day of the week, and any season of the year. Horsemen ride their steeds into town, show them off, order drinks from outside the bars and consume them on horseback, then move on to the next one, in the process extending their symbolic control, as ever, over the central spaces of the village. The stylistic canon to which these horsemen adhere is that of the classically attired shepherd described earlier: black corduroy or velvet trousers with boots and gaitors and a white shirt, sometimes with the colourful traditional costume sewn by local artisans. Horses are brought into town most frequently at festival time – especially the village patron saints' day of Saints Peter and Paul in June, and during the week of festivities surrounding the Assumption of the Virgin Mary in mid-August. The participation of the riders is central to organized processions on these occasions, but, beyond the more solemn religiously sanctioned performances, they also participate in *sa vardia*, a skilled form of horse racing that includes feats of trick riding within the built-up spaces of the village. Young men gain recognition for their equestrian skills and hair-raising stunts, which include kneeling and standing on their horses at full gallop, or locking arms and forming pyramids of three riders on two untethered horses, likewise at full gallop. *Sa vardia* attracts many visitors from neighbouring towns and villages, and the spectacle creates a moment of collective effervescence for participants and spectators alike. However, by introducing the sights, smells, and sounds of rurality into the central spaces of Orgosolo, these riders call attention to an image of local culture that is strongly inflected by the pastoral identity. As such, they are met with ambivalence. Following *sa vardia*, young men will ride their horses, many of them not sufficiently trained to ride safely in crowds, into the busy streets and narrow alleys, causing unease among pedestrians, wreaking havoc with vehicular traffic (see Heatherington 1999). Aside from defecating everywhere, horses sometimes kick cars and even people, and accidents and mishaps are frequent. In sum, this causes everyone but the hardiest (and hardest-drinking) to flee the streets of Orgosolo.

For many such young men, the home is a place principally reserved for meals and rest, where few waking hours are spent. Once shepherds spent much of the year away from the village to herd livestock in the commons and, in the winter months, on the lowlands; today, they spend much of their time in homosocial settings in or near the village. The term, *Paese dei balocchi* (Land of Toys), is often used, tongue-in-cheek but with acerbic overtones, by some Orgolesi to describe the nature of local life as they see it. This Italian term, intended to designate a societal tendency toward light and irresponsible behaviour, has its origin in Carlo Collodi's allegorical 1883 fable, *The Adventures of Pinocchio*, and refers to the fantastical village to which the wooden protagonist is lured in his attempt to escape the Odyssean ordeals that would transform him from a puppet to a human boy (a metaphor, of course, for the transition from boyhood to manhood). The diversions in question concern the limitless ways in which responsibility can be evaded, and all that this entails – namely, a lack of seriousness and gravitas, discipline, tenacity, self-denial, planning for the future, and so on. "We live in the *Paese dei balocchi*," I was told more than once. One poignant observation, shared with me during the February carnival celebrations in 2002, is hard to forget: "We eat, we drink, we amuse ourselves, and we pilfer our old mothers' and fathers' pensions to do it. Don't delude yourself, Antò, this place is fallen from the grace of God."

This pessimistic understanding of community, though genuine, is not complete. Intense sociability among men and the feasting and merrymaking that characterize it encompass conceptions of proper behaviour and deportment for the male sex. Men may cavort and socialize for many hours on end, seemingly not engaged in any productive undertaking, then return home at night only to begin the routine anew the next day. This demonstration of social identity primarily takes place at bars – the salons of the marginalized, one local woman called them – where young men spend a large portion of their free time. More than just centres of amusement, they are places where the performative element of *balentia* is most clearly observed, where social ties are recreated, and where social reputations are upheld and put on display. To everyone else, however, these are merely sites of merriment, where the responsibilities of real life are suspended and where young men trade their duties for their desires. The ends to which recognition for toughness, machismo, for performative excellence – for being a *balente* – are put to use remains difficult to ascertain for non-shepherds, especially if the mastery of such traits occurs in a context of leisure, in which one glass of beer follows another in an interminable series of rounds.

Male Sociability and the Bar

There is general agreement in Orgosolo that bar life can be difficult. However, it is essential for most non-elderly men to pay regular visits to these centres of male sociability, where being publicly noticed is part of the process of obtaining social recognition. This is especially the case within the pastoral sector, particularly for young, umarried men whose bar attendance is most regular and frequent. The willingness with which young men are required to offer themselves up to public scrutiny makes frequency of bar attendance a subject of criticism, both among regulars and nonparticipants. "We like to be in the company of friends," one is often told, or "we are amicable, we like to spend time with others and *fare amicizia* [make new friends]." Such statements are often proffered with the rejoinder, "but you can't let yourself get carried away." Getting "carried away" in this context refers to the overconsumption of alcohol and, more generally, to the amount of time spent in bars. Although the rules of conduct vary, highly discernible patterns of interaction repeat themselves in all of Orgosolo's bars, making it possible to ascertain guidelines to proper behaviour. Despite the numerous bars in Orgosolo, each catering to different tastes, there are consistent and clearly defined rules of social exchange that define all interactions in these spaces (Sorge 2009). We must therefore highlight the role of these exchanges, both verbal and symbolic. To enter a bar is to enter a public space – and, consequently, to subject oneself to scrutiny – with the intention of engaging in ritualized transactions structured by pattern of speech, tone of voice, and overall demeanor appropriate to the setting. Proper bar etiquette requires a measure of discretion, politeness, and reserve, yet also raised voices, boisterousness, and posturing. The atmosphere of the bar tends toward ambivalence. It is both an arena of amicable exchange and cordiality as well as of agonistic rivalry and suspicion, at once convivial and competitive and reflective of the strain perennially felt in Orgosolo between self-interest and social solidarity. It is a place where mundane rules of social interaction are replaced by a set of fluid expectations, necessarily volatile and subject to negotiation, and often dependent upon the interpersonal dynamics of those present as well as upon the level of alcohol consumed. Orgolesi in bars tell tales, argue, joke, gossip, interrogate, exchange information, and talk about politics, sports, the weather, women, and nothing at all. The structures of verbal duelling are heavily laced with irony, wit, innuendo, double entendres, ambiguity of meaning, and the quick rejoinder. To enter a bar is to enter a playing field where the intent of interaction centres in part on the ability to successfully undermine one's interlocutor, display one's own eloquence, and establish social precedence.

The exchange of drinks usually proceeds at a relentless pace, particularly in the evenings. A momentary lull in conversation occurs whenever someone enters a bar; strangers are usually greeted with prolonged stares, followed by an amicable or cool greeting (or sometimes no greeting at all). Ordering a beverage is *de rigueur*. "Only spies and the sick do not drink," I was often reminded, and paying for a drink after establishing a rapport with a regular client is virtually impossible; in my experience, any insistence was usually rebuffed with the phrase "don't worry" or "you're my guest." A patron who is a member of the community proceeds differently. He is known to be a local, and greetings are exchanged in accordance with his relationships to those already present. If his friends are in attendance, then he will sit or stand with them by the bar and engage in the reciprocal exchange of beverages, usually small glasses of red wine or *mesu birras* – stemmed Belgian-style tumblers half-filled with local *Ichnusa* brew – which are ordered every few minutes so that all members of the group are not excluded and payment of rounds is roughly equal. Those who are not solvent cannot hope to participate fully in this form of exchange, and numerous bars in Orgosolo routinely ban unreliable clients from establishing a monthly tab. The *scroccone* (sponger) and the *miserabile* (miser) are in the unfortunate position of having hospitality bestowed upon them, and their failure to pay, a result either of insolvency or reluctance, places them in a subordinate position to those who can. To have only one drink is normally impossible, and to drink alone is unusual. A rapport is established with the exhortation to accept a drink, known as s'*invitu*. "*Piha una cosa* [Take something]!" is the standard phrase expressing a host's desire to inaugurate an exchange that may last for a few minutes or several hours. The refusal of s'*invitu* due to unwillingness to engage in dialogue may be construed as a rebuff. As such, any refusal must be accompanied by a justification, as well as an apology. Refusng s'*invitu* in order to attend a previously scheduled engagement or to attend to a task requiring immediate attention is acceptable, but of course must be followed by a quick exit. To remain in a bar after having refused *s'invitu* amounts to a possible solicitation of rancour, especially if a drink is later accepted from someone else or purchased and consumed by oneself. The guest's appeal to physical ailment serves no purpose, because someone who is unfit to consume alcohol may still request a non-alcoholic beverage, of which every bar is well stocked. While the amount of alcohol consumed in any single night can be quite considerable, displays of drunkenness are not well tolerated. Recognition is bestowed upon those capable of consuming significant amounts of alcohol without appearing too ine-briated. Staggered gait, slurred speech, vomiting, and general incoher-ence are symptomatic of an absolute failure to engage maturely and honourably with one's fellows, while hearty approval is bestowed upon those can who drink heavily but who are capable of retaining coherence. It is ignoble to be expelled from a bar, and avoiding these centres of male sociability is hardly an option for it implies an accep-tance of social demotion.

Despite the many similarities in patterns of socialization found throughout all bars in Orgosolo, clients tend to frequent a limited set of establishments. By and large, shepherds, forestry workers, tradesmen, and athletic youth only frequent bars that cater to their own associates and peers, and will even go so far as to avoid others. Sets of prominent, or at least known, friendship groups also frequent specific bars, and only out of convenience will they enter and take refreshments in estab-lishments where they are not regulars. Bar owners know their clientele very well, and establish an atmosphere they know will be welcoming to their clients. Sports bars will always have a large-screen television showing sporting events, with athletic paraphernalia on its walls; smoking tends to be discouraged.[11] Shepherds' bars, on the other hand, are more spartan in décor, and favour playing music in lieu of tele-visions, usually traditional highland tenor singing and various styles of Sardinian folk music. Young shepherds are usually found in the *bar del centro* (centre-town bars, also known as shepherds' bars, or *tzilleros 'e sos pastores*), and as a general rule will not patronize bars known to cater to different occupational classes, where they will not find the style of sociality that reflects the habitus they have come to adopt and exem-plify. The atmosphere of the shepherds' bars is of a very particular type, and these establishments, prominently clustered in the centre of the vil-lage, are locally renowned as spaces to avoid unless one is part of the cohesive pastoral occupational group. Town functionaries and young professionals attend an even more restricted number of bars, ones that are quieter, more urbane, and well stocked with more expensive imported products (such as the few mixed-sex establishments). These have an atmosphere notably less confrontational and agonistic than the shepherds' haunts. This is the pattern seen throughout the Sardinian interior, where most bars are exclusively male social spaces; in the low-lands and coastal towns and cities, the notion that women should not go to bars is a thing of the past.

Being the principal centres of male sociability, bars are both defined and pervaded by the social and occupational personalities of their patrons. So too are the spaces immediately beyond their front doors, with the entranceway to the bar serving as a space subject to definition by those who are most closely contiguous to it. Tables and chairs placed outside the front doors and alongside the perimeter transform the public space beyond the bar into a claimed area, used – and hence defined – by the paying clients of the bar. A bar ceases to be a self-contained space when this occurs, and its patrons lay claim to observing and commenting the passing scene. Such monopolization of public space is most notable among the *bar del centro*, to the occasional discomfort of passersby. The running commentary on community life so central to interactions in public spaces makes tangible the perspectives of members of different social categories, with most of it so closely interwoven with the fabric of daily life as to render it, at the level of shared perceptions, essential to any form of sociability - it is just "what we do," they say, and one may sometimes hear the old Italian proverb, uttered with humour, "the village is small, people talk." Spur-of-the moment jibes and gossip in face-to-face communities such as Orgosolo, much of it directed towards seemingly oblivious passersby, is constant. The casual words express judgments about proper decorum and behaviour, and much of this gossip inevitably follows group and occupational lines. Gossip is also a performative act, wherein the intention of the speaker is to identify and proclaim himself as a holder of standards highly estimated among the actors present. Max Gluckman (1963) emphasizes that gossip reinforces in-group identities because it is typically directed towards those very members who make up the group. Within Orgosolo they also reinforce in-group identity precisely by being directed externally, towards those who are excluded. In the present context, gossiping might be viewed as an actor's plea to social others for their recognition of symbolic capital held and esteemed.

Shepherds engage in more than occasional gossip, and their observations and commentaries directed towards non-shepherds are particularly noteworthy, for the latter do not share in the former's universe. When shepherds make jibes and comments directed at non-shepherds, or vice-versa, the words become an expression of assertion of social difference, and therefore take on a particular meaning. This can be observed in the way in which people go about their daily rounds, always careful to act in a manner commensurate with their status. Therefore, as my friends and informants, both within and outside the *ambiente pastorale* (pastoral setting), regularly talked and gossiped, specific patterns of social cleavage emerged.

Some examples will illustrate this. My friend Serafino always drove straight through the central portion of the Corso Repubblica without stopping, usually remaining tight-lipped and bemused as he observed the socializing that took place. On occasion, a friendly greeting would compel him to stop his car and reciprocate in a ritualized or stereotyped exchange of *sas novas*, casual news, with an acquaintance or associate. When I asked him why he never frequented these bars, he replied, simply, "I don't go there." When nudged for more, he acceded: "Not that I have anything against the people there, it's just that I never go. I don't know the bar owners, really, and I don't know many of the clients. Anyhow, it's a world unto its own, where the shepherds go! As long as I'm not a *buzzuru* [ruffian], or a *peddone* [from *pedde*, the goatskin capes once worn by shepherds], I don't think I would be all that welcome, you know." Another casual conversation with Daniele, the shop owner, reveals a similar attitude. He and his wife, Pasqualina, have two young children, and actively avoid the main strip in the evenings: "It's impossible to even take a walk after a given hour," he once told me. "There are speeding cars everywhere, drunk people, not the place to go and have an *passegiata* [evening stroll] with your wife and small children." When I asked him where he did prefer to go, he said Nuoro, the local provincial capital 25 kilometres away: "It is not as bad there. They close the Corso [Garibaldi] to all traffic in the evenings. And the people are different, more *tranquilli* [easygoing]." As in the village of Telemula (a pseudonym used by Ayora-Diaz [1993]) in the neighbouring Ogliastra district, shepherds in Orgosolo claim the central public spaces. Unlike in Telemula, however, Orgosolo has nothing resembling an evening *passegiata*, as gruff and hard-drinking men, mostly shepherds, have appropriated village spaces in the evenings altering the atmosphere to the point where these spaces are disagreeable to everyone else (see Ayora-Diaz 1993:255–6). On another day, I was in a car with Francesco and Maria Antonia, young professionals living in Cagliari but on a summer visit back to Orgosolo. The Corso Repubblica is a major thoroughfare within the village, and all local traffic must, in one way or another, be directed along a stretch of it, forcing everyone to drive past the cluster of shepherds' bars on a regular basis. A singular quip offered by Maria Antonia and the smirk on Francesco's face spoke volumes: "As you can see, Antonio, all the best ones have stayed." The context of this quip should be noted: we had been discussing their lives away from Orgosolo and the question of whether they intended to return for good one day. Their answer at the time was ambivalent; they missed their families, but they did not miss the *ambiente,* ambiance. Giovanna, a member of the town council and small businesswoman, offered a different view of the young shepherds of the bars on the Corso Repubblica:

> Some people tell me these young men do nothing good with their lives. It's true, in a way. But in the end, who can blame them? They don't have much, they don't ask for much, and yet they are who we are. They give Orgosolo its fame. They're charming *mascalzoni* [scoundrels], they look and stare at you but who do they hurt? Me, for my part, I like walking down the Corso and seeing them that way. They almost seem like Mexicans, with the dreamy gaze, and if you say hello to them, they sometimes just furl their brows, like you have even noted yourself. They do it to me, too, you know. All they need is sombreros! The tourists love them!

Appropriately enough, Giovanna is the *assessore al turismo* (town councillor for tourism). Salvatore, owner of a sports bar away from the town centre, provided a more strongly worded opinion when I asked him rather candidly whether his establishment catered to any shepherds.

> Shepherds? Here? Do you see any? No, they don't come here much, obviously. And it's better that way. They always drink too much and cause trouble. And the way people are here, is that when they drink, they get litigious. They lose their heads. And the problem is that these *balentes* carry knives, guns, and before you know it, it's me who could end up in trouble if I have these types around. At any rate, I don't like drunkards, and I don't hesitate to kick them out. And that way I make enemies. It's a thankless job! Do you see the mess every night on the Corso? That's what it could be like here if some kinds of people started showing up. You know, maybe I don't get as many clients as other bars, but the clients I do have are good. I'm happy the way I have things now.

With her characteristic verve, Silvana, who obtained a university degree in Milan, who now works in Nuoro, and whose only relationship with Orgosolo is to use it as a place to rest and sleep in the evenings, speaks her mind about the topic of the shepherds' bars:

> You probably shouldn't spend much time in those bars. The people will close ranks when someone like you appears. And you won't be shown genuine hospitality then. All you will find is people not really interested in your presence, and if they have anything much to say to you, it will be with the idea of amusing themselves at your expense. You won't notice this, because they'll hide it from you, but you go in, order something, and start chatting. They'll chat with you, but when you look the other way they'll make faces and gestures at one another, as if to say 'What's this type doing in here? When is he leaving?' There are other people to talk to anyway if you want to know interesting things about Orgosolo.

On the other hand, shepherds' criticisms of non-shepherds are tinged with condescension, for these other Orgolesi – although they may be friendly acquaintances or even relatives – have been led astray from a purer calling. This criticism is directed towards the appearance, habits, and values of non-shepherds. Generally, they do not voluntarily partake of the sociability of shepherds' circles, nor are they integrated into these circles for reasons of occupation, lifestyle, and habitus. Therefore, they rest beyond the strict moral-cum-stylistic imperatives to which the conduct of shepherds must conform. Sometimes questions of appearance are brought to the fore as examples of what *noi pastori* (we shepherds) are not. Therefore, on a bright Sunday afternoon, Gonario, one of my casual acquaintainces and a secondary entry point into the world of pastoralism, motioned towards a passerby with a movement of his chin as we were leaning on a wall outside of the *bar del centro*. "Look at that one," he whispered with a sneer. The individual he was referring to was a thin, tall young man with whom I was not acquainted, maybe in his mid-twenties, with longish hair; he was walking along with two other young women. "He is wasting so much of his time with girls," says Gonario, "that he is starting to look like one."[12]

Such spontaneous commentary directed towards passersby is constant, and the casualness with which judgments are made towards both outsiders and cosmopolitans reflects an attitude of "endosociality" (Ekholm-Friedman and Friedman 1995), which separates these localists-among-the-localists from all others. This separateness is also manifested on a sartorial level. As Umberto Cocco and Giampiero Marras put it, the dark velvet or corduroy outfit worn regularly by shepherds in Orgosolo and other highland villages, is a symbol of resistance against urbanity, emblematic of "a warrior struggling not only against hostile nature and his competitors on meagre pastures, but all of civilization with all of its styles, including vestiary ones" (2000:34).

My own difficulty in entering into this inner circle of localists can serve as an example. Simply put, my research among localists and cosmopolitans required me to straddle the expectations of both. My scholarly persona distanced me from localists, as it aligned me with cosmopolitans. Yet many of the questions I wanted to pursue required that I become familiar with numerous individuals from a broad cross-section of the population. Getting to know localists required me to adapt to their habits and conditions, engaging them on their own terms. Although this is not an unsusual demand of ethnographic fieldwork, it can be challenging in its resultant appearance of indeterminate affiliation. I harboured suspicions that some Orgolesi found it unbecoming of a scholar to spend his time among shepherds in the bars, cantinas, and pastures, drinking, smoking, and eating. What could they possibly teach me? Likewise, associating with cosmopolitans kept me away from my shepherd friends, one of whom intercepted me one day as I was walking to the library to meet a town councilor. Gesturing towards my more-formal-than-usual outfit, he humorously asked, "Are you heading to court?" To the library, I replied. "Ah, leave that be, you'll go tomorrow; today you come with us!" With those words, he led me into the nearest bar, and offered me a drink. I left after a brief time in order to make my appointment, with the assurance that I would return a few hours later, which I did, resulting in a long evening of boisterous socializing that I had earlier intended to avoid. Over the course of that evening, a few of the men in the clique I had become acquainted with taunted me, in good-natured fashion, about my sartorial choices. I had not changed my outfit from earlier, and was still wearing a shirt and jacket, rendering me conspicuous. "You're not embarrassed being seen with us here, are you, Antonio? So elegant as you are!" Some of the patrons who did not know me inquired whether I was a town hall employee or a police officer. They were slightly disarmed when they learned I was a harmless anthropologist; while plying me with drinks, they interrogated me on my real reasons for being in Orgosolo.

The statements made candidly by shepherds in informal contexts indicated a profound realization of the deeper distinctions between themselves and outsiders, more so than comments about other people's outward appearances did. "We shepherds think and act a certain way, we maintain the old values of tenacity in the face of hardship, we are unpretentious, we preserve the old ways, and so on. We are, in other words, the real Orgolesi." This claim is begrudgingly accepted with an equal measure of condemnation and admiration on the part of a large number of Orgolesi only a generation or two removed from the pastoral economy. At the same time, shepherds and non-shepherds are each for the other a frequent target of mockery, despite shared membership in the local community and the ties of kinship that frequently unite them. The opacity of local reality underscores the difficulty in ascertaining the standards by which the *balente* is to be judged, and, for that matter, of what *balentia* even consists. This is a source of concern, and a subject of scrutiny and evaluation in a context in which people's judgment speaks loudly to contrasting ideals. Furthermore, as a differential process of esteem allocation, *balentia* should serve as a ready indicator of status hierarchies. However, when there is little agreement as to what a *balente* is even supposed to be, the observer is often left wondering where the lines are drawn. The best approximation of the local dynamics at play is found in the suggestion that we are dealing with two highly divergent representations of what constitutes proper standards of masculine behaviour worthy of esteem. Therefore, two broad social categories generally seem to offer themselves up as representative of divergent standards. On the one hand are the localists, whose habitus and ontology revolve around the recreation of an earthy locality. Their most staunch exemplars are the shepherds, who are exclusively male and traditionalist. On the other hand are the cosmopolitans, young men and women whose normative orientations are informed by a more individualistic set of values, and whose sights are directed outward, toward a more globally connected ecumene. Each of these two social categories, discerned here with a heuristic intent, are defined by their own distinctive life-worlds, and the opposition between the two is striking. The following chapter considers the various facets of the distinction between localism and cosmopolitanism by reprising and elaborating some of the themes explored earlier.

5
Divergent Visions

Sardinia is incorporated into a modern nation-state that is a member of the G8 group of nations, the North Atlantic Treaty Organization (NATO), the European Union (EU), and, as of 2002, this supranational organization's economic and monetary union. At the national level, Italy has employed a standardized national language since unification in 1861. Orgosolo, therefore, and the Barbagia district in which it is located, is certainly not immune to any of the great currents, contemporary and historic, that have shaken the rest of Italy, Europe, and the world over the past several generations. Everyone owns television sets, radios, and telephones. Even personal computers are no longer rare commodities. Effective literacy is the norm, and daily newspapers and magazines are widely circulated. Most of the consumer products available in Milan, Naples, and Rome are also available in Orgosolo or in the nearby provincial capital of Nuoro. Networks of communication are well-developed and ease of transportation is now taken for granted.

Despite this, Orgosolo is emphatically and unmistakably a distinctive locale, distinguishable from neighbouring villages, to say nothing of other towns or cities in Sardinia or on the Italian mainland. Orgosolo is not singularly unique, however; its study can tell us much about rural communities elsewhere on the island, and subsequently about the wider social system of which it is part, which notably incorporates both halves of a sociological duality: localism and cosmopolitanism. This chapter examines the dynamics of this duality, and outlines how ideas, values, and images that originate from beyond the community are locally engaged. Preceding this duality is the classic divide between the Great and the Little Traditions, with localists and cosmopolitans corresponding with distinct cultural styles that embody contrasting aesthetic and value orientations. As we will see, localists' understanding of cosmopolitan lifestyles is tinged with ambiguity, and evaluated according to standards that are no longer normative in Orgosolo. I suggest that the localist-cosmopolitan dynamic is a byproduct of a longstanding tension between local rural culture and identity and the larger, encompassing urban-based culture, and that traditionalism constitutes an alternative to cosmopolitan aspirations and the increasing dominance of urban-based values in the twenty-first century.

Great Traditions and Little Traditions

The full incorporation of the Sardinian central highlands into a nation-state occurred only within the modern era. Before the General Enclosures Act of 1820, the distribution of wealth, while not entirely equitable, was not so unbalanced as to give rise to a class system. Rather, differing household sizes permitted relative accumulation of precarious and moveable wealth in the form of livestock, and the only property owned by anyone was the familial dwelling. No social or occupational classes ever took root, even following the enclosures that enabled some households to claim greater shares of real estate from which they are today still modestly benefiting. The absence of titles and any such formalities of social hierarchy within day-to-day interactions is noteworthy, and measurable differences in material wealth do not necessarily signal deep social cleavage.[1] This is reflected in the local architecture, which consists of comfortable and spacious houses built in a modern style in the newer parts of the village as well as stylistically uniform granitic stone structures – damp, dark, and uncomfortable – in the old quarter, by now mostly abandoned.

As Robert Merton (1957) has shown, small localities commonly incorporate their members differentially via inclusion into these two conceptual categories depending upon their degree of commitment towards their community of origin and residence. For Merton, whether one was a "localite" or a cosmopolitan depended upon social networks. A localite preserved strong ties within the community, and the bulk of his or her daily interactions revolved around issues of more or less local relevance. The cosmopolitan, by contrast, was outward-oriented, and tended to anticipate, or at least envision, life away from the local community of origin. The former had a strong desire to stay put, whereas the latter more easily welcomed uprootedness. "If the local type is parochial, the cosmopolitan is ecumenical" (Merton 1957:393). While I will not directly adopt this approach, which is heavily reliant upon the single variable of "commitment" to the local community, I will retain the terminology and preserve some original definitions and connotations. The issues of parochialism and ecumenism retain their relevance to the present case.

The dualism of cosmopolitanism and localism has been reformulated and its relevance to anthropological theory highlighted by Ulf Hannerz, who recognized that the process of globalization has witnessed an increasing interconnectedness of local cultures, leading to the emergence of a global ecumene (Hannerz 1989, 1990, 1992). Within this global ecumene, there are locals and cosmopolitans, each showing a variable degree of competence with cultural forms not "properly" their own and a general if distinctive openness towards other ontologies. In Hannerz's own words, "cosmopolitanism is first of all an orientation, a willingness to engage with the Other. It is an intellectual and aesthetic stance of openness toward divergent cultural experiences, a search for contrasts rather than uniformity" (Hannerz 1990:239; cf. Driessen 2005:137). Such a view is relevant to the contemporary period; even within the context of rural highland Sardinia – so often represented, usually by outsiders, as a place of stability and tradition – cultural flux and flow strongly challenge notions of cultural boundedness (Hannerz 1987; Stade and Dahl 2003). Yesterday's internally undifferentiated hamlet is today's universe in a microcosm, divided along numerous lines, consisting of diverse social categories, and home to a people who are aware of the ease with which they can shape their own destinies, make their own lifestyle choices, and actively construct identities by borrowing from a plethora of symbols and values originating both from within and outside the local setting. Orgolesi today are not united by a common ethos, habitus, or world view. Instead, they may elect to engage with more than one set of orientations, emanating from either the rural setting or urban centres on the island, or even from beyond regional and national cultural traditions altogether.

Whereas we could once safely speak of the Sardinian highlands as a strictly rural sector exemplifying a Little Tradition, existing on the periphery of larger urban centres endowed with an administrative and clerical infrastructure and therefore exemplifying a Great Tradition, the current reality does not allow us to posit such a clear-cut distinction.[2] As Jack Goody (2001:474) suggests, the distinction between Great and Little refers significantly to "higher" and "lower" cultural forms within a single stratified social order, to an attachment to a literate and a non-literate tradition, respectively.[3] Localism and cosmopolitanism are nothing new within the Mediterranean, in that differentiation in styles of life has long been an entrenched feature of the region. But what has changed is that, first, such differentiation no longer has a clear territorial dimension, and, second, popular and elite cultural forms have become unmoored from their seating within a coherent civilizational tradition. We may say that cosmopolitans in Orgosolo are adepts within the Great Tradition, except that this Great Tradition is not necessarily specific to the Mediterranean ecumene as it comprises much more than the exalted form of a single cultural system. The need among the Sardinian elite and middle class to exhibit adherence to an urbane lifestyle is a direct product of this, and not, as Peter Schweizer (1988:218) suggests, a possible consequence of the island's geographic isolation and distance from mainland urban centres. At any rate, the evaluative connotations of "higher" and "lower" have today lost some of their relevance, and we may continue to speak of Great Tradition (insofar as we may speak of "Great" and "Little" at all) as incorporating a fair amount of decontextualized cultural capital emergent from the wider global ecumene – a world characterized by greater transnational flows than the more distant past. The Great Tradition was embedded within a civilizational ecumene, not an all-encompassing world system of instant communication and rapid flows. Therefore, villages that may have been far-flung, laterally insulated, and difficult to access in the past, are today part of mass-media and mass-consumption societies. They are incorporated into much wider networks with which they are often synchronized as well. For example, Orgolesi of my acquaintance have enjoyed opportunities to vacation throughout much of Europe, North and South America, Southeast Asia, and North Africa; they make extensive use of consumer credit and drive Swedish cars and Land Rover sport utility vehicles. They listen to the latest Italian- and English-language pop music, watch American blockbusters, wear baseball caps and play softball, drink Dutch and Belgian beer, shop in supermarkets and large discount retailers in Nuoro, obtain diplomas from technical schools, get university degrees, and so forth. Not all such Orgolesi have left or intend to leave their natal village for good. Many elect to stay, or, if they were away for a time, to return. Some have opened up clothing or furniture stores, bars, and other shops, and intend to live out their lives with, in some instances, foreign spouses and, in a couple of cases, children adopted from Eastern Bloc countries. In the weekly solar markets set up in the main piazza we no longer find only Sardinian vendors from other towns and villages, but also North African and Senegalese men selling socks and undershirts, leather wallets, key chains, cigarette lighters, laser pointers, and various other trinkets, as well as Polish emigrés sitting behind makeshift stands retailing inexpensive Russian cameras.

The presence of immigrants – documented or undocumented, refugees or migrant labourers – is not unique to Sardinia or even to the rest of Italy. Rather, the last two decades have witnessed an increased transnationalization of space within cities and towns throughout the European Union as a result of new arrivals from the global south.[4] Nonetheless, within rural central Sardinia, foreigners remain a rarity, and are widely perceived to be temporary guests whose time in Italy will be limited, rather than permanent residents with an emotional investment in what they see as their country of adoption. According to official figures, immigrants from within and beyond the European Union constitute approximately 1.7 per cent of all legal residents in Sardinia, and as of late 2011 numbered 31,101. Of these, 2,724 resided in the province of Nuoro (ISTAT 2011). At the time of writing, three foreigners, all female caregivers and unknown to the author, live permanently in Orgosolo. Within the province of Nuoro, a majority resides in the capital (the city of Nuoro) as well as in the towns of Macomer, Siniscola, and Orosei. Most foreign residents in Sardinia are Romanian nationals, and include large numbers of Chinese, Senegalese, and North Africans who work as behind-the-scenes labourers in the hospitality sector, itinerant merchants, and, in the case of some Chinese immigrants, shopkeepers. As in other mountain communities, this reality is not easily apprehended within Orgosolo, and the stance of locals towards new immigrants is not always hospitable. Itinerant Senegalese vendors are occasional targets of mirth and joshing. Known as *vu cumprà* ("wanna buys") for their mispronunciation of the interrogative Italian phrase *vuoi comprare?* (you want to buy?) typically called out to passersby, they move through the village centre quickly with their wares, stopping occasionally to chat or banter with locals, and spend only two or three hours in town as part of their daily rounds. Itinerant vendors are tolerated because of their evidently benign commercial activity.

Much less well tolerated are Roma, who arrived in Sardinia in modest numbers by the year 2000, on the heels of the European Union elimination of border controls with the creation of the Schengen Treaty Area. Several local informants related accounts of annoyances and disturbances that resulted from the ephemeral presence, in recent years, of Roma panhandlers passing through Orgosolo. Alleged petty thefts and the disposal of food given in charity raised the ire of local people, who would make it clear that Roma were not welcome in Orgosolo. I never encountered any Roma in Orgosolo at all. As one local man told me, "they know they are not welcome here." In Orgosolo, the domination of the central public spaces by localist traditionalists renders it difficult for outsiders to gain acceptance as social fixtures, and, on more than one occasion, I heard, over casual conversation, expressions of xenophobic sentiment directed towards Chinese migrants settling, opening shops, and conducting business locally, something that had occurred in the nearby town of Macomer by 2001. These sentiments were expressed by the dominant public personas within Orgosolo; namely, localists who wished to preserve the image of a stable, culturally homogenous community. Outside of the tightly knit communities of the central Sardinian highlands, however, young herders from other countries are an important source of labour in large stockraising operations in Sardinia and throughout Italy. Much like Sardinian migrants from the highlands who, from the postwar period until the present day, have laboured as shepherds and dairy workers on the Italian mainland, these new migrants, many from non-European Mediterranean countries, have been filling positions undesirable to the mainstream Italian workforce for more than two decades (Pardini and Nori 2011:6–7).

Goody (2001:477) suggests that an inherent element in the dynamic between the Great Tradition and the Little Tradition is a two-way communication that often manifests itself as a two-way rejection, "with the upper throwing out what they consider as lower and the peasantry objecting to some of the foppery of the court." An analogous dynamic plays out today whenever localists in Orgosolo reject the embellishment characteristic of urbanity and much of what is perceived as foreign in general. The transnationalization of public space within Orgosolo has witnessed a corresponding emergence of an emotional commitment to tradition. For instance, from the early 1990s onwards, the importance of village festivals has grown substantially. The mid-August festivities surrounding the Assumption of the Virgin Mary have become a week-long extravaganza organized by a village-wide committee made up of thirty-year-olds. This committee, known as the Leva dei trentenni (Thirty-year-old age set), provides the opportunity, to all local men and women who are thirty years of age, to assist in the organization of the various events, religious or secular, intended to involve as many members of the community as possible. Also, in the spring of 2002, the very first Festa del pastore: Protagonista della montagna (Celebration of the Shepherd: Protagonist of the Mountain) was organized to showcase the artisanal crafts of the rural heritage. About a dozen stations are set up in courtyards throughout the village, showcasing ironwork, wine-making, carpentry, silk weaving, spinning, and needlecraft as well as locally prepared foods, such as cheese, honey, and bread. This celebration of tradition is born out of fear that highland culture is not being passed on to the next generation, and that the crafts and skills requiring long apprenticeship may soon be lost. Some local people deem such cultural elements, which are perceived to embody traditional culture and the genius of a unique people, as in need of preservation.[5] Many kinds of artisanal craftsmanship, such as weaving, shoemaking, carpentry, wrought-iron work, and saddlemaking, have largely fallen by the wayside throughout Sardinia. The Festa del pastore was organized and sponsored by the town administration, and reflects a commitment to tradition common to those who are removed from the pastoral way of life. But in the end there is no real consensus on the matter of cultural preservation within Orgosolo, just as there is no complete agreement on what is even a desirable way of life.

The rupture in expectations that shapes this dissensus in vision at the local level is not recent, and ultimately finds its origins in the full incorporation of this marginalized region into the social, political, and economic structures of the nation-state. Numerous Sardinian scholars argue that the national system of formal education was central to the legitimation of the structures and relations of modernity, and for the spread and entrenchment of a universal script–based national culture. As such, the introduction of formal schooling was a harbinger of great changes to come. Sardinian anthropologist Michelangelo Pira (1978) proposes a dialectical dynamic between what he calls *scuola ufficiale* (literally "official school," which is the formal, state-mandated, system of education) and *scuola impropria* (irregular, non–state mandated, unofficial folk systems of education). Some kind of system of imparting knowledge to younger generations is essential to any society, and peoples not fully incorporated into hegemonic political formations possess solely emic systems of expertise, of mastery over technical aspects of production, and of ethics, all of which constitute, in their totality, the lifeways of autonomous communities. This emic knowledge is the natural outgrowth of any social formation, and in Sardinia its pedagogical profile consisted of the relationship between *mere* and *theracu* (master and apprentice), distinguished from one another only by age (Pira 1978:377). Formal schooling aims to supplant this system, owing to a set of relations overlain by multiple inequalities, most notably that of class. With this vision, its scope is the bowdlerization of pre-existing systems of emic knowledge, of value orientations, of autonomous lifeways.

What did *la scuola impropria* look like? Among the classic trades and in the pastoral sector, its system of conveying knowledge mainly comprised the relationship between master and apprentice, which allowed for the imparting of a total education that was practical not theoretical, grounded and not abstract, one that allowed the apprentice to accede to the status of *uomo fatto* (made man) – fashioned out of the raw material of youth, readied for the exigencies of life, and imbued with a moral and philosophical grounding particular to that world. Informal schooling here is the fount of the ethics and value orientations instilled in a young person, which marks him or her as a member of the moral community and which follows a productivist and communitarian ethos wherein each person consumes according to need and produces according to ability (Pira 1978:385). The *scuola ufficiale*, on the other hand, is organic to the urban bourgeoisie; its aims are dictated by the needs of these elite, who, from the nineteenth century onward, were positioned to control the reins of power within the ascendant modern state. The relationship between teacher and pupil is, in the official system of formal schooling, overlain by the ethos of master and servant; that is, it is characterized by the relations of compulsion that follow the penetration of a capitalist mode of production. Importantly for the present discussion, these relations also solidified social hierarchies that have always marked the urban-rural distinction.

The introduction of compulsory primary schooling in highland Sardinian pastoral districts led to the significant displacement of entire categories of thought, notably in the areas of gender and conceptualizations of space. In the pastoral sector, the ideal of male self-sufficiency was inherent in the successful practice of animal husbandry, which by necessity saw shepherds live away from domesticated village spaces for extended periods. To thrive, indeed to survive, the shepherd had to master the precarious balance between his conceptual domestication and wildness. The *saltus* – in Sardinian, *su sartu* (pasture lands) – are an undomesticated space conceptually counterpoised to the domesticated space of *sa bidda* (the village), where women, children, the elderly, and physically disabled men, who could become craftsmen, lived and worked. The learning imparted to the shepherd made him into a man, cast him into the ideal archetype, and instructed him in the mastery of his environment, but it was only a partial domestication that did not annul his true, predomesticated, untamed nature inherent to his maleness. After all, the shepherd, according to the old local turn of phrase, must know to live and thrive *solu che fera* – alone like an animal. The village space, on the other hand, is domesticated space, where civility, docility, and the refined graces of proper socialization govern social relations. Exiled from the space of culture, men could indulge their affinity for wilderness and nature, whereas women, who presided over the cultured space of the community, exemplified refinement, civility, and *mansuetudine* (tameness). According to Pira's interpretation, culture is *una cosa de 'eminas* – a thing of, or belonging to, women (1978:382). In Orgosolo, some of my local interlocutors, men as well as women, drew a clear binary opposition between the sexes that equated maleness to nature and femaleness to culture, presenting a situation that diverges from the more common, ethnographically grounded, supposition that equates maleness to culture and femaleness to nature (Ortner 1974). According to this formulation, the emic knowledge generated in the field, as opposed to the classroom, constituted the subaltern *lebenswelt* and gave the shepherd his indelible mark. This folk pedagogical reality is what Pira (1978:399) dubbed *l'università del Supramonte* (the university of the Supramonte) and jurist Antonio Pigliaru (2000 [1959]:318) called *scuola alla macchia* (school of the maquis); namely, a school of life that provided the source of the shepherd's rootedness, constituted the fount of his essence, mobilized the ethical system and concepts inherent in *su connottu*, and flowed into an identity that was fundamentally nonreflexive, at least in the absence of alternatives. The arrival of a system of compulsory primary education witnessed the possibility of co-opting local youth into the hegemonic cultural system and producing, locally, two contrasting social types – prototypes, as it were, of what I am here calling localists and cosmopolitans.

The distinction between social types caused great disruption to the community, the fallout of which is plainly discernible today. The world of the shepherd, marked by implicit, technical knowledge, not codified, would become regarded as a crude form of know-how born of haphazard experience, allegedly bypassed in cognitive superiority (and therefore prestige) by expert knowledge generated within proper schools, and thus superseded by it (see Angioni 2000:8). By the postwar period, the availability of alternative paths available to youth – a local life versus the pursuit of an education in the town – yielded a recognition on the part of age-mates of the profound differences among those who had chosen different paths, born simply of their

respective styles of education. According to Pira, here we find the origins of self-reflexiveness in the construction of personal identities. The
prospects of either social type are far from certain, and young men and
boys (women and girls are elided in Pira's analysis) now have choices
to make:

> I will be a shepherd vs. I will be a gentleman; I will sing and dance to
> rustic sounds ... vs. I will dance and sing to modern Italian music; I will
> dress like my father vs. I will dress as the schoolmaster; I will milk sheep
> vs. I will give lectures; if I should be unlucky I will become a bandit vs. if
> I am unlucky, instead of becoming a doctor or lawyer, I will become a civil
> servant. (Pira 1978:263)

This confrontation between two styles of life that exemplify the old
and the emergent order is represented poignantly in a classic autobio-
graphical account provided by Gavino Ledda (1975), who started off
life as an illiterate shepherd-boy to then end up a university professor
of linguistics. Ledda's famous *Padre Padrone* (*Father and Master*), published in 1975 and two years later adapted for the screen by directors
Paolo and Vittorio Taviani (Ledda 1977), provides an unflinching view
of the life of the shepherd – harshly represented as inelegant, miserable,
and downright feral – to which he was dragged after being pulled out
of primary school, against his will, by his domineering father. Ledda's
account epitomizes an extreme variant of the disdain felt by the urbanite
towards the shepherd, and the narrative is one of escape from a life of
rural idiocy by the transcendant force of his personal will. He escaped
his natal village of Siligo to join the military in his teenage years, and
there, with the help of an army comrade who tutored him, learned to
read and write. His natural curiosity would lead him to pursue a deeper
understanding of language, and his doggedness would allow him to
complete his primary and secondary education, enroll in university, and
fulfil his desire for a different kind of existence than the one he might have
lived otherwise. Anthropologist Michelangelo Pira himself travelled an
analogous path, but his theorization is, by contrast, measured and saga-
cious. An opportunity to reflect upon and compare his life path and education against the opportunities afforded by the pastoral lifeworld was
presented in the filming of a three-part documentary aired by the Italian
national broadcaster RAI in 1980 (Pira 1979). In the third part of *La festa,
la farina, la forca* (*The Festival, the Flour, the Pitchfork*), Pira interviews Libéri,
his childhood friend from the village of Bitti, who is now a middle-aged

shepherd. The footage, which unfolds in an *ovile* (sheepfold), presents some striking contrasts. Pira, the *signore* (gentleman), slender and gracile, wearing a grey suit, is seated on a low stool opposite Libéri, the *pastore* (shepherd), stout of build and rustic in manner and appearance. Their conversation is an attempt to recognize in their respective experiences, knowledge, and personas the modern reality of Sardinia, characterized as it is by a profound divide between languages, cultures, codes, and lifeways. Libéri and Pira both speak their native dialects, but this similarity highlights the fact that only one of them is truly conversant with the larger, hegemonic order represented by urbanism, by formal knowledge, by the consumer society, and, of course, the Italian language. Libéri, for his part, is a holdout under siege, aware of the precarity of his cultural world, of his marginalization, and of the dwindling likelihood that many boys and young men would really want to live a life like his. This theme – of the life choices made by Sardinian youth, namely, whether to pursue the rural life or to obtain accreditation for a profession that will lead them away from their natal community – is so central to the contemporary concerns of local people throughout Sardinia that documentarist David MacDougall also picked up on it. His acclaimed film, *Tempus de Baristas* (*Time of the Barmen*) (1997), centres on the relationship between a father and teenage son in the village of Urzulei in the early 1990s. Its title speaks to the widespread malaise expressed by one central figure in the film, who laments that the time of the shepherd is over and the time of the barman has arrived. That is, we inhabit a hedonist age or, as alternatively stated, a leisure society, that apex of western civilization represented by the sunbather who drinks cocktails on the beach – an image that is immediate to all Sardinians owing to the proliferation of beach resorts on the island's coasts.

The sorting of lifestyles into two broad categories clearly has historical precedent, and the terms *localist* and *cosmopolitan* represent the ideal-typical ends of a continuum that in actuality witnesses some variation. Among other things, this distinction captures the centrality of stylistic competence in self-presentation, but its significance extends beyond this.[6] That is, to be a cosmopolitan or a localist is about more than convincingly embodying and performing a given style within a given setting, for style is itself a referent to a whole set of values, orientations, and understandings of one's place within what is today an increasingly transnationalized regional and national arena. As Ayora-Diaz (1993:287) noted for nearby Telemula in the early 1990s, lifestyle and career choices made by young people each have their own binding standards, and whether the preference is for a "modern" or "traditional" path, the actor must develop a grasp of the divergent expectations that will lead to social success in either sphere. The patterns detected here are classic ones, but also persistent, and are born of a rupture in styles of life due to momentous social transition, unlikely to be mended anytime soon. Rather, we appear to be presented with a scenario, the broad outlines of which are by now deeply engraved at the level of collective representations, whereby a past orientation and future orientation in performative styles as well as personal ethics are juxtaposed with one another, giving scope to a diversity of choice that is unprecedented in historical terms. Having noted some of the key trappings of cosmopolitanism and localism, we might consider the two domains in which the contrast is articulated most unmistakeably: representations of civic identity, mutual stereotypes, and respective views of the outside world.

Symbols and Aspirations

Both cosmopolitanans and locals share an emotional commitment to Orgosolo, seeing in the mountain landscape surrounding their village the physical symbol of their cultural uniqueness. The mountains, and the shared history of dissidence vis-à-vis the outside world, are key to local perceptions of self, even if cosmopolitans and localists differ in their understanding of the past. For the former, a spirit of romanticism reigns, whereas for the latter, this opposition to the outside world constitutes a surviving reality. Despite this difference, both groups are recognized as rightfully "belonging" to Orgosolo, even if, as we will see, some urban-oriented individuals occasionally claim to want to live elsewhere, thereby affirming the cosmopolitan image they wish to project. However, localist and cosmopolitan visions of Orgosolo – what it is or what it should become – differ markedly. This internal schism reflects a folk-urban dichotomy, one that is steeped in complexity. We are presented with a continuum that incorporates all Orgolesi, ranging from those who have never left home, to others who were away and have returned for good, to those who return to visit regularly, as well as those who, by force of circumstance or by preference, only visit infrequently. These latter by necessity fall mostly beyond the scope of present considerations, as direct access to their views is difficult as a result of their absence in a study concentrated on a single fieldsite. What remains apparent is a differentiation along lines of inward versus outward orientation, which is openly expressed through everyday practices that effectively underscore respective understandings of what it means to be Orgolese. Beyond actual practice and performance, it is also common to encounter claims that there are "correct" and "incorrect" representations of civic identity, as well as more and less desirable ways of acting and relating within the social arena.

Localists subscribe to a strong communitarian ethic, but are not at the same time ethnic nationalists, even if they do self-consciously live according to locally perceived traditional and conservative standards. On the other hand, cosmopolitans (or those who at least identify as such) have usually had at least some sustained contact with the outside world through travel, work, or study. Their stylistic competence is akin to that which characterizes most Italian urbanites, and on the whole their appearance and manners do not render them conspicuous in any large Italian city. Some may express nostalgia about the world that they have left behind or about the "traditional" highland culture from which they originate but do not actively partake. Hence, it is not rare to encounter college-educated or urban-oriented professionals – those people, in other words, who never have been and never will be shepherds – wearing the classic corduroy outfit once customary among rural herders.[7] There is a striking difference easily observed between those who engage in pastoral production and those who do not: the former have stained or worn outfits and scuffed boots, whereas the latter do not. Cosmopolitans do not wear the classic black or dark brown shepherd's jacket and trousers for work in the pastures, but only on festive occasions, as a way of declaring their ties to a cultural heritage. However, setting aside the unelaborated, passive acceptance or rejection of discourses of cultural authenticity, cosmopolitans' competence in adopting various styles still does not permit them to effectively embody the habitus characteristic of rurality. Conversely, localists have limited skills outside of the local rural context, and are unambiguously marked as belonging to that sector. Simply put, one walks and talks as either a shepherd or as an urbanite, and it's not easy to switch styles.

This differentiation of styles meshes with avowed preferences as well as perceptions of the relative merits of urban versus rural life. More than this, the concepts of urbanity and rurality provide a ready-made and widely available basis for ordering the world. We find some noteworthy terminology of identity in the local vocabulary, employed to designate the exemplary personas of the cosmopolitan and localist ideal type. The Italian term *cittadini* (sing. *cittadino*, urbanite) is often used by localists, with mild derision, to refer to men and women who work within the tertiary or the public sector, either in Orgosolo or in

nearby Nuoro, whereas the term *paesani* (sing. *paesano*, villager) desig-
nates those who have lived within Orgosolo for all or most of their lives,
do not have a higher education, and embody a rural habitus reflected in
their dress, locution, and demeanour. The moniker *paesano* itself incorporates the more specific designations of *operaio* (manual worker) and
pastore (shepherd). The dividing line between workers and shepherds
is, in many cases, fluid. Several men divide their time as *servo pastori*
and seasonal forestry workers, or have bought and sold small herds of
livestock, mostly sheep, while several men keep pigs, sheep, or goats
to supplement their income and provide their families with meat and
cheese. Luca, a mason and cement worker, kept some thirty sheep and
a few goats (whose milk he mixed to make his own unusual but tasty
sheep- and goat-milk cheese that he liked to call *pecorino caprino*), while
Gianfranco, a jack-of-all-trades, kept enough free-range pigs around
the oak forests outside of time to supplement his fluctuating income.[8]
Full-time shepherds, *sos pastores*, are the exemplary traditionalists, carriers of a proud heritage who have persisted in doing what once upon
a time most highland men did: keep and raise livestock. They are easy
to romanticize, but also liable to reproach. They both are, and are not,
what cosmopolitans wish them to be. They do not easily bend to cosmopolitan expectations, but at the same time are also rather obliging,
simply for being the metaphorical tableaux upon which cosmopolitan
Orgolesi project their own understanding of the heritage they claim for
themselves. Among the notions central to the rural idyll is a view of
country life as one that is close to nature, characterized by a cleanliness
of spirit and a closeness of relations structured by reciprocal obligations
upheld on an ongoing basis. The strong sense of community within
Orgosolo is purported to be great compared with what one may experience in urban centres. As Giovanna, the town councillor for tourism,
informed me early on in my stay, "Life here proceeds at a human pace
(*a passo d'uomo*). People will always have time for you, to speak to you,
to open themselves up to you. You won't find that in a big city, or even
in Nuoro." Despite such avowals, the rural idyll and the representation
of life in an unspoiled countryside evoke, for cosmopolitans, a bygone
ideal that is in many ways unattainable. Rurality, in other words, con-
jures up a view of the "traditional life" inevitably suffused with considerable ambiguity.

To cosmopolitans, shepherds are a conceptual "other" whose adherence to a way of life in some respects admired is not sufficiently desirable to be emulated. The continuity with the past that shepherds

purportedly represent speaks to their inability to capably succeed within the broader social system of which they are a part, and therefore with modernity as it is locally conceived. Their spoken Italian is passable, but marked with a heavy rural accent indicating a lack of extended contact with urban centres, where Italian is much more widely spoken in day-to-day interactions than it is in Orgosolo. Their locution, gait, and manner is emphatically local, and usually coupled with a world view and a set of orientations, aspects of which cosmopolitans can and do find undesirable, retrograde, and in conflict with their own. All of this is occasionally accompanied by a healthy dose of condescension. Among the numerous exclamatory remarks and statements of opinion regarding the habits and value orientations of *sos pastores*, and of life within the pastoral sector more more broadly, I have recorded the following statements, which, shorn from their context as a sampling of sorts, render them all the more poignant: "We're not all so backward here!"; "Their world [that of the shepherds] is sealed, like an egg"; "They [shepherds] only know what they know, they won't have much to say to you"; "My son spends too much time with my father that he has the delusion of one day becoming a shepherd, but I still have higher expectations of him!"; "I want my sons to get an education so they won't have to walk in boots encrusted with dung." These declarations were uttered by locals aspiring to upper middle-class respectability. As model neoliberal subjects, these are people who have managed to cultivate a refinement in context-free communication that renders them conversant with the expectations of urbanity. Unlike the prototypical localists, their bodies are not marked by the habitus particular to a single locality. In other words, these are statements that allow a glimpse into the social orientations of a category of people who are, or aspire to be, geographically, economically, and socially mobile.

Clearly, idealizations of country life are balanced by a set of trenchant criticisms. As we have seen, *paesani*, especially shepherds, drink too much, and spend unreasonable amounts of time in all-male settings, cavorting, eating and squandering time and money that would be better spent pursuing endeavours that result in self-betterment. Above all, they are seen as being unduly contented by a life structured according to well-known and reassuring expectations. In particular, the values of *balentia* are opposed by cosmopolitans – who think them anachronistic – and are ultimately a target of disapprobation. In the end, their positive evaluation of local tradition does not stay true to the values underpinning it; the cosmopolitan image of civic identity is genteel and pacifist, infused with an urbane spirit of universalism. Therefore, cosmopolitans do not view vendetta and aggressive masculinity – two elements central to the world of the *balente* – as part of authentic highland culture, and insofar as these have ever been normatively accepted or widespread, they are seen as an adaptive response to a cruel social order imposed from without and.[9]

Cosmopolitans in Orgosolo share the implicit view that the shepherds in their midst have proceeded, over time, to produce a narrative that stands in opposition to the world surrounding them. It is an opposition that is at once admired, but also understood as a quixotic struggle doomed to ultimate failure. Whether this presents an accurate portrait of reality is beside the point, as the more immediate matter (to them) centres on their perception that shepherds – localists par excellence – *sono rimasti indietro* (have been left behind). Stories of how difficult it is for shepherds to find spouses, for example, are legion, and, in addition to providing a running commentary on their de facto marginal status, bring to the fore the prominent gender dimension involved. As Battistina, a single woman in her late twenties, candidly noted to me, "Women don't care to marry shepherds, or at least they shouldn't. But some impressionable younger girls really do like the *balentes* and so they marry them and then pay the consequences." The time spent away from home, often in all-male settings, and the drinking habits that can end up costing young families a small fortune, are cited among the reasons why many women are reluctant to pair with shepherds. Stories and gossip recounted in intimate settings relate how "antiquated" and coercive masculinity complexes affect the well-being of those women married to shepherds, who suffer abuse and frequent inattentiveness, with shepherds who disappear for days on end without any explanation. The urbane woman does not easily tolerate this classically masculinist comportment, and is apprehensive of its myriad entailments. The model of a tight, emotionally supportive relationship between conjugal partners has slowly spread throughout rural Sardinia, as well as elsewhere in Italy, but its first champions were inevitably censured by their communities. Married men risked their masculinity if they were seen in the company of their wives in public outside of special occasions; however, according to Assmuth (1997:243), women have succeeded in gradually persuading their husbands to embrace a new model of relations between the sexes. This is not the case everywhere, though; husbands and wives do not frequently go out together in Orgosolo, and dating or married couples most often spend time together in public in larger towns such as Nuoro, where any norm of separation of men and women has long abated in favour of new forms of sociability between the sexes. Young single women in Orgosolo who aspire to a cosmopolitan lifestyle, but do not have the means to move away and live elsewhere, frequently stay at home in their spare hours, fully aware of the limited opportunities locally of finding a mate who conforms to the standards they have come to expect. The daughter of a retired millwright, Michelina, is one such young woman who never succeeded in coming to terms with the reality of the paucity of single men who could accept her own career ambitions and the fact that she was employed locally as a store manager – a not insignificant feat for a woman younger than thirty years of age. Michelina spends her days working long hours, and retires in the evening to her parents' house where she lives. Most of her Sundays are spent with family or catching up with friends during house visits. Most women's sociality unfolds within the domestic sphere, and excludes men, just as most men's sociality unfolds within the public spaces, and excludes women. Men generally do not do house visits, just as women generally do not socialize or spend time in bars. While this does not entail a diminishment of the significance of women's roles within the community, or of men's roles within their households, it does reinforce their respective marginalization from those spheres and hinders prospects of creating spaces within which it is possible for men and women to meet. Meanwhile, the central social spaces of Orgosolo are dominated by men like Martino, a shepherd in his mid-forties who, like many of his unmarried peers (and like Michelina), also continues to reside with his parents. His own perspective on things is rather clear:

Women *vogliono stare tranquille* [want to be at ease]. A shepherd can't give a woman the life she wants – nice clothes, cars, vacations, money in the bank. It is not that we're dying of hunger, but we have not so much to spare. And because we are away for so many hours during the day, and when we come back we're filthy ... Well, you know, we're not the delicate men that women want these days.

As evidenced by such a statement, young shepherds within the pastoral milieu must be capable of straddling expectations, something that does not come naturally when the expectations are difficult to reconcile and incorporate incompatible lifestyles. In practice, one can only be effectively competent in one performative style, as styles are part and parcel of a habitus and cannot easily be donned or removed like an article of clothing. In general, cosmopolitans' style changes are part of a performance intended to parody or mimic localists, much like their mirthful imitation of the robust speech patterns and guttural sounds made by shepherds when greeting someone or when surprised at something. Similarly, localists themselves are not indifferent to what they may consider to be the more curious aspects of the habitus of cosmopolitans, and freely mock the gestural flopping of wrists and lilting of verbal tone, cocking their heads back in imitation of a pompous urbane demeanour. The lines of division appear the most clear when one encounters declarations that Orgosolo would benefit from more of its inhabitants spending time away in a larger centre. As I was told by a local schoolteacher, "When someone lives in Cagliari for some time, and then returns to Orgosolo, he brings here a sense of civility, of culture. It's a beautiful city, the best of Sardinia, and Sardinia's face to the world. When people go live there and come back they return as better people."

The city, however, is not unambiguous to cosmopolitans either. It is at once a place of anomie as well as a point of conceptual orientation insofar as it allows for individual personalities to flourish and permits, for many who are willing to travel, a respite from the atmosphere of the local community.[10] Notwithstanding the personal freedom and opportunity it affords, both positive and negative connotations pervade the cosmopolitan view of the city. Women and men who leave Orgosolo often come back with sad tales of life in urban centres – homelessness, street violence, prostitution, anonymity, loneliness, and so on – but at the same time tend to adopt the deportment and behavioural refinement of urbanites. Home, to them, is still Orgosolo. However, they perceive local values, as well as local, arbitrary notions of common sense, as some of "several sources of personal meaning" (Hannerz 1990:248). As cosmopolitans themselves might phrase it, they are not prisoners of the world out of which they emerged. This places them in a somewhat problematic relationship to the locals in whose midst they live.[11] Within Orgosolo, the oft-heard claim *"qui c'intendiamo bene"* (here we understand one another well) may be fiction, as cosmopolitans and localists, especially those ideal-types who stand at seemingly opposite ends of the spectrum, do not interact very much as a matter of course, and inhabit strikingly distinct worlds.

Ambivalence and Rejection

In the eyes of villagers who have never left Orgosolo, especially shepherds, cosmopolitans have forsaken an authentic identity in favour of urbane artifice, and have adopted a sheen of superficial refinement and affectation that stands at odds with localist expectations of simplicity and modesty. We may say that their way of being is infused with a spirit of consumerism, much like that of urbanites, and that their aesthetic preferences are driven by a desire to appear polished and refined. They are beholden to individualism and a career-oriented dynamism premised upon a positive engagement with a refined economy of taste, necessarily marking them as part of a theoretically emergent category that is oblivious to its less than ostentatious origins. If to cosmopolitans, the city is a place to which ambiguous feelings attach, to localists it is altogether the antithesis of the good life. Cosmopolitans, with their urban orientation, are considered by localists as rootless and shifting, and not easy to fathom. Their limited knowledge of country activities and sometimes minimal residence within the village do not necessarily constitute a barrier to acceptance within the community – they remain Orgolesi by origin, after all – but they do place cosmopolitans at a remove from networks of exchange and interaction. To localists, cosmopolitans' ties to the outside world, be they personal or professional, signal a split in their alliances and priorities and detract from social contact with other resident Orgolesi, indicating an overall indeterminacy of character. Within the localist framework, however, determinacy of character is marked by pedigree and rootedness.[12]

The nearby provincial capital of Nuoro, being a focal point in the lives of numerous outward-oriented Orgolesi, is not free from condemnatory remarks by localists either. As a rural centre that emerged as a city relatively recently, becoming populous mainly as a result of administrative necessity, Nuoro, with its occupationally specific neighbourhoods, has retained some of its original flavour. Nuoro-born shepherds still reside predominantly in San Pietro, farmers live in the Seuna district, and absentee landowners and the merchant *petite bourgeoisie* reside along the main Corso Garibaldi. Unlike many other highland settlements, Nuoro is characterized by longstanding occupational specializations that set it apart from Orgosolo. Overlaying this older substratum is a set of institutions such as art galleries, museums, and theatres that cater to a non-local resident population that has arrived from all corners of Sardinia and Italy to fill the many posts in both public institutions and the private sector. Italian is much more widely spoken here than it is in Orgosolo, where proficiency can vary considerably. A rural-urban divide is striking to the outside observer, but the urbanity of Nuoro is played down, if not altogether negated, by localists within Orgosolo (some of whom proudly boast how they never go there) and by recorded statements, frequently uttered, to the effect that Nuoro is no city at all, but an overgrown village whose residents think they live in a great metropolis. The implication of such a view, or its subtext, is of course that the Barbagia is, or should be, a unitary entity whose inhabitants share a common history and set of values that stand opposed to the outside world. Therefore, the ease of communications within highland Sardinia to which I have at several points already alluded has not necessarily broadened horizons as much as refined local meanings and distilled localist self-definitions.[13]

As far as shared identity and categories of belonging are concerned, the frame of reference narrows greatly when considerations of other rural centres arise. Village pride, or what is known in Italian as *campanilismo*, trumps allegiance to the wider subregional category of Barbaricino. Campanilismo, from *campanile*, or bell tower, refers to a sense of exclusiveness felt by the inhabitants of a village; a church's bell tower is therefore as "tall" as villagers' awareness of their perceived distinctiveness vis-à-vis other settlements within the region. Orgolesi, most notably localists, proudly proclaim their hospitality to be greater than that found anywhere else on the island; their food is better, heartier, and healthier, and always more *genuino* (genuine, authentic), than what is found elsewhere; the women of Orgosolo are said to be the most beautiful, strong-willed, and virtuous of all women within Barbagia and the men most tenacious in the face of adversity. In addition, Orgolesi often proclaim the particular local variant of *su sardu* (the Sardinian tongue) to be *chiuso* (closed), marking it as particularly distinctive compared with what is spoken elsewhere and nearly impossible for outsiders to learn. Much mirth was had at my own expense whenever the subject of mastering *s'orgolesu* (the local dialect) would arise. As if to underscore the difficulty, or, better yet, the impossibility, of ever learning to speak *s'orgolesu*, which has many aspirated sounds, various interlocutors would enjoin me to recite a nonsense tongue twister, made up, appropriately, of aspirated words: *"uril'a 'e pol'u pil'ao, intril'a in tres tril'os 'e 'el'u"* ("folded ear of swine, braided in three concentric circles"). The alleged impossibility of outsiders to ever fully master the local tongue is a central element of the distinctiveness of Orgosolo.

Daily transactions among local men, women, and children unfold in
s'orgolesu, while standard Italian is the language of officialdom: of interactions and transactions with outsiders of various kinds, including legal
authorities and agents of the state, and of formal schooling. Children in
Orgosolo are all taught the local dialect from a very young age, and
many will learn Italian principally at school. There is a clear dividing
line between Italian and the local variant of *su sardu*, and situational
code-switching occurs only in contexts in which the local dialect does
not have ready equivalents for technical Italian terms that derive from a
wide range of domains, from abstract concepts to sports terminology to
the names of auto parts, etc. All common terms, including food names,
food preparation techniques, geographic descriptors, kinship terms,
named activities within the pastoral economy, and material objects pertinent to it, as well as all concepts pertaining to any mundane aspects of
daily life, are spoken in Sardinian. The outsider who wishes to live and
study in Orgosolo has to master at least a basic vocabulary and syntax
in order to interact naturally with local people. Failing this, the host will
forever find him or herself in the mentally taxing situation of translat-
ing everything, or alternatively speaking in Italian, for the sole benefit
of the guest. An ability to communicate – or, at least, get by – in the
local dialect, marks a transition point for the guest. My earliest attempts
to speak in *s'orgolesu* won the admiration of my interlocutors, some of
whom, jovially, blurted out the insincere compliment, "You have been
here so long, you even speak *s'orgolesu* better than we do!" The insin-
cerity, of course, resides in the fact that no one who is from outside the
village can ever learn its tongue very well, if at all. Every village has its
own unique dialectical style that identifies the community to outsiders
and envelops it within an exclusive linguistic space (Bandinu 2001:128).
Orgolesi – and indeed people from countless villages of their own – are
proud of their claimed ability to note minimally distinct sounds and
pronunciations in the Sardinian spoken by outsiders, and some of my
friends were particularly talented in pinpointing the geographical origins of their intelocutors after they uttered their first sentences. Dialect
is a primary marker of difference tied to a geographically rooted identity that is specifically unique to particular villages. Dialect *is* locality.

It is not surprising that despite a widespread pride in the distinctiveness of Sardinian dialects, implementation at the federal level of
official provisions for the preservation of minority languages through
primary and secondary instruction has not led to the development
of Sardinian-language education programs in schools on the island.[14]

While the preservation of *su sardu* is widely regarded as a social good, the existence of innumerable local dialects, many not fully mutually comprehensible – southern lowland and central highland variants are especially different from one another – would require a privileging of one region over others, and lead to a standardization and elevation of a single dialect into a literary language, which would then be imposed throughout the island. This possibility is alarming and objectionable to those communities, such as Orgosolo and countless others like it, that hope to preserve distinct linguistic forms. As such, all variants of the Sardinian tongue remain resolutely local, and there is little interest anywhere on the island for the implementation of a curriculum of language instruction in a standardized variant.[15] Besides, as Giulo Angioni (2001) points out, the concept is altogether bewildering to those islanders, especially in the lowlands and in the cities, for whom Italian has been a mother tongue for centuries, and whose families have not spoken any variant of the Sardinian tongue for generations.

In conjuction with a pride in the uniqueness of their local tongue, many Orgolesi localists believe that they are the real Sardinians, unmixed with other historical populations – Latin and non-Latin – who conquered and administered the island in centuries past. According to an oft-expressed local notion, the position of Orgosolo in this respect stands in stark opposition to that of Mamoiada, which, at less than 10 kilometres away, is the village closest to Orgosolo. Mamoiadini, localist Orgolesi are fond of saying, are not even Sardinians at all. Instead, they are believed to be descendants of ancient Roman soldiers or, in other versions of local lore, descendants of nineteenth-century Italian tree-cutters and railway workers. According to one folk theory, ancient Roman legions established an important headquarters near Mamoiada, and the erstwhile authorities let their soldiers help themselves to the local women. As my friend Angelo put it, "Mamoiada was the *bordello dell'Impero Romano* (whorehouse of the Roman empire). The Romans took all the local women, mixed them up with the prostitutes they had brought with them, and used them all to satisfy their appetites." As the story goes, of course, the Roman legions never did capture Orgosolo, as it much more capably defended its territory from incursion; furthermore, it succeeded in dealing with the external agents as a sovereign and equal people. The apparent historical failure of Mamoiada to defend the honour of its women is reflected in the related localist myth about the looseness of women in Mamoiada and a prevalence of *cornuti* (cuckolds) within that village today. They are also said to speak Italian to their children, rather than their Sardinian tongue. Within the localist imagination, Mamoiada is an exceptional case for a highland centre, notwithstanding, or perhaps because of, its cultural and geographic proximity.[16]

A Rapprochement

Localists in Orgosolo are politically and ideologically disinclined, and are generally disengaged from organized politics as a result of their cynicism towards the aims and ambitions of the political class (Heatherington 2001). However, their commitment to an ethos of dissidence is complemented by the perspectives of more cosmopolitan members of the community who espouse an understanding of history that constructs the locality as distinct from all surrounding towns and villages. The *campanilismo* of Orgosolo is closely tied in with diverse aspects of local self-image, and it is within this area of public discourse that we note less striking differences between the views of localists and cosmopolitans. The singularity of Orgosolo is a widespread supposition among most Orgolesi. The common ground found in social memory relates to historical experiences that are not necessarily as remote as antiquity, but that centre on resistance to external forces, ranging from the antibanditry campaigns at the end of the nineteenth century and again in the 1950s, to the protests against the establishment of a military training range on the commons territory in the late 1960s, to the local opposition towards the creation of a national park that would swallow up large tracts of the village commons. Together, these periods were formative to Orgosolo for the way in which they illustrated how Italian government policy may be at odds with local interests. Local perceptions of these events expose the widely felt antagonism towards the Italian state for its heavy-handed exercise of authority.

The proposed construction of an artillery firing range in 1969, for example, impressed upon highland Sardinians the sense that the Italian state considered Sardinia a land to be governed without concern for local interests. Orgolesi declared their intent to reject such a government manoeuver by occupying the site of Pratobello en masse. As a result, supposed plans for a permanent base were scrapped in order to avoid a confrontation between locals and the Italian military, but only following completion of some planned military exercises. In this, as in numerous other aspects of local history, everyone has an opinion, which, however, may or may not coincide with the perspectives espoused by some self-appointed experts on local affairs. As in other towns in Sardinia (see Schweizer 1988), Orgosolo has a small activist minority that has effectively positioned itself as the arbiter and elaborator of local historical accounts by placing them within a wider frame of reference informed by a Marxian dialectic. More particularly, these are universalists inspired by the writings of fellow Sardinian and key figure of twentieth-century Italian thought, Antonio Gramsci, and see it as their role to champion the causes of subalterns both at home and abroad.[17] We may trace the genesis of this small group of progressivists to the Circolo Giovanile (Youth Circle) of the mid-1960s, an association initially formed by members of both the youth wing of the local chapter of Azione Cattolica, a national organization for lay Catholics, as well as local Young Christian Democrats. In early 1967, during a general meeting convened to work out various details in the founding charter, young members of the local chapter of the PSIUP (Partito Socialista Italiano di Unità Proletaria [Italian Socialist Party of Proletarian Unity]), who had by then enrolled in large numbers and consequently formed a de facto majority within the Circolo, elected to do away with the membership age limit of thirty years. Dominated by young (and now not-so-young) activists driven by the spirit of dissident protest, the membership of this association adopted an overtly anticlerical stance and would quickly become the target of disapprobation on the part of Don Giovanni Sanna, the parish priest at the time, for stridently opposing the construction of a new church on the Corso Repubblica – the Chiesa Parrocchiale Santissimo Salvatore – in the spring of 1967. This signalled an emerging divide between more traditional elements within the village and the local representatives of leftist internationalism. The present-day contours of the distinction between localists and cosmopolitans contain elements of this earlier divide within the community.

The Circolo Giovanile animated a thriving muralist campaign beginning in the summer of 1967, itself a formative period for the wider international student movement. The inspiration for the rise of the mural as a characteristic form of popular expression within Orgosolo is credited to Francesco Del Casino, an art teacher in the local middle school and a key member of the Circolo Giovanile who arrived some years earlier from Tuscany. The themes incorporated within these murals communicate indignation at the plight of the global working poor, and, quite importantly, the trials and tribulations faced by the people of Orgosolo, represented as an oppressed proletariat within their own, somewhat more restricted, historical and national context. Of the almost 200 murals adorning the village walls, we find one that depicts coal miners huddled together, embellished with the caption, "If I had known what the life of a miner was like, I would gladly have chosen the life of a fugitive for one hundred years rather than submit myself to such work." Another depicts a stoic Native American chief, head held high, holding a scrap of paper and surveying the land around him, with the caption, "The white man brought a piece of paper and said to sign it. Later, when we learned English, we realized that with that document they were able to take our land away." Yet another shows a young man in the path of a rolling tank in Tiananmen Square, with the words, "This was the day the mandate of heaven was lost." While many of the images depicted in these murals do not relate directly to Sardinian history, their avowed sympathies stand as symbolic expressions of rural Sardinian marginality. Other murals tellingly express the ideological spirit that drove Del Casino and his associates. A depiction of a uniformed Che Guevara is accompanied by an inscription, derived from the goodbye letter written to his children in 1965, which entreats them to cultivate a moral commitment to revolutionary values: "Above all, be always capable of feeling deeply within your heart any injustice committed against anyone, anywhere in the world. This is the most beautiful quality in a revolutionary."

Murals that depict the trials and tribulations of Orgosolo range across all eras of Sardinian history. One mural figures a battle between Nuragic warriors and ancient Roman soldiers, another a shepherd in traditional garb being carted away by the *carabinieri*, a third, captioned "Caccia grossa a Orgosolo" ("Big game hunt at Orgosolo"), is a painting of an existing 1899 portrait of *carabinieri* posing proudly with the corpse of a slain bandit, and in another we see a scruffy handcuffed shepherd captioned with a verbose inanity derived from Alfredo Niceforo's work on the stunted crania he deemed characteristic of the inhabitants of Sardinia's "criminal zone." A local community's social memory of resistance towards external forces may effectively reinforce its identity in opposition to outsiders (Fentress and Wickham 1992), even if, as in this particular case, those who expressed that opposition were themselves inspired by outside ideas.

It is by now clear that the articulation of social memory through mural art has long been the exclusive domain of a small, educated minority that has succeeded to position itself as the official voice of the community. This quasi division of labour lies at the root of some degree of contention insofar as how and to what ends the past is represented. For example, in the 1990s a new group of mural painters – a friendship clique composed mostly of young women and known by the name Le Api (The Bees) – produced a mural featuring the landscape of Pratobello with neatly made beds, with the caption "Sweet dreams on mattresses of Pratobello." This was, according to one member of this no-longer-active group, a tongue-in-cheek jibe against what they perceived to be the self-righteous moralism of an old guard that proclaims to have acted as the awakeners of a local population dormant on a dreadful occasion of government infringement of customary land use rights. This mural was whitewashed in short order, and has now become part of the local lore about the seriousness with which the aging members of the now defunct Circolo Giovanile take themselves. However, despite this generational divide, the younger mural painters and aging 1960s activists alike remain far removed from the world of the shepherds. Therefore, beyond this cosmopolitan category of internationalist and socially mobile mural painters we find the localists who behold the whole phenomenon with some bemusement. These latter adhere to the view that mural painters have appropriated representations of the past for self-serving and narrowly propagandistic purposes, unduly extracting mileage from their previous idealism by framing aspects of local history for tourist consumption. The original mural painters have at any rate by now become *sistemati* (settled), that is, comfortable and wealthy. They enjoy white-collar employment and considerable security, while the remaining young Orgolesi who continue to paint are regarded as upwardly mobile and urban-oriented cosmopolitans, a college-educated class of loafers with pretensions to artistic distinction. In reality, they only sell an image of Orgosolo to outsiders, and in doing so effectively exclude those whom they apparently deem to be the true and authentic Sardinian highlanders.

As an example of the sensibilities expressed by contemporary mural painters, it is useful here to examine the case of one group of friends who, in July 2008, convened in the preparation of an unusual mural that has become among the most photographed images of Orgosolo since its creation. The "Enjoy Orgosolo" mural is located at the main northern entrance into town, and is styled after the trademarked Coca-Cola logo. However, the inspiration behind this ironic design was the famous Trio Sarajevo, a group of Sarajevo-based graphic design artists who, at the height of the Balkan War in 1993, painted a mural that highlighted the plight of a city under siege. That image has circulated widely, and presented an especially poignant image after it was damaged by a mortar blast. What did such a mural intend to signify, placed in relative proximity to a bullet-riddled road sign at the main entrance to Orgosolo?

When I asked one member of this group how he came up with the idea, his response deemphasized any possibly profound intentions: "*Ci divertiamo soltanto*" [We're just having fun]. There is a mural like this in Sarajevo, and it's famous ... [and] you know, Orgosolo is little like Sarajevo, an open-air shooting range. Maybe it will become famous here, too." Painting began at night, and by dawn the mural was finished. The reason for working at night was simple – the image was produced with design software, and projected onto a blank wall with a projecter connected to a laptop computer, all powered by a gas generator. The painters were mostly unknown to me, but included one young man I knew in passing from my earlier fieldwork in 2002 and 2003, who had since lived and travelled widely in Thailand and also in Canada, where he claimed to have worked for some months as a chauffeur and personal assistant to a wealthy Italian-Canadian businessman in Montreal. The clique also included the person who invited me to attend the event in the first place, namely my old friend Ballore, the eccentric town barber whose shop proudly displays images of Che Guevara, Osama Bin Laden, and a scrap metal statuette of Don Quixote. This gathering of friends was a jovial affair, and the bright red mural stands as an ironic pop culture reference that hardly registers with most local folk.

Mural painting does not hold the same ideological significance that it did forty years earlier, and current painters are inconspicuous members of the community who, unlike their forebears, have not publicly adopted a stance of activism. Private home or business owners sometimes commission a mural on a facing wall, and the exchange of cash involved is felt by many local people to defeat the original purpose of mural art as a form of protest. "It's all for the tourists now," one man told me. With regard to the localist view of the founding members of the Circolo Giovanile, it is not unambiguous; it is accepted that these painters and activists are to be accorded a degree of respect, however grudgingly, for their earnest attempts to disseminate beyond the borders of Orgosolo the truth about the historical suffering experienced locally at the hands of the Italian state. Thus, such a recorded statement as, "They are all *sessantottini* ["sixty-eighters," people who were active in the 1968 international student movement] who are stuck in the past! They served some purpose back then, but now they are just ridiculous!" is counterbalanced with many other localists' suggestions that they are to be respected for their knowledge of local history and strong commitment to Orgosolo. They remain, for all intents and purposes, unofficial but effective local ambassadors, cosmopolitans who are firmly rooted in their locality of origin and committed to its fortunes.

In sum, we can discern here the broad outlines of a dynamic of social cohesion that unites all members of the local community. The dissident identity of highland Sardinia is alive and well despite a divergence of lifestyles and ontologies. The play of identities involved, in being defined as worldly and cosmopolitan versus authentic and localist, reflects Appadurai's (1996:48) claim that in late modernity "groups are no longer tightly territorialized, spatially bounded, historically unselfconscious, or culturally homogeneous." At the same time, this fact should not blind us to historical antecedents, for highland Sardinia has long been incorporated into a civilizational ecumene in which the distinction between exalted and folk cultural forms was strongly expressed. Today this distinction is iterated through a reformulation of the distinction between the Great Tradition and Little Tradition to one that signals incorporation into a wider, global ecumene. As such, some elements of the localist-cosmopolitan distinction are not new; while standing in an apparent dialectical relationship, the different visions inherent to these divergent ontologies lose at least some of their salience when collective village identity is refracted through social memory. We are presented then with an exaltation of the vernacular through different registers – the localist and the cosmopolitan – reflecting, in their respective ways, an equal measure of awareness of the violent acts visited upon the locality throughout history.

6

Cohesion and Community

An image of a dissident highland pastoral community steadfastly resisting encroachment from the outside world has both persisted through time and also undergone numerous permutations. It is a contested notion that suggests a reconfiguration of identity dynamics in the present through the lens of the past (Giordano 2012b). Recognition of the persistence of the past in the present is central to appreciate elements of contemporary life, as is the question of social integration within Orgosolo, an examination of which provides a wider perspective on the tone and temper of social relations within the community. The following considers the role of the individual and the nuclear family and examines patterns of kinship, friendship, and sociality with the aim of understanding the mechanisms by which a sense of locality and community are created and preserved.

This will be an exercise in circumspection requiring a critical view of a commonplace understanding of local realities. This includes the classic elements of a stereotyped view of life in rural Mediterranean communities as consisting of cloistered households that are in a constant state of siege vis-à-vis the outside world, offering a singular refuge from the agonistic torment that characterizes the public sphere. Taken to its extreme, such stereotypes represent the "Mediterranean myth," a widespread set of preconceptions and reifications that do not spare highland Sardinia. One may well wonder how social existence could at all be possible were such conditions to prevail to the exclusion of opposing, centripetal tendencies. Concurrently, a rejection of this myth should not necessarily entail the suggestion that centrifugal forces do not present obstacles to social integration at the community level. Interpersonal competition, dissimulation, gossip, and slander are part of mundane interactions, the salience of which should not be disregarded.

The various informal local-level sodalities to which people belong provide a point of departure in the consideration of how networks of integration are structured and patterned. This chapter begins with an exploration of the basic unit of social organization – the nuclear family household – and considers how a range of ties extending beyond this basic economic unit act as a complex web, bringing together members of the local community and those beyond it. I argue that patterns and rituals of sociality, as well as the range of structured expectations that condition social life, conspire to express an emphatic sense of local distinctiveness. To this latter theme, the question of hospitality is examined as an example of a boundary-creating system of transactions that preserves the symbolic coherence of the community and acts as a defining element within constructs of local identity.

The Family

Relationships that extend beyond close family are precarious, and subject to severance and transformation in ways that blood ties are not. Within Sardinia, as elsewhere in the Mediterranean, a certain structuring of honour values makes the primacy of the nuclear family tangible, and lends social relationships their particular tenor. In an ideal-typical mass society of individuals where family bonds are superseded by elective affinities and by impersonal obligations based on single-interest relationships, honour values have become divorced from a focus on status linked to familial descent, and because of this cease to have great social relevance. This is especially the case in large cities.[1] Life in an urban setting is vastly different from life in a face-to-face community. Although assumptions regarding the character of social relationships in rural versus urban settings have been the subject of numerous cogent reanalyses and criticisms,[2] a folk-urban continuum is observable within the current context, especially in the selectiveness of relationships and degree of anonymity possible in urban spaces. Therefore, compared with face-to-face communities, large urban centres permit an unmooring of honour values from their fount, and as such these cease to be housed in the looking glass of the nuclear family household. They may enter into the sphere of personal morality, becoming a matter of private self-conception, part of an identity or persona fashioned independently of heredity and descent. On the other hand, where conceptions of honour colour day-to-day interactions, they necessarily become subject to public scrutiny. Although it is erroneous to suggest that the nuclear family should without exception be regarded as the only social unit to command allegiance, in some places its role in housing socially normative values makes it the most tangible point of reference and indeed primary unit of social identification. However, counterposing any ideal-typical image of familial versus civic orientation within a society, like the related opposition between "traditional" and "modern," presents a false dichotomy. While elements of the foregoing analysis emphasize a tendency towards social fragmentation and its attendant characteristics of circumspection and distrust, we would do well to balance this characterization with a description of some antitheses, and therefore complete the synthesis that constitutes social reality. To do this will require an exploration of one end of this spectrum, namely, the family-centric orientation characteristic of local life, and its significance to cultural self-conceptions.

The American sociologist Edward Banfield (1958) coined the term *amoral familism* in his attempt to explain the vagaries of social life in a village in the Italian region of Basilicata. Viewed as the normative orientation in Montegrano, amoral familism was believed to be responsible for the apparent fragmentation of the community along nuclear family lines, and allegedly undermined community integration, cooperation, and civic feeling. More than this, the supposed lack of civic spirit in Montegrano was reflected in the ease with which villagers would undermine, deceive, or sabotage fellow townspeople, or, at best, display only indifference and apathy towards their plight. To Banfield, the nuclear family in Montegrano was the overriding focus of all allegiances, with any ties beyond it necessarily fragile and existing only insofar as they might serve to further the material interests of individuals and their immediate families. The end result of this ethos was grinding poverty and economic underdevelopment, itself a byproduct of a lack of civic spirit and an inability to cooperate for the greater good. The amoral familism thesis provided an explanation of peasant behaviour and served as a predictive model that singled out cultural factors as the culprit of all social, economic, and political disadvantage.[3]

Contrary to the simplistic amoral familism model, we may venture the assertion that a familistic orientation – loosely defined as a special regard for one's own family – is ubiquitous owing to the simple givens of life. However, the family, be it nuclear, blended, or extended, is not the only unit to which an individual belongs, and an understanding of its centrality to social organization should not hypothesize social frag- mentation and divisiveness as a necessary byproduct. Historically, a larger unit to which highland Sardinians, along with most rural Ital- ians, owe loyalty today is the *comune* (village).[4] In cases where there are no other structurally defined units (such as lineages or age sets) mediating between the nuclear family (the smallest unit of member- ship) on the one hand and the village (the largest unit of membership) on the other, various mechanisms counteract fragmentation along nuclear family lines. General and balanced forms of reciprocity can and do characterize many non-family relations within "atmostic-type" rural Mediterranean settings, such as Andalusia (Gilmore 1975), rural Greece (du Boulay and Williams 1987), and even Montegrano, which Banfield originally believed represented a case of deeply entrenched amoral familism, but which was reassessed and represented very dif- ferently in the work of Italian sociologist Alessio Colombis (1997). In central Sardinia, voluntary organizations, in addition to neighbourly relations, affinal and dyadic ties, and friendship networks all provide the rich foundations of sociality that cannot go unnoticed. Numerous affiliations add tone and texture to daily life, and their rules and pat- terns prescribe the rhythms of a coexistence that conveys an image of community beholden to a system of values pronouncedly opposed to an ethos of amoral familism. These associational ties will be considered later in this chapter, however, following a discussion of the household and its position within the community.

The Household

A household unites the sexes into the local community's basic social unit through generally well-defined roles for its members, and until recent times in Orgosolo this was the only sanctioned institution per- mitting the union of the sexes. Furthermore, a household also unites the assets and wealth of both husband and wife.[5] There are few clear or stated rules of inheritance, residence, and marriage in Orgosolo, but patterns can still be discerned in all of these areas. Neolocal residence is most common, and the establishment of a new household is generally marked by the marriage of a man and a woman and their relocation into a *domu* (house) of their own. Incuding the extended family into the household is uncommon, with the exception of aged or ailing widowed parents who can no longer manage alone. Therefore, the dissolution of a household occurs with the passing of the elderly, whereupon the house is either sold and the proceeds distributed equally among all sons and daughters, or alternatively purchased and inhabited by one of the children who secures a loan for payment to his or her siblings. Likewise, private gardens adjacent to the village are divided and distributed equally to all offspring. Among shepherding households, a system of anticipatory inheritance ensures that newly married sons receive a share of livestock so that they may engage in remunerative pastoral production and therefore be capable of providing for their new families. The personal interests of individual children as to the distribution of an estate are frequently considered, and arrangements are often contingent upon these. One local widow – Serafino's mother, Carmelina – inscribed into her will that all her children were to receive either an equal share of her few hectares of land or cash payment, but only so long as their allotments were sold to the other siblings at current market value. Partible inheritance often results in the subdivision of arable lands into tiny parcels viable only for the most meagre output of produce or grapes for wine, until eventually these plots are merged again through transactions among siblings and cousins. Conflicts can and do arise whenever the ideal of partible inheritance is not followed closely, or payments for the purchase and use of the natal household are not made reliably. As such, the dissolution of the natal household may occasion states of animosity and malaise among siblings. The corporate unity of any nuclear family is therefore not perpetual, but dependent upon its status as a unit of consumption and, to a lesser degree today, of production.

Households are "mother-centred" and "mother-ruled," and the women of a household recreate the society in a microcosm. They dress, feed, and impart a moral education to their children, contribute to the provisioning of the household, manage the finances, and represent the family to the outside world. The proverb *ube no b'hat 'emina no b'hat domo ne manera* (where there is no woman there is no home and no grace), underscores the centrality of women in the collective representation of domesticity, warmth, wholesomeness, and, in sum, of culture itself (Cambosu 1954:127; see Oppo 1990:498). Furthermore, women are not cloistered from view, but have a definite presence in the public sphere. For instance, the solar market, held once a week in Orgosolo's central piazza, is principally attended by women acquiring provisions, exchanging news, and meeting with friends. A walk into the post-office or bank branch often rendered me the momentary focus of a hushed scrutiny on the part of elderly and middle-aged women, there to cash pension cheques, pay bills, expedite parcels, and patiently while away the time by exchanging local news. This public prominence of women probably has historical precedence, which is to be expected where transhumant stockraising was the dominant economic activity until recent times and men were compelled to tend their herds in distant pastures for several months at a stretch. The possible implications of this reality are not lost on local people, and the notion of Sardinian matriarchy (*matriarcato sardo*) informs local ideas about the historic structure of highland society; as a result, it has received some treatment, albeit limited, in the regional ethnography (see Pitzalis 1978). Although actual evidence of matriarchy is lacking, there was, until the end of the nineteenth century, a uxorilocal bias in the highland shepherding villages of the Gennargentu massif (Oppo 1990), as well as a history of onomastic plurality, before a patrilineal system of filiation was instituted in law by the end of the eighteenth century (Murru Corriga 2000:165). The conspicuously high status of women, reflected in their relative autonomy and in their role of representing their families to the outside world, was sometimes presented, by my more anthropologically inclined interlocutors, as residual of an ancient system of matrilineal descent that once prevailed. To illustrate this, one man asked me to pay special attention to local conversations: "People here know one another through [i.e., by reference to] their mothers. When two people speak to one another about a third person, and that third person is not known to one of them, then the other will say, 'he's the son of so-and-so.' If it ever happens to you [that you observe this], listen carefully, and you will see that so-and-so is always a woman." There is wide consensus that Sardinian women are not subordinate to men, at least not in an obvious sense, but rather are central figures in the community, as well as central figures in the primary institution in society – the nuclear family (Angioni 1989:193ff.).[6]

In contrast to bars – those classic centres of male sociability previously examined – the domestic sphere remains a decidedly feminine space (see Magliocco 2006:28–31). This is a lived ideal, not an abstract one, and is manifested on the most basic sensory levels. The bar, *cantina* (cellar), *cuile* (herding station), piazza, and ubiquitous *chisina rustica* (rustic kitchen) to a greater or lesser extent exclude women. These places are neither warm in winter nor comfortable in summer; their atmospheres are suffused with an aroma of alcohol (beer or fermenting wine) and tobacco; and, in the case of sheepfolds, cellars or rustic kitchens are crudely furnished and inelegantly arranged. A guest entering any such spaces is immediately offered, without great formality, a serving of wine or beer and, if he is entering a rustic kitchen – a gathering area often located adjacent to a workshop or a herding station, furnished with roughly hewn wooden benches, a table, and a hearth for cooking roasts – will be entreated to help himself to meat prepared over a fire, seasoned only with salt, to be eaten on a plastic dish with no cutlery other than a *lesoria* (a folding blade, the shepherd's knife). A guest entering a home, on the other hand, is invited to the kitchen or dining room, and, if a woman of the house is present, served sweets, such as individually wrapped chocolates or pastries, espresso coffee poured in delicate cups and presented on a tray, or a liqueur, often a myrtle berry–infused local specialty, served in crystal glassware. The home, in other words, is a warm and comforting space, refined in manner, clean, tastefully furnished, and often scented with the aroma of cooking and with the fragrance of an oak fire in the hearth. The hearth itself, often located in the kitchen, constitutes the most intimate and conceptually feminine area within the home from which men should maintain their distance; it is unseemly for any man to covet the warmth of a hearth by sitting close to it. Only women and the elderly may do this, and a younger man who hunches in front of glowing embers is a figure of contempt. An unusually priggish boy, who spurns his mates, stays home, and is unwilling to adapt to life among men is sometimes referred to as a *chisineri*, after *chisina* (kitchen).

Since the end of the Second World War, growing occupational differentiation and a greater range of career and employment opportunities for younger generations have resulted in a decline in residency within the village. Likewise, greater wealth created opportunities to construct houses in underveloped areas north and west of the village, away from Haspiri, the oldest continually inhabited part of Orgosolo. Evidently, houses inherited from deceased parents frequently remain unsold and unused for lengthy periods, or languish in various stages of renovation for the eventual use of younger generations.[7] Ease of transport in the village is made possible by the ubiquity of automobiles, which, to the disapproval of hardier older folk, are often used for the shortest errands of even only a few hundred metres.[8] This increased mobility obviates a preference for contiguous settlements, and today the purchase of houses and selection of sites for the construction of familial homes is reliant upon price and location, including reputation of potential neighbours, more than anything else.

Despite these changes, the ideal of home ownership persists; the family home should be owned, not rented. It houses husband and wife and all children until marriage, comprises the social unit within which intimate family life is lived, maintains cohesion of its occupants through the apportioning of male and female roles, and represents the public identity of its individual members that is projected to the rest of the community. These continuities, taken together, form a comprehensive whole insofar as the structure and position of the household is concerned. Therefore, throughout Orgosolo, young men and women who intend to marry and remain within the village tend to do so only once they have succeeded in securing home ownership for their future families, either through personal means or with parental assistance. Until that time, a couple will continue to live at home, often well into adulthood.[9] Consequently, there is no shortage of unfinished houses in various stages of construction throughout Orgosolo. Viewed at a distance from any direction (but especially from the north), the village resembles a large construction site, with grey concrete or terra cotta brick structures of uneven size and shape, awaiting completion. If the means are available and when there is intergenerational consensus, a male head of household may, over the space of several years, engage in the construction of a house intended to accommodate as many of his children and their spouses as possible in the years to come. While this is not the norm, it is also not uncommon. For instance, my friend Pietro Salis, aged but energetic and an accomplished mason, purchased land in the undeveloped southwestern fringe of the village, and, over the space of fifteen years, completed a spacious three-storey house with the help of his four sons. Added to his other house in an older, more settled, part of Orgosolo, all the combined living spaces will provide an eventual home and hearth for three generations of the Salis family. There is no normative expectation of patrilocal postmarital residence, however, and in the end children often have ideas of their own. Stories abound of young people who had left Orgosolo many years earlier to attend university or to work elsewhere, only to create lives for themselves in their new cities and towns and stay away for good. Likewise, village endogamy was customary until the postwar period, but is less common today, especially among men and women who have spent considerable time away from the community.

The separation of the sexes is noteworthy in Orgosolo. "Going out," understood as eating in a restaurant, attending a performance, seeing a film, or engaging in any other public activity together, is not *de rigueur*. As with most highland villages, Orgosolo has no movie theatre or playhouse. An auditorium is found next to the library, but it is rarely used for performances of any kind. There are, however, four restaurants. Two are attached to hotels and serve up traditional fare to tourists, one is more modern and provides a formal setting and extensive menu, and another is a typical pizzeria. The formal restaurant, *Montiblu*, is owned and operated by a young couple and frequented by other young Orgolesi and visitors whose tastes suggest urban preferences. Many (but not all) of these are returnees who have spent time away from the village for work or study. Pizza is not a classic Sardinian staple, but is widely appreciated and eaten. Therefore, the pizzeria is the only restaurant to see brisk business by locals. Even then, though, most of the clientele appears only during the lunch hour and consists of town hall functionaries, staff from the nearby clinic, and students from the middle school. In the evenings the atmosphere is sedate. It is always easy to find a free table, and the few diners mainly consist of young groups of friends or unmarried couples. Local bars, on the other hand, do not want for customers, day or night, and these are frequented, as we have seen, almost exclusively by men.

Men's and women's roles within the household differ, and this is reflected in patterns of social interaction outside of the home. Together, they unite the two complementary streams of male and female honour into the household, the principal structural unit within the community, and in their daily interactions they are tasked with upholding their personal and familial reputation. Contrary to the model of amoral familism, the ability to claim a solid position for the household is assured through the establishment of social ties extending beyond it, especially where the labour market does not provide for the fulfilment of all material needs. Women's roles are instrumental in ensuring positive neighbourly relations, and feminine forms of sociality are central to securing and maintaining networks of reciprocal ties. The Roman Catholic Church remains an important locus of activity in this regard, and women of many ages regularly attend Sunday mass and visit together afterwards, or else with their children participate in activities held by the local chapter of the Azione Cattolica, the large national association of lay Catholics.

House visits and the friendships that evolve through longstanding ties are integral to an important aspect of local cultural reproduction: the procurement and preparation of food. The preparation of local specialties (biscuits and cakes, such as *urilletas* and *papassini*, pastas, and festive season breads, such as *maloreddus* and *pane de sa Candelaría*), especially during Easter, Christmas, and Carnival, is often a cooperative effort among groups of women. On a more mundane scale, food provisioning for the household sometimes involves the bulk purchase of fresh meat, from which sausages and a variety of cuts are prepared and divided among all those who participate in the collective endeavour. Every household is also stocked with *pane carasau*, crisp rounds of wafer-thin bread made with durum wheat flour and stacked in neat piles. This bread, a staple without which any highland Sardinian pantry would be incomplete, is eaten daily with a wide variety of foods, especially cheese and cured meats. Its production is, or should be, local, and it is baked communally by female heads of household, occasionally with the assistance of their children. Place of production is a point of pride in considering the inherent qualities of this food. Although *pane carasau* is found throughout the Barbagia, and is made everywhere using similar techniques, the bread produced within each village varies subtly. The thickness, texture, taste, colour, and aroma allegedly mark each village's *pane carasau* as the very best there is. To appreciate this symbolic centrality of communally baked bread, we may agree with Heatherington's observation that food production in Orgosolo is informed by a local discourse of authenticity and is dependent upon the following of strictly interpreted traditions, deviations from which render the products undesirable (2001:333–5).[10]

Once made, *pane carasau*, like many other food products, is circulated widely among households via informal networks of exchange. More than this, however, pane *carasau* is the focal point in a network of social exchange informed both by positive reciprocity as well as mutual respect between and among households, embedding the household in a set of structured expectations as to its role in the process of social reproduction. The women who cooperate in the preparation of *pane carasau* share affective ties of many years' duration. Therefore, attaching a monetary value to this foodstuff does an injustice to its symbolic value as well as to the communal spirit that underlies its production and consumption. As such, bread is life; it is affect and sentiment (Counihan 1999), as well as community and identity, and its cooperative preparation maintains an ethos of locality as a property of social life (Appadurai 1996). This is especially the case with *pane carasau*, which until recently was not consumed by lowland Sardinians and was totally unknown to some parts of the island, and certainly to the rest of Italy. Today, however, several brands of *pane carasau* are available in Orgosolo's grocery stores, arriving ready-made and packaged in shiny plastic wrap from bakeries in Nuoro, Dorgali, and other larger centres that have commercial bakeries or cooperatives. Orgosolo itself has no bakery, but anyone wishing to acquire locally made *pane carasau* has the option of visiting any of two known but unmarked addresses of private homes to do this; even if it is bought with cash, it is still at least better than what is produced elsewhere and sold in stores. Nonetheless, local stores do manage to sell their product, and stock it rather conspicuously for easy access to buyers. As Carole Counihan (1999) has shown for the larger western Sardinian town of Bosa, the acquisition and consumption of bread has become a more commercial and individualistic activity than is locally considered ideal. This has also become true of *pane carasau* in Orgosolo.

Frequent house visits, announced or not, from friends and neighbours are a regular feature of daily life and central to structures of sociality among female heads of household. Such visits are central to the maintenance of affective ties and the reaffirmation of friendships, and in their aggregate constitute a social support network for women. They can also be a mixed blessing, as they often require a degree of formality that some may find stifling. House visits are supposed to be a pleasure, a break from daily routine and an opportunity to share good company, but whenever outsiders are admitted into the home one ceases to be completely at ease and must instead act with circumspection. Rules of hospitality not followed with the requisite grace can backfire through gossip. How a home is kept can easily enter the public domain, for one can never know what a guest will say to others about what they notice about one's domestic sphere during a friendly visit.

The manner in which this tension is expressed day-to-day may be illustrated by observations made following a quiet lunch I was invited to on a warm Saturday afternoon at Ignazio and Elsa's house. A light lunch was served, and once it was eaten and the table cleared, Elsa cheerfully announced, "*Cari miei* (my dears), I need to clean up today, you'll forgive me, won't you! I have some guests coming later." This was a polite way of saying, "please go." Ignazio: "Clean what? You cleaned just the other day." With an expression of amusement, he turned to me and said, "She's obsessed with cleaning." Elsa's reaction was unexpected: "And you're a slob! Coming in here with your boots and smoking and spilling ashes and never putting things away and making a mess whenever you move! You know I expect company tonight, don't you? And you know how it is if they end up finding this place such a mess, no?!" "Take no notice," Ignazio says as we walk out. As my friend later explained it, there was a larger meaning behind that interaction. Of course, Ignazio provides an emphatically male perspective:

Always, when guests come over Elsa gets anxious. She worries too much what they will think. But then women are like that. They all worry because they know that as soon as they turn their backs, everyone is talking about them. You should see them all on Sunday morning outside the Church! They're like so many hens!"

How well a household is provisioned is also a matter that passes easily from the private into the public sphere. The longstanding institution of *sa Candelaría*, held on the last day of December, sees the community engaged in a merry ritual of reciprocal visiting and well-wishing, and represents a temporary abeyance of ill feeling or even enmity among families and households. In the morning, households open their doors to welcome groups of children carrying white pillowcases to be filled with treats. The children visit homes throughout the village to recite the refrain, *"A nois la dazes sa Candelaría?"* ("Will you give us the Candelaría?"), a plea for an offering that can take the form of sweets, candies, cookies, cheeses, cured meats, money (previously small bills, but now euro coins which come in larger denominations), and fruits. In the past, the *pane de sa Candelaría*, a festive bread made purposefully for the occasion, was the principal offering. Informants suggested to me that today the occasion is more lavish than it used to be. Only women of the house provide *sa Candelaría*, and how much they provide does not go unnoticed. Most of the provisions for this event are purchased, and one family informed me that they had spent more than a hundred Euros for the occasion, which afforded enough goods to fill the trunk of their small car. But this seemed boastful; after all, much fun is had at the expense of households that children report to be miserly or its dwellers lacking in grace. Children are less aware of the delicateness of such matters, and unknowingly act as live conduits in the flow of information within the community. The evening of this same day sees a different kind of merriment. Groups of young men visit the homes of couples married during the previous twelve months, and bring greetings of success in the year to come. Once again, offerings flow in the direction of the guests who continuously arrive in small cliques until the wee hours of the morning. Wine and spirits and a rich assortment of festive treats are prepared, courtesy of the young wives, and are consumed by numerous small groups of men over brief stays of usually less than an hour.

Local people claimed that *sa Candelaría* harks back to an earlier period of scarcity and material deprivation. According to local explanation,

it served as a levelling mechanism, allowing those who were less fortunate to have access to a measure of the wealth possessed by those
who were more fortunate. The understanding was, of course, that in
subsequent years the tables might be turned. A different interpretation is provided by Cosimo Zene (2005, 2007), for whom this institution exemplifies a socially centripetal ritual of gift-giving that serves
as a counterpoint to the socially centrifugal mechanism of exchange
inherent in vendetta. Additonally, being centred on the home, the ritual
of *sa Candelaría* highlights the central role of women in social life as
givers of sustenance, reconcilers of conflict. Its reconstitution of tradition reinforces the cultural boundaries of the community, while the very
joyousness of the occasion conceals any realities of dissensus within the
community, reinforcing moral boundaries. In sum, an image of the rural
idyll is recreated, if even for a short time.

   According to some local people, *sa Candelaría* has changed considerably over time. Wealthier families once upon a time saw large processions of well-wishers on the eve of the New Year. These latter would
arrive, masked and shrouded so that their identity may be concealed,
carrying lanterns or candles (hence the evident origins of the name
Candelaría), to request offerings. This is no longer an accepted part of
local tradition; however, an analogous practice occurs frequently in
Orgosolo's bars during the February carnival celebrations. Masked
revellers, or *maimones* (mummers), who act with considerable anonymity, will enter bars with a harlequin flourish, speak in falsetto tones,
air public secrets, act erratically, then request libations from the non-
masked patrons. Much of the clientele reacts with consternation or
simply holds its peace, agreeing or not to purchase drinks for them;
interacting with unknowns in this way is not to everyone's liking, and
for obvious reasons.[11]

   The conceptual solidity of the home – its cleanliness, its members'
cohesiveness, and its ability to recreate valued aspects of material
culture and gracefully bestow hospitality – is gauged by the community, and in turn acts as a measure by which a family is judged
and ranked within a hierarchy of esteem. In short, women uphold
the integrity of the household, secure social connections with other
female heads of household, and project its public face outward to the
rest of the community. This is particularly the case following marriage, but even unmarried daughters are expected to contribute to this
ultimate goal. The role of unmarried women in securing the esteem

of their households is to a greater degree oriented towards their circumspect and judicious behaviour when they are away from home.
While they do not face considerable restrictions – young women in
Orgosolo enjoy a great degree of mobility and freedom – they are
expected to refrain from engaging in activities that may be regarded
as untoward, such as drinking or smoking. While dating is common,
it is not to be taken lightly, and serial dating is unknown. Potential
mates and spouses are not assigned in any system of arranged mar-
riages, but courtships, which often last several years, are subject to
considerable scrutiny. Courtships present opportunities for households to appreciably widen their networks of social relations, and
parents thus take considerable interest in the romantic involvements
of their children. In general, unmarried members of a household represent their families to the community, and their habits and manners
speak to the values imparted by their parents. However, sons and
daughters often have ideas of their own, as witnessed by the row of
steamy-windowed cars parked most nights along the main provincial
road just beyond village limits.

Beyond the Household

Friendships follow a definite life course. Following marriage, the free
and easy relationships previously enjoyed among young adults cease to
be central to their everyday lives (Magliocco 2006:35; cf. Reed-Danahay
1999). Friendship ties become formalized and subject to a wider reassessment of life priorities. The frequency with which young women
together take the evening *passeggiata* (promenade) diminishes, as does
the spontaneity that comes with young age. This is less pronounced
among men than among women, since men, married or not, will spend
a far greater deal of time outside of the home.

Here we can take up the question we left behind earlier: is there
an underclass of men, engaged primarily in pastoral production and
working as occasional labourers, that is failing to fulfil the requirements
of successful manhood, working and sacrificing its own comforts in
order to build a future? Local views on the subject are not unanimous,
but instead point to a coexistence of more than one cultural model. One
local public figure suggested to me that the role that men play as representatives of their families is and has always been tenuous and uncertain compared with the role played by women in this regard. His point

of view, even if not universally shared, is fairly widespread throughout Orgosolo, and for this reason, and also because of its comprehensiveness, merits extensive citation:

> The women of Orgosolo are very public, but the men have never carried the responsibility of representing the family until recent times, or at least not much, and because of this they don't do it very well. After all, they used to not live in the village very much, and so obviously their roles [within the village] were limited. So, if you've travelled around, I'm sure you have already noticed, men here are different from men in many other parts [of Sardinia]. They are sullen and taciturn, while instead it is women who have a monopoly on social grace. It seems to me that changes in the pastoral economy within the last generation have not changed [or have not been accompanied by a change in] attitudes. The men, it looks like they just came in from the pastures, and after a generation they still carry with them that spirit of the mountains. It is as if they brought the countryside into the village, if you know what I mean. They think they're shepherds but they are not. They only play the part, and so they're never well turned-out, they're slovenly and gruff, just like shepherds, and the problem is that their women do nothing to ensure otherwise. They don't help them to keep up a respectable appearance.

When I asked him why this should be the case, my interlocutor confidently, and with a strong sense of annoyance at the state of affairs he had just diagnosed, suggested that it was due to a lack of communication between the sexes:

> Men and women speak little and spouses hardly know one another! Men leave in the mornings and come back at night, and only go home when they have had enough to drink. This lack of communication in Orgosolo is a real cultural problem, heh! Unemployment is chronic here, and in the end people don't do much to remedy their own situation. The fact that the shepherd of Orgosolo is a *pelandrone* [loafer], and not a very elegant one either, who drinks and stays away from home, just perpetuates his condition. It looks to me like they just resign themselves to their fate.

Such an understanding of local life does not reflect any one particular social position, but rather accounts for a fairly wide cross-section of the local population. It is not rare to hear analogous complaints among Orgolesi who, in particular, are not engaged in the pastoral economy. However, it is not an opinion a shepherd or even a labourer, especially if underemployed and younger than forty years of age, is likely to express. Few deny that there is a shortage of opportunities for employment. Contract work in small home repairs and construction projects, or as *servo-pastori*, or even seasonal stints in the tourism industry provide local men with only an unsteady source of income. As for forestry work, it is a mixed blessing, as we have seen.

My focus here is on those localist men who engage in the small politics of everyday life, who retain access to what Frederick Bailey (1971:4) calls the "fund of common knowledge about all members of the community," and whose reputations constitute part of that fund. Perhaps the most conspicuous local institution of which they are a part is the ubiquitous informal friendship clique, *sa cricca*, a tight association of mates who drink together, eat together, cooperate in collective endeavours, look out after one another's interests, and share a collective status and reputation as part of that group. Especially among young men, participation in the most intensively public spaces of village life is mediated by membership within such a sodality. Membership is voluntary, tends towards exclusivity, and depends upon the observation of more or less strict rules of conduct. For instance, one does not jump from one *cricca* to another, and to do so could demand severance of all ties to the previous group. Similarly, one does not seek excuses to absolve himself from the cooperative responsibilities of the group, or refuse assistance to anyone who needs it. Membership can certainly be coercive, which is cited by some as a reason why some people may decide to never be part of a *cricca*.

Comprising a loosely ordered set of egalitarian relationships, the *cricca* emerges spontaneously out of long-term interactions extending back many years, often to shared experiences in primary and secondary school or to growing up in the same neighbourhood. Being an informally structured unit, new members may join or others sloughed off, usually for reasons of personality incompatibility. One *cricca* to which I gained access and from which I benefited in terms of developing social ties of my own consisted of ten men, close in age except for its eldest and most prominent member, Cristolu, who was in his early fifties and affectionately regarded by other members of the group as a father-like figure. They were a motley crew, consisting of seasonal forestry workers, independent swineherders, and some construction workers who became acquainted over the space of several years by force of association: frequenting the same bars, working at similar occasional jobs, and sharing various interests, after which (most importantly) a shared spirit of affinity emerged. As Gianfranco, a member of this sodality, once affirmed, "These guys are great, we get along well and we look out for each other." To be attentive to the needs of these social others, as noted above, is of central importance to the propagation of the sodality. This cricca cooperated on many undertakings: the butchering and preparation of large quantities of meat for sale on regional markets as well as for personal provisioning, the harvesting of grapes for wine, the collection of fallen timber on the commons, the construction of a rustic kitchen, and the replacement of brakes on a small truck used by one man in his work as a swineherd. "We are very *'fai-da-te* [do-it-yourself]'" Gianfranco told me during a particularly intensive period of shared work lasting several days. This particular group of energetic men, with all their talents combined, were capable of accomplishing a great deal of tasks, and were clearly endowed with a strong sense of fellowship and commitment to their small collective.

All of the endeavours in which this group engaged were followed up with an *ispuntinu* (sumptuous picnic), a local custom that celebrates the importance of male commensal solidarity within friendship groups (see Papataxiarchis 1991). To the man for whom a job was executed fell the responsibility of acquiring foodstuffs for this large communal meal, usually consisting of pasta or boiled mutton with potatoes (*patate 'e peras*), in addition to roasted meat (piglet or veal) or pork sausages, as well as aged cheese, cured meats, bread, and generous quantities of wine and spirits. Typically held in a rustic kitchen, these feasts lasted well into the evenings, often followed up with a bout of drinking and socializing at a number of local bars (the French term *grande tournée* was popularly used to describe such such bar-hopping).

Deviation from the expected norms of participation in collective undertakings certainly resulted in annoyances, arguments, and in some cases ostracism of shirkers. A collective purchase of ten sheep from a local shepherd resulted in a fiasco when two of the participants from the previously mentioned friendship group – who were especially close with one another – contributed more than their fair share for the purchase but failed to be present for the slaughtering, cleaning, and preparation of the animals for their own provision. They were, as a result, allotted the two scrawniest carcasses, which were presented to them when they showed up, as inevitably they did, once all the work was completed and everyone was set to depart to a countryside rustic kitchen for the collective meal. As expected, they did not like this; they expected that their large cash contribution entitled them to the more substantial specimens. Their grievances, set forth without compunction, were doubly annoying to the coordinator of the undertaking and to the others as well. Much to their chagrin, their lack of collective participation in the work trumped their larger cash contribution. A vehement shouting match changed nothing, and, a few days later, Cristolu – the *primus inter pares* of the group – said to me,

> Did you see what happened the other day? It really upset me, and I didn't like how those two behaved after they just show up, all so cool and easy, once the work was done. Hard workers, really! Come on! What do they think, that the rest of us are at their service? From now on they'll do things on their own!"

Whether or not these two regained good standing and acceptance within the *cricca* – they eventually did, but not as very central characters – is beside the point. The risks of engaging with social others in collective endeavours might result in undesirable outcomes, such as feeling cheated of one's proper due. This was undoubtedly the case with the two men concerned, and was also the primary apprehension of the others. From this vignette we can easily detect a prevailing sentiment of the need for everyone to pull their own weight – any cooperative endeavour can only ever work if it is undertaken with the aim of benefitting all members of the group equally. In a sense, this is certainly the case; and while not all interactions that occur within the context of the *cricca* are purely instrumental, a degree of instrumentality, along with a fair dose of selflessness, combine to produce the cohesive compound that holds members together.

To choose not to be a member of a friendship group of this kind is to participate as an individual, and often less frequently, in the public centres of male sociability. It is to forego the cooperative spirit and the camaraderie upon which such intimate group ties are premised. One who goes out alone, for example, is frequently referred to, in the Italian term, as *un cane sciolto* (a stray dog). This is not necessarily a derisive term, and may be heard in self-description. Nonetheless, to be a *cane sciolto* is to be akin to a free-floating isolate, limiting individuals from accessing the key benefits of membership within an exclusive group that functions to advance the interests of its members. One is also more susceptible to treatment as an outsider; always deserving, of course, of the same courtesy as everyone else, but always the beneficiary of a diminished share of trust and confidence. While it is not an imperative that men belong to a *cricca*, many certainly do, and in it find great personal reward. The *cricca* fulfils both affective and instrumental needs, it ensures a more prominent standing within the community, it allows full participation in the flux and flow of village life, and it shows its members as emphatically public and unmistakably present within the community, placing them fully within the socially sanctioned male sphere.

Yet, for all of the local prominence of *sa cricca*, members do not always view one another as very close friends (*amigus*) so much as companions (*cumpanzos*). *Amigus* may or may not be found within a larger friendship group, but in any case "true" friendship is established through mutually exclusive dyadic ties. This is as much the case among the men as it is among the women of Orgosolo. But before we impose an analytic construct on local meanings of friendship, we would do well to consider the data by asking what Orgolesi, men and women alike, frequently ask: namely, what is a friend, and do friends exist?

Trust

Appearances manifested and patterns discerned through social interactions tell only part of the story. Locals' understanding of, and pronouncements on, the nature of human relationships within the village sometimes contradict these appearances, although they certainly complement the discernible patterns. A lack of certainty regarding the fidelity and trustworthiness of social intimates is matter of concern to many, and it is often expressed without hesitation. As one interlocutor, a bar owner whom I had come to know well over a period of many months, told me over a conversation about friendship:

> *Siamo tuttti di compagnia* [We all enjoy one another's company], and you can pass the time talking about the most unimportant things and really enjoy yourself doing it. But friends ... eh, friends are rare. You can say that we have many people we spend time with; you know, we have *conoscenze* [acquaintances] and *cumpanzos* [companions], but *amigus* [friends], we are lucky if we have even just one or two.

Asked what, exactly, is *unu amigu*, he replied: "A tomb. A friend is just like a tomb. He doesn't talk. What you tell him stays with him, and does not go [scattered] to the four winds. You can trust him." Another informant, a middle-aged woman and head of her household, suggested, "Friendship doesn't exist in Orgosolo. What we have instead are appearances. For example if I go out with Anna and Malena ... I know that when we part company they will talk behind my back, tell other people what I say. But I will never know that just by speaking to them." Yet another, this time my friend Pietro, the householder and mason: "I'm the friend of everybody and of nobody. I drink with others, I help people if they have need, but really, in the very end, I mind my own business." Obviously, there is some concern about what a friend really is, and much of this uncertainty relates to the problem of trust.

Matters of social integration and trust intersect very conspicuously, all the more so in a context in which a cultural ideal of equality markedly underlies all interactions and exchanges. This latter point needs emphasis. It is important to note, for example, that the nucleated village settlements within the Barbagia have no long-established systems of social inequality emanating from ascribed statuses. There has never been a landed gentry or aristocracy, no estates, no serfs, and no castes or despised trades. There are, correspondingly, no castles, citadels, manors, or villas. Such institutions and their trappings belong to a different social order – namely, the *polis* and its hinterland, the *campus* – altogether repudiated by the Barbagians, a people of the *saltus*. As such, the biblical axiom *nemo propheta in patria sua* (no one is a prophet in his own land) retains here a clear and immediate relevance. It is expressive of the central value of a local community that ill tolerates any pretensions to special status made by its own inhabitants. As a strict moral community, then, members may only claim recognition by acquiescing to rigidly defined expectations. An appearance of equality is highly valued, and any deviation from such provides an opportunity for criticism through gossip. As Anthony Cohen suggests, the characteristic refusal of many face-to-face communities to countenance displays of wealth or ostentation reflects a pragmatic egalitarianism or a "rhetorical expression of the integrity of the community" that exemplifies a desire for social harmony in day-to-day life (Cohen 1985:35). Therefore, numerous local authors who wrote small collections of poems or short stories were the butt of endless jokes, derisively referred to as "that learned man," or "our very own Dante Alighieri" in their absence. Someone who builds a house incorporating original, flashy, or foreign design elements will likewise be a target for censure. One young professional who commuted to the city of Nuoro for work every day regretted his purchase of a conspicuously expensive car, as it proved to be the focus of too much unwanted attention and curiosity, and was, he felt, a possible target for sabotage: "I always park my car in this garage at night. With the way some people are here I can never know if one day I'll start my engine and *boom!*" Such widespread scrutiny is often directed towards those who embrace tastes and preferences that set them apart from others, whose social style is skewed towards a cosmopolitan orientation or somehow lays claim to class superiority. In addition to triggering *invidia* (envy), it would appear that ostentatious consumption runs up against what Michelangelo Pira interprets to be a non-acquisitive disposition that ensures the maintenance of a degree of uniformity in statuses (Pira 1978:360).

Ironically, however, the zones of social encounter – bars, rustic kitchens, places of worship, and so on – are inevitably arenas of intense social competition. Here, self-presentation is central to all interaction, and as a result reputations may be made or lost. Although the game of one-upmanship is frowned upon, it has ironically been elevated to the level of cultural injunction. Yet it is a form of competitive jockeying that is aware of its limits, any breaching of which exposes the actor's true intentions. And so circumspection, self-restraint, and reserve are strongly valued traits, for they ensure if not the making of a reputation then its preservation. Likewise, the braggart is despised, as is the attention grabber and the preacher. On the other hand, to fulfil the requirements of one's station without fanfare, to assist a mate in need and to give of one's time without fuss, to be quick with an aphorism or a joke, and to have what we may call the gift of social grace – a spontaneous smile, even-handedness, and a modest but upright demeanour – is to ensure social success and the right to pride. Not speaking of oneself, one's projects, family matters, and transactions with third parties is the best course of action at all times. Knowing when to let one's guard down and allow entry into the most intimate personal spheres is seldom easy to gauge. Stories of false testimony retracted leading to the imprisonment of a criminal accomplice, machinations of informants who alert the authorities to planned ventures leading to arrests, and even homicides arising from betrayals of various kinds, evidence the darker side of this uncertainty and, as public secrets, provide much for everyone to ruminate upon.

Home and hearth and the inner sanctum of the domestic sphere remain the most inviolable spaces. Simple and unadorned outer walls shelter the family from prying eyes, and sometimes hide a not-insubstantial material wealth that is to remain out of public view. Lavishly furnished and expensively decorated interiors are not rare, and indicate a preference towards inconspicuous consumption. Public secrets in Orgosolo reveal the presence of local families that have amassed great fortunes through illegal means, such as large-scale livestock rustling or kidnappings for ransom, who appear to live no differently than any-one else in the community, but who are said to indulge in parallel lives in coastal resort areas or on the Italian mainland. The inner courtyard of the traditional house provided, until recent times, the only point where the public and the private could meet, where a glimpse of life within the domestic sphere could be provided to the trustworthiest of allies. Today, because resources allow for the construction of larger houses, the well-furnished living room serves this role. Antonio Pigliaru (2000 [1959]:224–30) too underscores the principle of the inviolability of the home, noting that it stands in opposition to the boundless countryside where treachery is to be expected. No mechanisms exist here to rectify an act of disloyalty or sabotage that affects the well-being of a house-hold and its inhabitants, except for blood feud. In the end, the integrity of the family and its well-being trumps any allegiance to actors from without, be they friend or not.

In terms of social integration, we may note the existence of almost tangible concentric circles of trust, at the centre of which is the nuclear family, then close blood relatives, thereafter friends and mates, and in the outermost ring, competitors and possible enemies (Bailey 1971:17; cf. Campbell 1966). Beyond this outermost ring are outsiders from beyond the moral community, unknowns who inhabit a surrounding world that is the source of aspiration or rejection and who, when pos-sible, are ritually incorporated as guests and placed in a subordinate position of accepting hospitality from a community that cannot incor-porate them as full members.

Hospitality and the Outsider

Hospitality is a sacred duty, and there is a noted proverb that suggests as much: *Dove c'è l'ospite, c'è Dio* (Where there is a guest, there is God). The injunction to be hospitable towards a guest, especially if the guest is an outsider to the community, is total and absolute, inescapable and non-negotiable. Hospitality has very precise meaning, entails very specific rules, and comprises more than just offering food and drink. It includes associated forms of commensal solidarity and the extension of personal sympathy to the social atom, without any overt calculation. Such an English-language phrase as "hospitality industry" would be regarded as bizarre, while of course what that term entails is certainly widespread throughout Sardinia and Italy, and has been for some time. There is another proverb, *il diavolo arriva dal mare* (the Devil arrives by sea), the meaning of which can be lost on no one. A widespread view of the outside world as hostile is frequently reiterated through accounts of resistance against imperious outside forces that have sought to subdue and control the Sardinian highlands, starting with the ancient Romans and extending into the contemporary period with the national government in Rome, with Saracen slave raiders, Genoese capitalists, and Spanish imperialists in between. These outsiders inevitably came from afar, and arrived by sea. It seems that outsiders may be the Devil, or God, or even both at once, but at any rate a source of possible danger, a figure whose presence never goes unnoticed. I suggest here that the rituals of hospitality directed towards such an outsider – the unknown – provide a glimpse into mechanisms by which the community, once again, defines itself vis-à-vis the outside world, subverts hegemonic structures, and effectively assists in the production of locality.

How then does one become a guest, and what is the process of incorporation? The observations that follow are limited to patterns discerned over the period of my own immersion into the community during my work in the field – namely, hospitality as practiced by men towards outsiders who are also men, which is structured by a set of well-established norms of social interaction. A stranger entering a bar in Orgosolo is seldom left to drink alone unless he is there only very briefly. In this case, a patron, who may or may not acknowledge his presence, will still pay for his drink. If the stranger lingers, he will be called over to a table of regulars or acknowledged by a patron standing by the bar, who will engage him in a formal, stereotyped interaction. Usually this interaction begins with an inquiry into the stranger's identity, and, if the interlocutor is especially cocky, is sometimes followed by a challenge: "You're a spy, aren't you?" An initially tense interaction, intended to unsettle the stranger and tacitly warn him that he is being watched, turns to jocular banter. The stranger partakes of every round offered by the company present, but is forbidden to pay. He is encouraged to drink at every round, and his glass must never be empty. Small glasses of local wine, spirits, or liqueurs, as well as beer, take an inevitable toll, but everyone is beholden to a definite standard of coherence as the rounds of drinks multiply. You should drink, but you should never get drunk. One who succeeds is admired, considered manly, strong, and a serious person worthy of possible respect, whereas someone who gets drunk is shunned as a weakling and a likely wastrel. In local terms, subjecting the stranger to interrogation while plying him with drinks is something known as *cuocere l'ospite*, cooking the guest, which refers to the transformative effect the practice has on the guest's status. Such an encounter is not always pleasant for the outsider, and he cannot help but sense a whiff of hostility in the air, mingling with a discordant tone of jocularity that inevitably accompanies his harassment. To sardonic laughter, he is *preso in giro* (taken for a ride). All subsequent encounters with those who initially subjected the guest to such an initiation are perfectly jovial and friendly. The guest is transformed.[12]

Ordeals that test the mettle of the stranger appear to share considerable cross-cultural parallels, from the Inuit studied by Franz Boas at the turn of the twentieth century, through to Julian Pitt-Rivers' more recent analysis of hospitality in Andalusia (1968), to Homer's *Odyssey*. The stranger is someone to be tested because of the very fact that he is an unknown. As Pitt-Rivers puts it, "He remains potentially anything: valiant or worthless, wellborn, well connected, wealthy or the contrary, and since his assertions regarding himself cannot be checked, he is above all not to be trusted. For this reason the charlatan is always, must be, a stranger" (1968:26). The ordeal he suffers transforms the stranger into a known entity, and serves as a vehicle through which he is introduced to his new status.

As I have already noted, men's participation in the most intensively public spaces of village life is most frequently mediated by membership within a friendship clique. Membership is based on a principle of voluntarism in which elective affinity plays a more important role than kinship; members of the *cricca*, like friends in general in Orgosolo, need not share any blood ties. The group's exclusivity relies on the observation of fairly strict rules of conduct. Most importantly, one does not move from one *cricca* to another. The internal solidarity of these groupings is precarious, and must periodically be reinforced through rituals of commensality, specifically *ispuntinus* (picnics) in the countryside or in cantinas. The aesthetic of these feasts centres largely on the kinds of foods consumed, all of which are produced locally and circulated within the informal market and conform to local expectations of culinary authenticity. Feasts include wines and spirits, roasted, boiled, or stewed pork, veal, beef, or ovine and caprine meats, heavy on offal like intestines, brain, lungs, liver, and heart and each with a unique method of preparation, as well as an array of aged cheeses, including such prized specialties as *casu marzu*.[13] There is a ritualized exchange interent to these feasts. When such foods are consumed by a gregarious male collective, with only the use of a knife and a plastic plate (or no plate at all), a profound sense of collective effervescence is generated and "the desiderata of male character" (Gilmore 1991:20) reproduced. Furthermore, these delicacies are all said to be very "strong," having unrefined textures and intense flavours that separate them from foods than can be appreciated by outsiders whose palates are accustomed to milder flavours. These foodstuffs express an emphatically local, rustic, highland identity. They are not available for purchase by most outsiders, and are not typically served to tourists (Satta 2001:120). The offering of these local delicacies to the bewildered guest, who is not accustomed to them, constitutes a rite of incorporation (van Gennep 1960) that sublimates his identity to that of the group, committing him to loyalty just as it commits the group to safeguarding his well-being.[14]

The guest is assimilated into male sociality, and learns to adapt his own identity to the group that absorbs him. The process of integration is complete once the guest is enjoined to participate in a gathering in full measure. "Pour us some wine, will you? You're one of us now!" These words were once spoken to me, in a tone of mirthful sarcasm, at a country picnic organized by a *cricca*. It was evident in the utterance that I, as a foreign-born guest with no deep ties to the community, effectively remained a displaced outsider, but one that was accepted into the sodality. That said, I was only conditionally integrated, surrounded by a barrier, protected, and made to witness and experience only the better, happier aspects of these men's lives: camaraderie, free spiritedness, and jovial effervescence.[15] Good, generous treatment of guests contributes to the collective honour of the sodality (cf. Abu-Zahra 1974:128). But the sodality is not an isolated entity; in their capacity as hosts, members of a friendship clique become representatives of the community and stand as guarantors of the community's reputation and renown as hospitable and cohesive. The friendship group is one of the primary and most important units to integrate and publicly confer a newfound status upon the guest. In contrast, private expressions of hospitality towards the outsider by members of a family or an individual interlocutor are far less elaborate and low-key than the boisterous feasts held by friendship cliques. As a result, an image of community solidarity is presented to the guest, who is spared the discomfort and feeling of insecurity that comes with knowing too much about local rivalries (Pigliaru 2000 [1959]:262ff.). In addition to indebting the guest to the host, the kind acts and gustatory delights that are the hallmark of hospitality also signify a moral advantage over the world of which the guest is a representative. Hospitality subverts the social, political, and economic dominance of the guest, and is the subaltern's mechanism for showcasing the best of what is local, assimilating the sentiments of the outsider to that of the community while maintaining the cohesiveness of the locality in the process.

Structures of hospitality in Orgosolo ritualize interaction with outsiders, integrate guests into a category that exempts them from the obligations of full participation in community life, and as such perpetuates the unity of the moral community vis-à-vis the outside world. In a time of unprecedented interconnectedness, the desire to maintain an image of bounded locality and distinctiveness is strong. In Orgosolo, the blurring of the community's boundaries frequently occasions a strengthening of its symbolic bases, and here, hospitality as a mode of transaction accomplishes that by focusing on the collective grace and honour of the community – the symbol of its wholeness.

Hospitality appears not only as a key element in the *constitution* of the local, but also serves as a technique for the actual *production* of the local (Appadurai 1996). Likewise, any appearance of opposition to the outside world, however conceived or expressed, represents merely one axis of locality, while the entire social complex, consisting of rituals, courtesies, kinship and friendship norms, conflicts, ambivalences and the entire panoply of daily interactions in general, provides the other. Put differently, the integrity of locality is maintained through the routines of social life (see Lambek 2011), so that life of the local does not only stand in explicit opposition to the that of the non-local, but is rather a result of the exigencies of daily living. This recreation of locality involves the energies of a variety of *dramatis personae*, and the community thereby "aggregates the individualities and other differences and provides the means for their expression, interpretation, and containment" (Cohen 1985:21). Therefore, as we have seen, Orgolesi need not all sing from the same hymn sheet to belong to the same congregation. The incommensurable values and goals of its members and the often discordant undertone to social life are the inevitable features of community life anywhere, and the locality renews itself every day by meeting this challenge. Lastly, the dynamic tension between the centrifugal and centripetal tendencies in social life reflects a deep awareness of the imperative of social cohesion, necessary to the maintenance of the community and locality.

7
Conclusion

The phrase *chentu concas, chentu berittas* is the Sardinian dialect version of the old saying, widespread throughout Italy, "a hundred heads, a hundred hats." The hundred hats, of course, are the hundred different ways the same number of heads think and feel. This expression is employed lightheartedly in reference to cases in which people do not see eye-to-eye on some particular matter, trivial or serious. It evokes an acceptance that individual preferences, opinions, and views will differ, but that in the end we must strive to coexist. The expression, pedestrian though it is, serves as a reminder that life in society is possible only with compromise, that, in sum, we are not all the same in thought and feeling.

This is all very conventional, as is the social machinery that is at first sight indicative of consensus and good relations in the face-to-face community yet that is ultimately geared to cloud much of what should elude the outsider anyway. It is a point of pride for Orgolesi to not co-opt outsiders into their personal antipathies and enmities, for they should be spared the burden of knowing too much about the disagreements and discords that characterize local life. As a result the many gestures of civility that are apparent everywhere, the spirit of neighbourliness that infuse social interactions and the many small exchanges of services, favours, and gifts that mark the passage of days, months, and years, create an image of tightly knit community. Yet, beneath this surface appearance lays a highly fractious parallel reality. I have shown that this double helix of consensus and dissensus constitutes the community, and its spatiotemporal embeddedness provides the context within which lives unfold. For Orgolesi, *sa bidda* (the village), with its houses and storefronts, roads and alleys, sounds and smells, and characters and personages is, for this reason, a central symbol of its inhabitants' collective self-definition.

Such a study as this, centred on a village community, might seem anachronistic in the early twenty-first century, a holdover from the age of structural-functionalist ethnography that conceived of peoples as bounded together in many discrete and self-contained units. This is by now a well-established critique, which salutarily warns of the dangers inherent to the concept of cultural area defined by lists of traits. The idea of the Mediterranean region as composed of seemingly homogenous, territorially bounded communities is certainly not useful for purposes of anthropological research, and never was, but the debate about whether such an approach really did inform ethnographic practice in the region is not likely to be resolved soon (Albera and Blok 2001). The perspective taken here suggests that the comparative ethnography of the Mediterranean guarded against a vision of homogeneity in the first place, as indeed comparativism necessarily takes heterogeneity as its starting point, setting all instances of the particular against larger backgrounds. An appreciation of this perspective underlies the last decade's rapidly emergent view of the Mediterranean as a complex assemblage. The region has variously been characterized as a "pluriverse" of competing and complementary values, religions, world views, and traditions (Zolo 2007), a "matrix" that enforces a coexistence of unity with diversity, universalism with particularism, and fundamentalism with tolerance (Morin 1998, 1999), a "cultural landscape" comprising multiplicity, contradictions, and paradoxes (Matvejevic 1999), a sea that binds together a "system of complementary differences" conditioned by history and maintained within a field of reciprocal oppositions (Bromberger 2006, 2007), a transactional field composed of family resemblances among its constitutive societies (Albera and Blok 2001), and, finally, a region defined by a history of contacts and clashes among the peoples and cultures that inhabit its islands and shores (Giordano 2001, 2012b). In this conception of the Mediterranean, there can be no isolated villages or self-contained units of any kind, outside history, lost to time, and easy prey to apparently reifying tendencies of a discipline defined by the pursuit of the traditional and the primitive. Nonetheless, a move away from perspectives of the Mediterranean as a cultural system became inevitable as a result of an increasing acceptance of claims that visions of regional unity constituted an exoticizing mission that served to create a distorting mirror through which Eurocentric ethnographers confronted themselves: "In this mirror we seek our own roots. We hope to discover the clear boundaries, which in modern society have become blurred, and to locate the past certainties, which for us have become ambiguities" (Dubisch 1995:201). According to Dubisch, Mediterrane-anist constructs assuaged Western male nostalgia of a mythic past in which men and women behaved according to our own projections.

This unfair reassessment of the aims of Mediterranean ethnol-ogy coincided with a critical turn in the discipline in the 1980s, when extant ethnographic representations of place-bound peoples fell under increased scrutiny on the part of theorists who called into question the methodology that had informed research since the Malinowskian revolution (see Clifford and Marcus 1986; Marcus and Fischer 1986). A move away from the methodologically bounded fieldsite would liberate us from the straitjackets of fieldwork, and give rise to new, mobile, multi-sited styles of research (Marcus 1995). Multi-site ethnog-raphy represented a permutation of world systems theory that further expanded Wolf's (1982) salutary call to contextualize the ethnography of so-called peoples without history within global historical processes. The spirit and aims of multi-site anthropology dovetailed with the eventual turn to mobility within the social sciences, in which movement and the "non-place" (Augé 1995) would become newfound objects of anthropological analysis (see Sorge and Roddick 2012). Likewise, James Clifford (1997) enthusiastically announced a post-locality mobility par-adigm that has forsaken roots in favour of routes – that is, the restless movements of people and objects, cultural dislocations, disjunctures, and ruptures. This critique has resonated throughout the discipline, and it is now a seldom-questioned commonplace that fieldwork based on long-term cultural immersion results in false constructions of boundedness that pre-empt the effective study of interconnections, movements, and flows. As Marcus (2008:4) suggests, "traditional methods à la Malinowski or Boas" are no longer adequate in our attempts to apprehend the complexities of late modernity.

This apparent assault on place, and the resultant unmooring of eth-nographic practice from the localized site (see Ferguson 2011), has been met in some quarters with an opposite reaction, summed up neatly in Fog Olwig's (1997:17) measured dictum that our studies of globaliza-tion must take care "not to overemphasize the global and transient character of human life on the loose." Clearly, emplaced human experi-ence and associated attachments to locality are not diminished in the twenty-first century, and the complex affinities that define sense of place are an expression of the social force of community that is especially salient in instances in which it is fused with elements of a collective identity (Basso 1996:87). Never a self-contained monadic entity, or even an ontologically secure thing, the highland Sardinian village nonetheless encompasses a population defined by its historical experience, brought together in response to external forces that, over the *longue durée*, have variously sought to control, regulate, and govern it according to principles that are exogenous to local systems. Orgosolo's experiences are not unique, but are in fact replicated throughout the Mediterranean region; as I suggested above, the lands bordering this inland sea contain no shortage of marginal populations that have taken refuge in mountainous terrains in order to evade political control and the violence of state societies that sought to establish their hegemony.

In this case, the highland Sardinian village represents a byproduct of a history that has generated a guarded but open, welcoming yet wary disposition towards the outside world. The creation of locality in Orgosolo is informed by this understanding of history, and has been constructed in symbolic opposition to the ethos believed to characterize the wider society. What is partly responsible for this is the sense – again, widespread throughout the Mediterranean (see Giordano 2006) – that history is a hostile and treacherous force that renders people the objects rather than the subjects of their own pasts. This is a prevalent notion in Orgosolo, and it strongly conditions the outlook of local traditionalists employed in the pastoral sector. These men's activities, centred as they are on the village and its territory, place them at the heart of the locality. Their espousal of *balentia* serves as a defining element of authenticity owing to its stance of dissidence vis-à-vis the outside world, even if, among non-shepherds, it is frequently believed to reflect little more than a corruption of the pastoral identity. Non-shepherds' perception of the non-local, specifically the universalizing aspirations of cosmopolitan actors, stands in sharp contrast to the parochialized forms of local identity that define the habitus of the shepherd.

An important aim of this study has been to gauge continuity and change over time in Orgosolo, and to assess local responses to circumstances beyond the community's control in order to comprehend the significance of some observable patterns. Notably, I have focused on the extent of continuity within the system of *balentia*, widely caricatured for its apparent incommensurability with the requirements of a hegemonic, modern nation-state and even with modernity itself. In addition, an outline of broad historical processes underscores how geography and landscape can condition social forms and enhances understanding of how geographical inaccessibility imparts onto local communities a spirit of opposition to the outside world. In sum, the resulting image is that of a cultural system that is both self-replicating as well as in a state of flux, flowing forth from an analysis of cultural history that points to the range of changes that have occurred in highland Sardinia since Italian unification in 1861. Agency and structure are given equal weight in this account, which takes as axiomatic the insight that people are not born into a world that they may shape independently of the givens of the past, because the past always conditions the structures of the present. This underscores the need to account for the range of factors that conspire to maintain those seemingly more "traditional" aspects of social life. Certain concepts of honour and honourable behaviour, various understandings of propriety, and discernible predispositions towards the outside world that characterize the social interactions of localist Orgolesi have been conditioned by circumstances that persist today. Outward-oriented cosmopolitan Orgolesi are, for their part, exemplars of all that is new, urbane, and refined, but between the two there is a grudging acceptance of the other's way of being.

The localist disposition towards the outside world is most visibly manifested in reactions to government attempts to impose laws onto a community that cannot tolerate the morality behind them. Throughout history we have witnessed numerous, often violent attempts on the part of agents of the state to impose onto rural highland shepherds a set of legal norms that offend local theories of justice and are incommensurable with indigenous mechanisms of conflict resolution. The longstanding preference in the Sardinian highlands has been for the preservation of a customary legal system premised upon a code of honour that regulates personal behaviour. I have contextualized Orgosolo by considering briefly throughout the text how a comparable range of phenomena have emerged throughout the Mediterranean region in predictable configurations, and how these in turn are the product of a range of historical constants.

Although violence is normative to and pervasive of social relations within agrarian society, it ceases to be so within industrial society, the citizens of which accept the full authority of the state and its legal apparatus. Where the means of violence are widely diffused, an ascendant state will actively seek to establish its own monopoly by divesting citizens of the means to openly engage in legal self-help. Yet why do honour systems, whose very credibility is premised upon the threat and practice of violence, persist despite such external pressures? For highland Sardinia, the answer to this question lies in the demands of pastoral production, in that honour values subsumed under *balentia*, and the concept of *balentia* itself, are the preserve of shepherds. Their lives are sharply distinguishable from those of Orgolesi who are not pastoralists, leading to a diagnosis of a localist cosmopolitan distinction within a community that was, less than a century ago, completely rural in its style of life and that, unlike today, comprised a single cultural model. But in its aggregate, the population of Orgosolo nonetheless continues to present a unity. The exemplary traditionalists – *sos balentes*, who are shepherds or at least self-consciously look and play the part – are both loathed and loved by the *cittadini*, those urbane locals whose outward-facing orientation reflects an adherence to an ethos and set of values that are inimical to the lives of localists. I have suggested that the best way to appreciate the contrasts between adherents to traditionalist and urbane outlooks, respectively, is to consider how they play out locally. An examination of family and household structures reveals that members of these two social categories do not live lives separate from one another. However, great differences are to be noted if we consider social norms outside of the family. An exploration of the broader significance of the coexistence of urbane and traditionalist cultural models is integral to this analysis, and ultimately the degree of openness towards the outside world reinforces this internal differentiation, which is strongly reflected in differences of dress, locution, and demeanour.

Difficult economic circumstances, paired with a widespread propensity towards an auto-essentialism that often casts local identity as a bygone form of pastoral highland culture and the romantic mystique that this entails, have a conditioning effect upon observable social forms. The *pastori finti* (pretend shepherds) – who to many are a target of disapproval, ridicule, or pity, and to one person I knew even a quaint tourist attraction – are in important ways a byproduct of unemployment. They are paired with a collective memory of a golden age of heroic pastoralism that always evaded and resisted outside political authority. Such a conception of the past is a legacy born of a history of violent acts long visited upon the locality, which in turn has generated those values I have subsumed under the term *balentia*. *Balentes* do not conform to the emergent neoliberal image of Sardinia as a technologically advanced region at the forefront of business and innovation. Such a vision was strongly propagated by Renato Soru – founder and CEO of Tiscali SpA, one of Italy's largest Internet and telecommunications companies – when he embarked on an ambitious program of digitization of schools during his tenure as President of Sardinia from 2004 to 2008, as well as the construction of a region-wide infrastructure that would ensure accessibility to high-speed Internet in every community on the island. Rather, the so-called pretend-shepherds have not become connected global citizens and aficionados of high-tech devices (although they do use cell phones, and portable Internet devices are becoming increasingly popular), but rather exemplify a habitus that is easily recognizable by the retired shepherd who spent most of his early formative years in the Università del Supramonte, that foreboding highland plateau in the common lands where one needed to quickly acquire the traits of tenacity and resilience in order to succeed as a herder. Often underemployed and not subject to anything like the physical hardships faced by their forefathers, modern shepherds have retained an outward appearance, comportment, and nomenclature that are unfamiliar to many non-shepherds, and for this reason appear as a conservative social element within the community. The forms of sociability in which they regularly engage was at one time only a rare diversion afforded to men upon their brief return to the village from the pastures during festive intervals in the annual cycle, when a long period of sober solitude was followed by a brief period of effervescent camaraderie. Today, bar owners see brisk business late into the night, and drinking begins early. Many insist that it never used to be this way, and that old patterns have been replaced with new, less desirable ones.

The apparent paradox of shepherds representing a past that is a source of collective pride, while concurrently symbolizing so much of what locals are ambivalent to or even embarrassed of, is a byproduct of a series of social changes that have culminated in the introduction of mainstream Italian understandings of "the good life." These changes have become a source of constant local negotiations in terms of individual and collective self-definitions, and have witnessed a proliferation of cultural ambiguities and uncertainties. Nonetheless, although a continuity of values and categories is discernible here, it is not untouched by the passage of time. Nor can it escape the concomitant acceptance on the part of many locals of other values and judgments emanating from urban centres. For the individual who is outwardly inclined, for whom the bulk of his or her social existence takes place outside of the local system, escape is a possibility. There is no shortage of such people in Orgosolo, but they are difficult to spot because they do not conspicuously adhere to local standards of sociality. Rather, their more socially distant lives are governed by other, more cosmopolitan, standards for which they feel greater affinity. These individuals may be salaried workers or professionals who commute to the city of Nuoro or other urban centres daily, or even locally employed shopkeepers, artisans, and members of the public administration who, for the most part, claim residence in Orgosolo but who either do not engage significantly with local life or limit such engagement considerably. These are not the *dramatis personae* that grace the streets of Orgosolo and animate the social life of the community. They inhabit Orgosolo, but do not quite live in it. Among the most visible members of the community we find the most marginalized people conceivable: young men with limited prospects, the rejects of a system that has rendered their ethos anachronistic, the heirs of a social order deemed barbaric. Nonetheless, in the end, I have managed to discern at least some agreement on the part of local people with regard to what it means to be Orgolese. Standards of hospitality and pride in shared traditions and, more generally, in Orgosolo's renown are widespread. On the part of cosmopolitans, we find a pride that is intellectually sustained and centred on an understanding of an idealized past, but that is not demonstrated on a day-to-day basis or embodied in action. Localists, on the other hand, do not concern themselves with avowals and reminiscences. To them, being Orgolese is about conforming daily to what they perceive to be the authentic social values of the past, which inevitably provides an alternative to the values of mainstream society in the era of late modernity. But for all their differences, cosmopolitans and localists find a point of convergence in a shared adherence to an image of community – an adherence rooted in the recollection of the past and in an awareness of their own transience as individuals.

Notes

1. Introduction

1 This dynamic is an old one, and was discerned by the Arab philosopher of history, Ibn Khaldun of Tunis in the 14th C., when he wrote of the distinction between *siba* (dissident hill tribalism) and *makhzen* (the state) (Issawi 1963:120-21; Gellner 1981:86-98). That civilizations can't climb hills is admittedly not a new discovery, but nonetheless serves as a reminder that can spur a novel way of apprehending the ecumene of those peoples that have existed on the margins of powerful state formations.

2 Throughout the Mediterranean, such cults of masculinity have been seen as comprising systems of male "honour-as-precedence" (Pitt-Rivers 1977).

3 Likewise, any understanding of honour and shame that simplistically assumes the parallelism represented in the formula "honour:shame// men:women" should be rejected out of hand. See Herzfeld (1980:446) and Wikan (1984).

4 A common explanation in Orgosolo for the lack of female cloistering, and indeed centrality of women in the public sphere, makes reference to the realities of the pastoral economy that would see men off into remote pastures for months at a time.

5 Several authors have noted the distinction between occupational sectors in central highland Sardinia, presenting parallels to own localist-cosmopolitan divide. Steffan Igor Ayora-Diaz (1993) examines occupational choices in the town of "Telemula," and writes about local discourses and judgments about "traditional" vs "modern" careers and the lifestyles they entail, David Lonergan (1984) considers the differences in sociability and friendship patterns among three categories of shepherds, artisans and labourers, and white collar workers in the village of "Bidda,"

while, similarly, Peter Schweizer (1988) developed the categorization of shepherds, workers, and intellectuals in his research on "Basilada."

6 Needless to say, this was not a topic about which it was wise for me to casually inquire, and the only information I could hope to obtain consists of public gossip and unsubstantiated opinions and guesses that already circulate within the public domain.

7 Cocco and Marras (2000) suggest that highland men's dress reflects a unique engagement with a local ethnic style (*stile etnico*) that distinguishes shepherds as as occupationally distinct and culturally authentic category. As Steffan Igor Ayora-Diaz (1993:283) has noted, conformity in dress and comportment among shepherds cannot be overemphasized. The young shepherd who wishes to stake a claim to individuality in his appearance will be the object of scorn, regarded as presumptuous and arrogant for adopting a style regarded as more refined than that of the shepherd.

2. Landscape and History

1 See Caltagirone (1989a, 1989b) for an extensive discussion of livestock rustling techniques, as well as measures taken to guard against it, including the range of district-specific styles of animal markings that are used.

2 The port at Tortolì-Arbatax was created in the mid-nineteenth century to service a nearby paper mill, while the artificial port at Olbia must be periodically excavated to maintain its depth of 7 metres (Cau 1999:328; Principe 1985:594).

3 In his brief treatment of the area, Braudel (1972:40) provides the following summation of differences between highlands and lowlands: "There was no tight urban network so no administration, no towns in the proper sense of the word, and no gendarmes either we might add. It is only in the lowlands that one finds a close-knit, stifling society, a prebendal clergy, a haughty aristocracy, and an efficient system of justice. The hills were the refuge of liberty, democracy, and peasant 'republics.'"

4 See Black-Michaud (1975:147ff.).

5 If this plaque, which has never been found, is accurate, then up to half of the highland population during that period may have been killed or enslaved according to one estimate. See Casula (1994:44).

6 Le Lannou (1941:124) writes that by the eighth century "le gouvernement byzantin acheva d'oublier qu'il possédait la Sardaigne" (the Byzantine government managed to forget that it controlled Sardinia).

7 See Cagnetta (1975:127ff.) for an extensive discussion.

8 Like the story of Cain and Abel, this theme is as old as antiquity: "Le nomade est un guerrier par nécessité, et, s'il descend dans la plaine, c'est moins poussé par un appétit de conquête que par le besoin de faire vivre ses troupeaux. Sa tranquillité ou sa fureur dépendent de l'herbe et de la pluie. Ses incursions sont de véritables transgressions d'origine climatique" (The nomad is a warrior by necessity, and, if he descends to the plain, it is spurred less by an appetite for conquest than by the need to feed his animals. His peaceableness or his fury is determined by the availability of edible grasses and by water. His incursions are transgressions born of weather conditions) (Le Lannou 1941:126; cf Masia 1992).

9 I never ceased to be amazed by the ability of numerous acquaintances and regular interlocutors, especially my friend Serafino with whom I travelled throughout numerous villages in the province of Nuoro, to deftly discern peoples' villages of origin on the basis of their speech. I only became aware of nuances of dialect toward the end of my research stay, and have only ever managed to develop the very modest ability to distinguish Orgolese from neighbouring forms of Sardinian.

10 Deledda's oeuvre also reflects no paucity of representations of highland Sardinia as beholden to an inescapable primitivism. The following passage is from her famed novel, *Colombi e Sparvieri* (*Doves and Sparrowhawks*): "The man of these mountains is still a primitive, and if he manages to steal a goat and to eat it with his friends or his family he will regard it as a successful undertaking. Even from him, a day or a week before, had been stolen a kid. Why shouldn't he make up his losses? And if you tell him that he has done wrong, he will get offended, and his rancour toward you will be that of a man from whom one has sought to deny a basic right. Segregated from the rest of the world, in continuous struggle with the few others who are his equals, often even with his relatives, or also his brother, the man of this village believes he has the right to mete out justice according to his own lights, with the weapons he possesses: physical force, astuteness, his tongue" (Deledda 1993 [1912]:463).

11 In 1883, 26,000 head of livestock were exported to France, but this figure would reach negligible proportions by 1888; so too did the export of wine plummet from a high of 433,000 litres in 1887 to 2,881 litres two years later (Clark 1989:271).

12 See Eric Hobsbawm (1969) and Anton Blok (1974) for their spirited debate on the question of "social banditry," and whether such a thing could exist.

13 We may ask, why? As Robert Nisbet (1990 [1953]:247) suggests, the establishment of an industrial economy undergirded by free-market principles only ever appears on the scene as a purely artificial

development, "brought into existence by the planned destruction of old customs, associations, villages, and other securities, by the force of the State throwing the weight of its fast-developing administrative system in favour of the new economic elements of the population."

14 See Regione Autonoma della Sardegna, Elezione del Quattordicesimo Consiglio regionale, 15 e 16 Febbraio 2009. A: Circoscrizioni provinciali. http://consiglio.regione.sardegna.it/Manuale%20consiliare/XIV _Legislatura/Tomo%20II/02a%20-%202009%20Quattordicesimo.pdf.

15 See Regione Autonoma della Sardegna, Elezioni 2009 (http://www .regione.sardegna.it/argomenti/attivita_istituzionali/elezioni2009/ risultati_comune.html), and Ministero dell'Interno, Elezioni 2013b. (http://elezionistorico.interno.it/index.php?tpel=C&dtel=24/02/201 3&tpa=I&tpe=C&lev0=0&levsut0=0&lev1=26&levsut1=1&lev2=53&le vsut2=2&lev3=600&levsut3=3&ne1=26&ne2=53&ne3=530600&es0=S& es1=S&es2=S&es3=N&ms=S).

16 See Ministero dell'Interno, Elezioni 2013b (http://elezionistorico.interno. it/index.php?tpel=C&dtel=24/02/2013&tpa=I&tpe=C&lev0=0&levsut0=0 &lev1=26&levsut1=1&lev2=53&levsut2=2&lev3=600&levsut3=3&ne1=26& ne2=53&ne3=530600&es0=S&es1=S&es2=S&es3=N&ms=S)..

3. On Barbarism

1 Pigliaru's claims do not apply to the present day, or at least not as well as they did to the post-WW2 period, when he gathered most of his data. As we will see, twenty-first century realities reflect a range of profound social and cultural transformations that ultimately present a more complex reality than before.

2 Conversely, where no intensive food production is found, as is the case in foraging societies, there could be no systematic accumulation of wealth; therefore, violence, stratification, and authority were neither pervasive nor normative to the social order. See Sahlins (1972).

3 Meloni (1996:120) further argues that honour codes necessarily justify and envision the enactment of vendetta, which, under circumstances of rapid social change, becomes instrumental in the commission of criminal acts that fall beyond the original spirit of the institution.

4 In the case at hand, the *balente* is not the standard bearer of the values of the local community, as the *pallikari* – a concept roughly analogous to *balente* among the Sarakatsani of Corinth – apparently were to theirs (Campbell 1964:278ff.).

5 The ineffable quality of "tacit knowledge" that Pierre Bourdieu (1977:27) sees as central to habitus applies to the performance of *balentia*; the

rules are never explicitly articulated, but are known by all, provide the background to everyday life, and are constitutive of individual agency.

6 Christian Giordano (2012a:20) provides a transactional view of honour values that I find very useful: "Honor in general, thus also honor in the Mediterranean societies, is not merely a moral code comprising values, norms, representations, and a set of practices, but rather a cultural idiom and a combination of social strategies found in several public arenas. Thus, honor in its various expressions in terms of representations and social practices alike is a phenomenon set up to highlight social differences (class and gender especially), and maintain, increase or restore status and reputation in order to define (better yet, redefine) the social identifications and auto-comprehensions of individuals and groups."

7 See Blok (2001:136-54) for a comprehensive discussion of the role of insecurity in the emergence of the Sicilian agro-town.

8 Their moral frustration is neatly expressed in Romans 7:19: "For the good that I would, I do not: but the evil which I would not, that I do" (cited in du Boulay 1991:46).

9 Furthermore, where village endogamy was the norm, livestock rustling was a form of exchange that could sustain sets of relations extending beyond the village, yielding a hypothesis as to the homologous link between livestock rustling and marriage (see Caltagirone 1989a:127-32).

10 The problem of outlawry was not restricted to Sardinia. Italy as a whole, especially the poorer south, faced a situation during this period in which public authority could not operate with any degree of efficiency due to claims to neo-statehood made by brigand chieftains through their assorted practices of extortion, racketeering, and localized maintenance of order. Such competing claims on the part of nonstate actors, some of which amassed small but dangerously armed and outfitted armies, could not be subdued with diplomatic tactics, but rather with offensive violence in excess of what they themselves could muster. See Bracalini (2001) and Scarcella (2001).

11 See Angioni (1989:221-46).

12 Euphemism for prostitutes.

13 Analogous to the present case, Elizabeth du Boulay (1976) describes the Greek village of Ambeli as a place where daily life is simultaneously intensely public and intensely private, where the effort to maintain privacy for oneself was counterbalanced by a desire to deny it for others. Thus, two neighbours meeting in the street will exchange the requisite pleasantries, followed by one asking the other, *Pou pas?* (Where are you going?), with the standard reply being *Poutheni* (Nowhere).

4. Anachronistic Men

1 Silvana knows of Giovanni through Belinda, the victim's sister, from her days as a student at a *scuola superiore* (senior high school) in the provincial capital of Nuoro in the 1980s.

2 For an extensive discussion of post-Fordism and its associated transformations in sexualities, see Lancaster (2003:306ff.).

3 See Caltagirone (1989a, 1989b) for a comprehensive examination of livestock rustling in the central highlands.

4 Philippe Bourgois (1996, 2003) documents a similar process among young Puerto Rican men in New York City.

5 Jaro Stacul (2003:101) records similarly scornful sentiments among Italian alpine villagers in the region of Trentino Alto Adige toward local folk who "went urban"; they "are often alluded to by their co-villagers as 'shit put on a stool' (*merda montada sul scagno*), on the grounds that they do not work at all and look down upon local workers."

6 At the start of the twenty-first century, the tertiary sector accounted for 70 per cent of the Sardinian workforce, while farming, fishing, forestry, and pastoralism together accounted for 8 per cent (Ruju 2006:171).

7 Emigration is another option. While Orgosolo, with its more or less stable population of 4,300 souls, has been spared the demographic shift away from rural centres, much of the rest of Sardinia, including both highland and lowland towns and villages, have not (cf. Magliocco 2006:25ff.; Ruju 2006:172; Tiragallo 2001). In neighbouring Corsica, high rates of migration away from village communities to coastal towns, but especially to the French mainland, have been a fact of life since the post-war period (see Ravis-Giordani 2001 [1983]).

8 ISTAT, Italy's national statistics agency, subsumes pastoral production under agriculture.

9 Selected aspects of this reality are sensitively depicted in David MacDougall's ethnographic film, *Tempus de Baristas* (1997).

10 This anxiety of masculine identity is by no means specific to Sardinia or even to Italy. Similarly marginalized young men the world over contend with analogous predicaments wherever similar kinds of socioeconomic transformations have occasioned a society-wide shift in gender sensibilities. Thus, young men in Ethiopia (Mains 2012), urban China (Jankowiak et al. 2012), and Georgia (Frederiksen 2012) who have not easily adapted to the economic realities of late modernity are frequently scapegoated as lazy troublemakers, idle preeners, and unreliable ne'er-do-wells (see Amit and Dyck 2012).

11 In January 2005, a nation-wide smoking ban in public places would include all bars and restaurants. The ban was successful, and now, to the chagrin but eventual resignation of many, Orgosolo's bars are, alas, smoke-free.

12 Recall that standards of sociability among shepherds are predicated upon a separation of the sexes. Local shepherds look askance at the idea that women and men can enjoy disinterested, non-sexual, relationships (see Satta 2001).

5. Divergent Visions

1 No families in Orgosolo can trace a membership within particular guilded or unguilded occupations to several generations in the past, as historically this was a socially undifferentiated hamlet of transhumant shepherds and not a rigidly stratified agrarian order with peasants and overlords. For a discussion of stratification in rural agro-towns, see Blok (2001:136–54), and Blok and Driessen (1984).

2 Once again, it is important to highlight that Orgosolo, or any other village in highland Sardinia, has never been isolated from the world beyond its horizons. There are no precontact Sardinian highlanders, at least not since prehistory.

3 The differentiation is also to be found in other spheres – music, artistic production generally, cuisine, and in the relationships between men and women.

4 See Stacul et al. (2005) for an extended comparative examination.

5 As Frederick Buell (1994:9) notes, such cultural revivals and their accompanying proliferation of asserted differences are widespread and recurrent wherever we observe an increase in global integration and ease of communications. See Beyer (1994:60ff.).

6 By contrast, in the work of James Ferguson (1999:82–122), the question of stylistic competence provides the key definition to the cosmopolitanism-localism divide, and, for that matter, captures most of its essence.

7 It is noteworthy that their occasional use of such an outfit is not the result of compliance extracted by localists who demand conformity to rigid local norms (cf. Ferguson 1999:110ff.).

8 Unlike other towns located at some distance from the central highlands, Orgosolo and neighbouring villages do not have an industrial working class, and therefore we do not find a fully developed class consciousness of the kind that one can expect of unionized factory employees. This presents a contrast with the situation found in "Basilada," (a pseudonym),

examined by Peter Schweizer (1988), which is located close to the large petrochemical installations in Ottana.

9 This view is widespread among the *intelligentsia*, having been gleaned from urban centres and set forth, for example, in the writings of the Sardinian archaeologist Giovanni Lilliu (2002), who has attempted to explicate the origins of what he calls the highland Sardinian *costante resistenziale* (steadfastness of resistance).

10 The nearby provincial capital of Nuoro is for many a place where a modicum of anonymity is permitted. Although it is not large by the standards of the more well-known Italian cities, or even nearly as large as Cagliari, Nuoro, at almost 40,000 inhabitants, is much larger than Orgosolo. It was proclaimed a diocese by Pope Pius VI in 1779, formally incorporated as a city in 1836, and became the capital of the newly created Provincia di Nuoro under the Mussolini regime. Nuoro has long attracted settlers from across Sardinia and Italy; as a result, it is a place where the arts flourish and where a plethora of restaurants, bookstores, cinemas, and nightclubs allow commuting inhabitants of many smaller centres to engage in an economy of taste that sets them apart from localists back home.

11 Hannerz puts the matter succinctly: "At home, for most cosmopolitans, most others are locals. This is true in the great majority of territorially-based cultures. Conversely, for most of these locals, the cosmopolitan is someone a little unusual, one of us and yet not quite one of us. Someone to be respected for his experiences, possibly, but equally possibly not somebody to be trusted as a matter of course. Trust tends to be a matter of shared perspectives, of 'I know, and I know that you know, and I know that you know that I know'. And this formula for the social organization of meaning does not necessarily apply to the relationship between local and cosmopolitan" (1990:248).

12 The anthropologist Gino Satta intuited as much when he reflexively noted how his own, somewhat translocalized existence was a source of consternation to some Orgolesi: "My own personal story was often perceived as an evident monstrosity: born in Cagliari to parents from Sassari, raised in Rome, and in Orgosolo on a doctoral bursary from the University of Naples, I seemed to incarnate the opposite of what is locally expected in matters of identity. Some less respectful interlocutors, on various occasions, jokingly tagged me and my condition with the less-than-honourable, but very significative, label: *burdu*, bastard" (2001:74).

13 For an examination of a similar dynamic within a southern Italian context, see Galt (1992:113ff.).

14 Details of this legislation are found in "Norme in materia di tutela delle minoranze linguistiche storiche," Legge 15 Dicembre 1999, n. 492. *Gazzetta Ufficiale* n. 297. http://www.parlamento.it/parlam/leggi/994821.htm.

15 By contrast, in neighbouring Corsica, instruction in a standard Corsican language is institutionalized in public schools (see Jaffe 1996; 2003).

16 This presents a likely instance of Freud's theory of the "narcissism of minor differences," the dynamics of which are examined within a Mediterranean context by Anton Blok (2001).

17 With reference to Basilada, Peter Schweizer (1988) describes such people as "intellectuals" within his tripartite division of the categories of shepherds, workers, and intellectuals. Here, my own analytical preference is to subsume the members of this group of progressive and engaged citizens under the broader category of "cosmopolitans." Running the gamut from shopkeepers, schoolteachers, town functionaries, and local *liberi professionisti* (independent professionals), they are not intellectuals according to any strict definition of the term.

6. Cohesion and Community

1 As the displaced protagonist in a modern Sardinian novel proclaims, honour in a large city (in this case, Milan) is a personal matter, not subject to the prying of others: "She indulged in her freedom. In walking in the streets without being observed. Criticized, perhaps. On the island everyone knows everything about you, she would say. They know what you do, whom you see, whom and what you like or do not like, what you think. They even know how much you have in your pockets. Pockets are transparent on the island, she would say. People judge and weigh you for what you possess and for the power you can demonstrate as having. Power counts for much in a world without power, but even more than riches and power what counts is 'honour'" (Giacobbe 1995:10).

2 See Lewis (1973), and Hannerz (1980:59–76).

3 A reformulation of this thesis would later appear in the work of political scientist Robert Putnam (1993), who diagnoses a high degree of civic commitment in northern Italy, but "less civic" and "uncivic" tendencies in the south and on the islands.

4 Herzfeld (2002:23) has pointedly noted that "in Italy every small *paese* is its own Athens," conceptually a city-state that serves as a reference point to its inhabitants for all that is desirable and commendable as far as customs, practices, values, and ideals are concerned.

5 These are administered jointly, as in the case of lands, or exclusively by the female head of household, as in the case of all wealth within the home. In cases in which male heads of household obtain all or most of their income through the herding of livestock, the responsibility for the management of herds falls to them, including the securement of nutrition, immunizations, shearing, and all transactions on local and regional markets for the sale of meat, milk, and cheese.

6 For extensive discussion, see Assmuth (1997).

7 Census data show that Orgosolo has 1,569 nuclear families, but 1,804 habitable houses (ISTAT 2001).

8 For a discussion of the rise and entrenchment within daily life of the regular use of the automobile within a northern Italian context, see Grasseni (2004).

9 This is unexceptional in Italy as a whole; country-wide, people marry late and have childen well into their thirties. The average age of new mothers in Italy is thirty-two years (ISTAT 2012), while in Sardinia it is thirty-three years (Regione Autonoma della Sardegna, 2013: Parti e Nascite in Sardegna). At 7.7 live births/1000 inhabitants, Sardinia also has a lower fertility rate than the rest of Italy, which stands at 9.3 live births/1000 inhabitants, while the province of Nuoro records 8.1 live births/1000 inhabitants (Parti e Nascite in Sardegna). An analysis of these statistics and the significance of their correlation with the ethnographic findings provided here is beyond the scope of the current study.

10 In Orgosolo and elsewhere on the island, the same standards are used in judging the quality of other foods, primary among them cheese and prepared meats. When produced according to traditional techniques of aging and curing, these foodstuffs are widely exalted as being authentic (*autentico*), genuine (*genuino*), and/or organic (*biologico*), clearly making use of bourgeois, urbane categories of culinary adjudication to herald the quality of local foods over mass-produced, commodified foods (see Ayora-Diaz 1993:238ff)..

11 During the 1930s, the Mussolini regime deemed the use of masks during carnival period to be unnecessarily detrimental to public security, and thus banned all forms of disguise.

12 See discussion in Satta (2001:173ff.).

13 This translates roughly as "rancid cheese," but the descriptor does not carry a negative connotation. To the contrary, the very mention of *casu marzu* fills diners with the anticipation of a perfect end to a meal. This well-loved delicacy consists of a round of sheep's milk cheese, pecorino, infested with the hatched larvae of the *Piophila casei*. Officially designated

as a tainted product, it is illegal to sell or purchase *casu marzu*, and it is therefore only acquirable through informal networks that exclude outsiders.

14 Such hospitality may be seen as comprising a gift, conceptualized here by Georg Simmel as an "imposition of identity." See Schwartz (1967).

15 Herzfeld's Cretans communicate the same message whenever they exclaim, to a guest, "As in your own home!" (1988:36).

References

Abu-Lughod, Lila. 1999. *Veiled Sentiments: Honor and Poetry in a Bedouin Society*. Berkeley, Los Angeles: University of California Press.

Abu-Zahra, Nadia. 1974. Material Power, Honour, Friendship, and the Etiquette of Visiting. *Anthropological Quarterly* 47 (1): 120–38. http://dx.doi .org/10.2307/3317030.

Albera, Dionigi, and Anton Blok. 2001. The Mediterranean as a Field of Ethnological Study: A Retrospective. In *Anthropologie de la Méditerranée / Anthropology of the Mediterranean*, ed. Dionigi Albera, Anton Blok, and Christian Bromberger, 15–37. Aix-en-Provence: Maisonneuve et Larose.

Amit, Vered, and Dick Noel, eds. 2012. *Young Men in Uncertain Times*. New York and Oxford: Berghahn.

Andreski, Stanislaw. 1968. *Military Organization and Society*. 2nd ed. Berkeley, Los Angeles: University of California Press.

Angioni, Giulio. 1989. *I pascoli erranti. Antropologia del pastore in Sardegna*. Naples: Liguori Editore.

Angioni, Giulio. 1998. Sardegna 1900: Lo Sguardo Antropologico. In *Storia d'Italia: Le Regioni dall'Unità a Oggi. La Sardegna*, ed. Luigi Berlinguer and Antonello Mattone, 1123–52. Turin: Einaudi.

Angioni, Giulio. 2000. Utilizzare i sapari locali? *La Ricerca Folklorica* 41 (41): 7–13 . http://dx.doi.org/10.2307/1479805.

Angioni, Giulio. 2001. Ingegneria Linguistica e Orgoglio Etnico. In *Limba Lingua Language: Lingue Locali, Standardizzazione e Identita in Sardegna nell'Era della Globalizzazzione*, ed. Mario Argiolas and Roberto Serra, 231–2. Cagliari: CUEC.

Angius, Vittorio, and Goffredo Casalis. 1992 [1833]. *III. Edizione anastatica, vol. II. Dizionario Geografico, Storico, Statistico, Commerciale degli Stati di S.M. il Re di Sardegna. Estratto delle Voci Riguardanti la Sardegna: Provincia di Nuoro*. Cagliari: Editrice Sardegna.

Appadurai, Arjun. 1996. *Modernity at Large: Cultural Dimensions of Globalization*. Minneapolis, London: University of Minnesota Press.

Assmuth, Laura. 1997. *Women's Work, Women's Worth: Changing Lifecourses in Highland Sardinia*. Helsinki: Finnish Anthropological Society.

Augé, Marc. 1995. *Non-Places: Introduction to an Anthropology of Super-Modernity*. London: Verso.

Ayora-Diaz, Steffan Igor. 1993. *Representations and Occupations: Shepherd's Choices in Sardinia*. PhD Thesis. Montreal: Department of Anthropology, McGill University.

Bailey, Frederick G. 1971. *Gifts and Poison: The Politics of Reputation*. New York: Schocken Books.

Banca d'Italia. 2013. *L'economia della Sardegna. Economie Regionali, no. 21*. Cagliari: Divisione Editoria e stampa della Banca d'Italia.

Bandinu, Bachisio. 2001. La Lingue della Differenza. In *Limba Lingua Language: Lingue Locali, Standardizzazione e Identita in Sardegna nell'Era della Globalizzazzione*, ed. Mario Argiolas and Roberto Serra, 125–38. Cagliari: CUEC.

Banfield, Edward C. 1958. *The Moral Basis of a Backward Society*. Chicago: The Free Press.

Basso, Keith H. 1996. Wisdom Sits in Places: Notes on a Western Apache Landscape. In *Senses of Place*, ed. Steven Feld and Keith H. Basso, 53–90. Santa Fe: School of American Research Press.

Bechi, Giulio. 1997 [1914]. *Caccia Grossa. Scene e Figure del Banditismo Sardo*. Cagliari: Ilisso Edizioni.

Beltrán, Gonzalo Aguirre. 1979. *Regions of Refuge*. Monograph Series, vol. 12. Washington, DC: Society for Applied Anthropology.

Beyer, Peter. 1994. *Religion and Globalization*. London: Sage.

Black-Michaud, Jacob. 1975. *Cohesive Force: Feud in the Mediterranean and the Middle East*. Oxford: Basil Blackwell.

Blake, Emma. 1998. Sardinia's Nuraghi: Four Millennia of Becoming. *World Archaeology* 30 (1): 59–71. http://dx.doi.org/10.1080/00438243.1998.9980397.

Bloch, Marc. 1961. *Feudal Society*. Trans. L.A. Manyon. Chicago: University of Chicago Press.

Blok, Anton. 1972. The Peasant and the Brigand: Social Banditry Reconsidered. *Comparative Studies in Society and History* 14 (4): 494–503.

Blok, Anton. 1974. *The Mafia of a Sicilian Village, 1860–1960: A Study of Violent Peasant Entrepreneurs*. Prospect Heights: Waveland.

Blok, Anton. 2000. *La mafia di un villaggio siciliano, 1860–1960: Contadini, imprenditori, violenti*. 2nd ed. Trans. Marina Bocconcelli. Torino: Einaudi, Edizioni di Comunità.

Blok, Anton. 2001. *Honour and Violence*. Cambridge: Polity.

Blok, Anton, and Henk Driessen. 1984. Mediterranean Agro-Towns as a Form of Cultural Dominance. *Ethnologia Europaea* 14:111–24.

Boscolo, Alberto. 1967. *Il Feudalesimo in Sardegna*. Cagliari: Fossataro.
Bourdieu, Pierre. 1966. The Sentiment of Honour in Kabyle Society. In *Honour and Shame: The Values of Mediterranean Society*, ed. J.G. Peristiany, 191–242. Chicago: University of Chicago Press.
Bourdieu, Pierre. 1977. *Outline of a Theory of Practice*. Trans. Richard Nice. Cambridge, New York: Cambridge University Press. http://dx.doi.org/10.1017/CBO9780511812507.
Bourdieu, Pierre. 2002. *Le Bal des Célibataires: Crise de la Société Paysanne en Béarn*. Paris: Editions du Seuil.
Bourgois, Phillipe. 1996. In Search of Masculinity: Violence, Respect, and Sexuality among Puerto Rican Crack Dealers in East Harlem. *British Journal of Criminology* 36 (3): 412–27. http://dx.doi.org/10.1093/oxfordjournals.bjc.a014103.
Bourgois, Phillipe. 2003. *In Search of Respect: Selling Crack in El Barrio*. Cambridge: Cambridge University Press.
Bracalini, Romano. 2001. *L'Italia Prima dell'Unità (1815-1860)*. Milan: Biblioteca Universale Rizzoli.
Brandes, Stanley. 1981. Like Wounded Stags: Male Sexual Ideology in an Andalusian Town. In *Sexual Meanings: The Cultural Construction of Gender and Sexuality*, ed. Sherry Ortner and Harriet Whitehead, 216–37. Cambridge: Cambridge University Press.
Braudel, Fernand. 1972. *The Mediterranean and the Mediterranean World in the Age of Philip II*. 2 vols. Trans. Sian Reynolds. New York: Harper and Row.
Brigaglia, Manlio. 1971. *Sardegna: Perchè Banditi*. Milan: Carte Segrete.
Bromberger, Christian. 2006. Towards an Anthropology of the Mediterranean. *History and Anthropology* 17 (2): 91–107. http://dx.doi.org/10.1080/02757200600624339.
Bromberger, Christian. 2007. Bridge, Wall, Mirror: Coexistence and Confrontations in the Mediterranean World. *History and Anthropology* 18 (3): 291–307. http://dx.doi.org/10.1080/02757200701389030.
Buell, Frederick. 1994. *National Culture and the New Global System*. Baltimore: Johns Hopkins University Press.
Cagnetta, Franco. 1975. *Banditi a Orgosolo*. Rimini: Guaraldi.
Caltagirone, Benedetto. 1989a. *Animali Perduti: Abigeato e Scambio Sociale in Barbagia*. Milano: CELT Editrice.
Caltagirone, Benedetto. 1989b. "Note sull'abigeato in Sardegna." *Quaderni Bolotanesi* 15: 129–73.
Cambosu, Salvatore. 1954. *Miele Amaro*. Firenze: Vallecchi.
Campbell, John K. 1964. *Honour, Family, and Patronage: A Study of Institutions and Moral Values in a Greek Mountain Community*. Oxford: Clarendon Press.

Campbell, John K. 1966. Honour and the Devil. In *Honour and Shame: The Values of Mediterranean Society*, ed. John Peristiany, 141–70. London: Weidenfeld and Nicolson.

Caro Baroja, Julio. 1963. The City and the Country: Reflexions on Some Ancient Commonplaces. In *Mediterranean Countrymen: Essays in the Social Anthropology of the Mediterranean*, ed. Julian Pitt-Rivers, 27–40. Paris: Mouton.

Casula, Francesco Cesare. 1994. *Breve Storia di Sardegna*. Sassari: Carlo Delfino Editore.

Cau, Luciano. 1999. Islands within Islands: Inner Isolation in Sardinia and Ireland. In *Insularity and Development: International Perspectives on Islands*, ed. Emilio Biagini and Brian Hoyle, 322–57. New York, London: Pinter.

Ciccone, Stefano. 2009. *Essere maschi: Tra potere e libertà*. Torino: Rosenberg & Sellier.

Clark, Martin. 1989. La Storia Politica e Sociale (1847–1914). In *Storia dei Sardi e della Sardegna*, vol. 4, ed. Massimo Guidetti, 243–86. Milano: Jaca.

Clastres, Pierre. 1974. *La Société Contre L'Etat: Recherches d'Anthropologie Politique*. Paris: Les Éditions de Minuit.

Clastres, Pierre. 2010 [1980]. *Archaeology of Violence*. Trans. Jeanine Herman. Los Angeles: Semiotext(e).

Clifford, James. 1997. *Routes: Travel and Translation in the Late Twentieth Century*. Cambridge, MA: Harvard University Press.

Clifford, James, and George Marcus, eds. 1986. *Writing Culture: The Poetics and Politics of Ethnography*. Berkeley, Los Angeles: University of California Press.

Cocco, Umberto, and Giampiero Marras. 2000. *Una Moda Fuorilegge: Il Fascino del Pastore in Velluto, la Riscoperta di uno Stile Etnico*. Naples: CUEN.

Cohen, Anthony P. 1985. *The Symbolic Construction of Community*. London, New York: Routledge. http://dx.doi.org/10.4324/9780203323373.

Collodi, Carlo. 1999 [1883]. *Le Avventure di Pinocchio*. Milano: RCS Libri.

Colombis, Alessio. 1997. Invece del Familismo: La Famiglianza. In *Famiglia Meridionale Senza Familismo: Strategie Economiche, Reti di Relazione e Parentela*, ed. Benedetto Meloni, 382–408. Catanzaro: Meridiana Libri.

Commissione Parlamentare d'Inchiesta sui Fenomeni di Criminalità in Sardegna. 1972. Camera dei Deputati, V Legislatura. Istituita con Legge 27 Ottobre 1969, No. 755. Doc. XXIII, No. 3-bis. Roma.

Counihan, Carole M. 1999. Bread as World: Food Habits and Social Relations in Modernizing Sardinia. In *The Anthropology of Food and Body: Gender, Meaning, and Power*, ed. Carole Counihan, 25–42. New York: Routledge.

Davis, John. 1977. *People of the Mediterranean: An Essay in Comparative Social Anthropology*. London: Routledge and Kegan Paul.

Day, John. 1968. *Villagi Abbandonati in Sardegna dal Trecento al Settecento*. Paris: CNRS.

Deledda, Grazia. 1993. Colombi e Sparvieri. In *I Grandi Romanzi di Grazia Deledda*, ed. Marta Savini, 438–584. Rome: Newton e Compton.

Deledda, Grazia. 1995. *Tradizioni popolari di Sardegna: Credenze magiche, antiche feste, superstizioni e riti di una volta nei più significativi scritti etnografici dell'autrice sarda*, ed. Dolores Turchi. Rome: Edizioni Della Torre.

Della Marmora, Alberto. 1997 [1860]. *Itinerario dell'Isola di Sardegna*. Trans. Maria Grazia Longhi. Nuoro: Ilisso Edizioni.

Demartis, Salvatore Angelo Maria. 1899. Spirito di Obbedienza e zelo nel dovere. In *Circolari della Parrochia di Orgosolo. 1843–1903, Cassetta no. 2*. Circolare no. 108, 139–42. Archivio Parrochiale di Orgosolo.

Deutsch, Karl. 1966. *Nationalism and Social Communication*. New York: MIT Press.

Driessen, Henk. 2005. Mediterranean Port Cities: Cosmopolitanism Reconsidered. *History and Anthropology* 16 (1): 129–41. http://dx.doi.org/10.1080/0275720042000316669.

du Boulay, Juliet. 1976. Lies, Mockery, and Family Integrity. In *Mediterranean Family Structures*, ed. John G. Peristiany, 389–406. Cambridge: Cambridge University Press.

du Boulay, Juliet. 1991. Strangers and Gifts: Hostility and Hospitality in Rural Greece. *Journal of Mediterranean Studies* 1 (1): 37–53.

du Boulay, Juliet, and Rory Williams. 1987. Amoral Familism and the Image of Limited Good: A Critique from a European Perspective. *Anthropological Quarterly* 60 (1): 12–24. http://dx.doi.org/10.2307/3317394.

Dubisch, Jill. 1995. *In a Different Place: Pilgrimage, Gender, and Politics at a Greek Island Shrine*. Princeton: Princeton University Press.

Ekholm-Friedman, Kajsa, and Jonathan Friedman. 1995. Global Complexity and the Simplicity of Everyday Life. In *Worlds Apart: Modernity through the Prism of the Local*, ed. Daniel Miller, 134–68. London: Routledge.

Elias, Norbert. 1982. Civilization and Violence: On the State Monopoly of Physical Violence and its Infringements. *Telos* 54: 133–54.

Elias, Norbert. 2000. *The Civilizing Process: Sociogenetic and Psychogenetic Investigations*, 2nd ed. Oxford: Wiley Blackwell.

Escobar, Arturo. 2001. Culture Sits in Places: Reflections on Globalism and Subaltern Strategies of Localization. *Political Geography* 20 (2): 139–74. http://dx.doi.org/10.1016/S0962-6298(00)00064-0.

Fabian, Johannes. 1983. *Time and the Other: How Anthropology Makes its Object*. New York: Columbia University Press.

Fadda, Paolo. 2002. Il doppio destino della Sardegna tra nuove fabbriche e vecchi ovili. *Sardegna Economica* 4 (2): 37–45.

Fentress, James, and Chris Wickham. 1992. *Social Memory*. Oxford: Blackwell.

Ferguson, James. 1999. *Expectations of Modernity: Myths and Meanings of Urban Life on the Zambian Copperbelt*. Berkeley, Los Angeles: University of California Press.

Ferguson, James. 2011. Novelty and Method: Reflections on Global Fieldwork. In *Multi-Sited Ethnography: Problems and Possibilities in the Translocation of Research Methods*, ed. Simon Coleman and Pauline von Hellermann, 194–207. London: Routledge.

Fiskesjö, Magnus. 2012. Outlaws, Barbarians, Slaves: Critical Reflections on Agamben's *Homo Sacer. HAU* 2 (1): 161–80. http://dx.doi.org/10.14318/hau2.1.009.

Floris, Francesco. 2002. *Storia della Sardegna*. 2nd ed. Rome: Newton e Compton Editori.

Frederiksen, Martin Demant. 2012. Good Hearts or Big Bellies: Dzmak'atsoba and Images of Masculinity in the Republic of Georgia. In *Young Men in Uncertain Times*, ed. Vered Amit and Noel Dyck, 165–86. New York, Oxford: Berghahn Books.

Funnell, Don, and Romola Parish. 2001. *Mountain Environments and Communities*. London and New York: Routledge.

Furesi, Roberto, Fabio A. Madau, and Pietro Pulina. 2013. Technical Efficiency in the Sheep Dairy Industry: An Application on the Sardinian (Italy) Sector. *Agricultual and Food Economics* 1 (4).

Galt, Anthony. 1992. *Town and Country in Locorotondo*. Fort Worth: Holt, Rinehart and Winston.

Geertz, Clifford. 1973. *The Interpretation of Cultures: Selected Essays*. New York: Basic Books.

Geertz, Clifford. 1983. *Local Knowledge: Further Essays in Interpretive Anthropology*. New York: Basic Books.

Gellner, Ernest. 1981. *Muslim Society*. Cambridge: Cambridge University Press.

Gellner, Ernest. 1983. *Nations and Nationalism*. Ithaca, NY: Cornell University Press.

Gellner, Ernest. 1988. *Plough, Sword, and Book: The Structure of Human History*. Chicago: Chicago University Press.

Gellner, Ernest. 1997. *Nationalism*. London: Weidenfeld and Nicolson.

Giacobbe, Maria. 1995. *Gli Arcipelaghi*. Rome: Biblioteca del Vascello.

Gibson, Mary. 1998. Biology or Environment? Race and Southern "Deviancy" in the Writings of Italian Criminologists, 1880–1920. In *Italy's 'Southern Question': Orientalism in One Country*, ed. Jane Schneider, 99–115. Oxford: Berg.

Giddens, Anthony. 1987. *The Nation-State and Violence: Volume Two of a Contemporary Critique of Historical Materialism*. Berkeley, Los Angeles: University of California Press.

Gilmore, David. 1975. Friendship in Fuenmayor: Patterns of Integration in an Atomistic Society. *Ethnology* 14 (4): 311–24. http://dx.doi.org/10.2307/3773234.

Gilmore, David. 1982. Anthropology of the Mediterranean Area. *Annual Review of Anthropology* 11 (1): 175–205. http://dx.doi.org/10.1146/annurev.an.11.100182.001135.

Gilmore, David. 1984. Andalusian Anti-Clericalism: An Eroticized Rural Protest. *Anthropology* 7:31–44.

Gilmore, David. 1991. Commodity, Comity, Community: Male Exchange in Rural Andalusia. *Ethnology* 30 (1): 17–30. http://dx.doi.org/10.2307/3773495.

Giordano, Christian. 2001. Europe: Sociocultural Overview. In *International Encyclopedia of the Social and Behavioral Sciences*, vol. 7, ed. Neil J. Smelser and Paul B. Baltes, 4917–23. Oxford: Pergamon. http://dx.doi.org/10.1016/B0-08-043076-7/00863-9.

Giordano, Christian. 2006. Mediterranean Region. In *The Brill Dictionary of Religion*, vol. 3, ed. Kocku von Stuckrad, 1201–9. Leiden: Brill.

Giordano, Christian. 2012a. The Anthropology of Mediterranean Societies." In *A Companion to the Anthropology of Europe*, ed. Ullrich Kockel, Máiréad Nic Craith, and Jonas Frykman, 13–31. Oxford: Blackwell. http://dx.doi.org/10.1002/9781118257203.ch2.

Giordano, Christian. 2012b. Anthropology Meets History: Investigating European Societies. *Anthropological Journal on European Cultures* 21 (2): 20–34. http://dx.doi.org/10.3167/ajec.2012.210204.

Gluckman, Max. 1963. Gossip and Scandal. *Current Anthropology* 4 (3): 307–16. http://dx.doi.org/10.1086/200378.

Goody, Jack. 2001. The Great and Little Traditions in the Mediterranean. In *L'anthropologie de la Méditerranée / Anthropology of the Mediterranean*, ed. Dionigi Albera, Anton Blok, and Christian Bromberger, 473–89. Aix-en-Provence: Maisonneuve et Larose.

Graeber, David. 2011. *Debt: The First 5,000 Years*. Brooklyn: Melville House Printing.

Gramsci, Antonio. 1975. *Quaderni del Carcere. Edizione Critica dell'Istituto Gramsci*. Torino: Einaudi.

Grasseni, Cristina. 2004. Blessed Be the Car! Routes, Memory and Identity in a Mountain "Enclosure" *Journal of the Society for the Anthropology of Europe* 4 (1): 24–36.

Hall, John A. 1994. *Coercion and Consent: Studies on the Modern State*. Cambridge: Polity Press.

Hannerz, Ulf. 1980. *Exploring the City: Inquiries Toward an Urban Anthropology*. New York: Columbia University Press.

Hannerz, Ulf. 1987. The World in Creolization. *Africa: Journal of the International African Institute* 57 (4): 546–59. http://dx.doi.org/10.2307/1159899.

Hannerz, Ulf. 1989. Notes on the Global Ecumene. *Public Culture* 1 (2): 66–75. http://dx.doi.org/10.1215/08992363-1-2-66.

Hannerz, Ulf. 1990. Cosmopolitans and Locals in World Culture. In *Global Culture: Nationalism, Globalization and Modernity*, ed. Mike Featherstone, 237–52. London: Sage Publications.

Hannerz, Ulf. 1992. The Global Ecumene as a Network of Networks. In *Conceptualizing Society*, ed. Adam Kuper, 34–56. London, New York: Routledge.

Hannerz, Ulf. 2010. *Anthropology's World: Life in a Twenty-First-Century Discipline*. London: Pluto.

Hayek, Friedrich A. 1978. *New Studies in Philosophy, Politics, Economics and the History of Ideas*. Chicago: University of Chicago Press. http://dx.doi.org/10.7208/chicago/9780226321288.001.0001.

Heatherington, Tracey. 1999. Street Tactics: Catholic Ritual and the Senses of the Past in Central Sardinia. *Ethnology* 38 (4): 315–34. http://dx.doi.org/10.2307/3773910.

Heatherington, Tracey. 2001. In the Rustic Kitchen: Real Talk and Reciprocity. *Ethnology* 40 (4): 329–45. http://dx.doi.org/10.2307/3773880.

Heatherington, Tracey. 2010. *Wild Sardinia: Indigeneity and the Global Dreamtimes of Environmentalism*. Seattle: University of Washington Press.

Hepburn, Eve. 2009. Explaining Failure: the Highs and Lows of Sardinian Nationalism. *Regional & Federal Studies* 19 (4–5): 595–618. http://dx.doi.org/10.1080/13597560903310378.

Herzfeld, Michael. 1980. Honour and Shame: Problems in the Comparative Analysis of Moral Systems. *Man (N.S.)* 15 (2): 339–51. http://dx.doi.org/10.2307/2801675.

Herzfeld, Michael. 1988. *The Poetics of Manhood: Contest and Identity in a Cretan Mountain Village*. Princeton: Princeton University Press.

Herzfeld, Michael. 2002. Towards an Ethnographic Phenomenology of the Greek Spirit. In *Political Uses of the Past: The Recent Mediterranean Experience*, ed. Jacques Revel and Giovanni Levi, 13–26. London: Frank Cass.

Hobsbawm, Eric. 1969. *Bandits*. London: Weidenfeld and Nicolson.

Horden, Peregrine, and Nicholas Purcell. 2000. *The Corrupting Sea: A Study of Mediterranean History*. Oxford: Blackwell.

Issawi, Charles, ed. 1963. *An Arab Philosophy of History: The Prolegomena of Ibn Khaldun of Tunis (1332–1406)*. London: John Murray.

ISTAT (Istituto Nazionale di Statistica). 2001. *Annuario Statistico Italiano*. Roma: Istituto Poligrafico e Zecca dello Stato.

ISTAT (Istituto Nazionale di Statistica). 2010. Censimento Generale dell'Agricoltura. Consistenza degli allevamenti (Numero di aziende per zona altimetrica, classi di superficie per tipo allevamento [tutte le voci tranne api e alter allevamenti] classe di giornate di lavoro totale aziendale). http://dati-censimentoagricoltura.istat.it/?lang=it.

ISTAT (Istituto Nazionale di Statistica). 2011. Cittadini Stranieri. Popolazione residente al 31 dicembre (dati ricalcolati a partire dal Censimento) e bilancio demografico dal 9 ottobre al 31 dicembre 2011 Regione: Sardegna. http:// demo.istat.it/str20111009/index.html.

ISTAT (Istituto Nazionale di Statistica). 2012. Natalita e Fecondita della Popolazione Residente. http://www.istat.it/it/archivio/74300.

Jaffe, Alexandra. 1996. The Second Annual Corsican Spelling Contest: Orthography and Ideology. *American Ethnologist* 23 (4): 816–35. http:// dx.doi.org/10.1525/ae.1996.23.4.02a00080.

Jaffe, Alexandra. 2003. Misrecognition Unmasked? "Polynomic" Language, Expert Statuses, and Orthographic Practices in Corsican Schools. *Pragmatics* 13 (4): 515–37.

Jankowiak, William, Robert Moore, and Tianshu Pan. 2012. Institutionalizing an Extended Youth Phase in Chinese Society: Social Class and Sex Differences in the Pursuit of the Personal and the Pragmatic. In *Young Men in Uncertain Times*, ed. Vered Amit and Noel Dyck, 79–110. New York, Oxford: Berghahn Books.

Lai, Franco. 1998. Il Pastoralismo e la Formazione dei Confini Comunali nella Sardegna Centro-Orientale. *La Ricerca Folklorica* 38 (38): 75–82. http:// dx.doi.org/10.2307/1479954.

Lambek, Michael. 2011. Catching the Local. *Anthropological Theory* 11 (2): 197–221. http://dx.doi.org/10.1177/1463499611407397.

Lancaster, Roger. 2003. *The Trouble with Nature: Sex in Science and Popular Culture*. Berkeley, Los Angeles: University of California Press.

La Nuova Sardegna. 17 May 1899. Trecento e piu arrestati nei circondari di Nuoro e di Ozieri. 9 (132): 2.

La Nuova Sardegna. 11 July 1899. Un conflitto tra carabinieri e latitanti. 9 (185): 2.

La Nuova Sardegna. 12 July 1899. Gli scontri nel territorio di Orgosolo: Quattro latatanti uccisi. 9 (186): 2.

La Nuova Sardegna. 1901. Un grave conflitto fra carabinieri e latitanti: La morte di Lovico. 11 (197): 2. Daily newspaper, published in Sassari, Sardinia.

La Nuova Sardegna. 2002. Freddato dai killer davanti alla chiesa. 116 (335): 1.

La Nuova Sardegna. 2003. I carabinieri sbarcano in forze a Lula. 117 (27): 1.

La Nuova Sardegna. 2007. Hanno fermato il cuore di un poeta. 30 December 2007. http://lanuovasardegna.gelocal.it/regione/2007/12/30/news/ hanno-fermato-il-cuore-di-un-poeta-1.3299953.

La Nuova Sardegna. 2008. L'Appello dei Marotto: Basta con il sangue. 7 January 2008. http://lanuovasardegna.gelocal.it/regione/2008/01/07/news/l-appello-dei-marotto-basta-con-il-sangue-1.3300003.

La Nuova Sardegna. 2008. Ancora sangue a Orgosolo. Dopo Marotto altre due omicidi. 5 January 2008. http://lanuovasardegna.gelocal.it/regione/2008/01/05/news/ancora-sangue-a-orgosolo-dopo-marotto-altri-due-omicidi-1.3299989.

Le Lannou, Maurice. 1941. *Pâtres et paysans de la Sardaigne*. Tours: Arrault.

Ledda, Alberto. 1971. *La Civiltà Fuorilegge: Storia del Banditismo Sardo*. Milan: Mursia.

Ledda, Gavino. 1975. *Padre Padrone*. Milano: Feltrinelli.

Ledda, Gavino. 1977. *Padre Padrone*, VHS, directed by Paolo Taviani and Vittorio Taviani. Italy: Radiotelevisione Italiana (RAI).

Lei-Spano, Giovanni Maria. 2000 [1922]. *La Questione Sarda*. Nuoro: Ilisso Edizioni.

Lewis, Oscar. 1973. Some Perspectives on Urbanization with Special Reference to Mexico City. In *Urban Anthropology*, ed. Aiden Southall, 125–38. New York: Oxford University Press.

Liber Chronicon Orgosolo. 25 November 1954. Archivio Parrochiale di Orgosolo.

Lilliu, Giovanni. 2002. *La Costante Resistenziale Sarda*. Nuoro: Ilisso.

Lison-Tolosana, Carmelo. 1966. *Belmonte de los Caballeros: Anthropology and History in an Aragonese Community*. Oxford: Oxford University Press.

Livy (Livius), Titus. 1976. *Livy with an English Translation, in Fourteen Volumes*, vol. XII, books XL–XLII. Loeb Classical Library No. 332. Trans. Evan T. Sage and Alfred Schlesinger. Cambridge: Harvard University Press.

Loi, Pierangelo. 2001. *Bardane e Sequestri: Eventi-Notizia tra Centro e Periferia in Sardegna*. Cagliari: CUEC.

Lombroso, Cesare. 1876. *L'Uomo Delinquente*. Turin: Bocca.

Lonergan, David F. 1984. *Sociability and Friendship in a Sardinian Village*. PhD thesis, Pennsylvania State University.

Macdonald, Sharon. 2012. Presencing Europe's Pasts. In *A Companion to the Anthropology of Europe*, ed. Ullrich Kockel, Máiréad Nic Craith, and Jonas Frykman, 233–52. Oxford: Blackwell. http://dx.doi.org/10.1002/9781118257203.ch14.

MacDougall, David. 1997. *Tempus de Baristas*, DVD, directed by David MacDougall. Berkeley: Berkeley Media LLC.

Magliocco, Sabina. 2006. *The Two Madonnas: The Politics of Festival in a Sardinian Community*. 2nd ed. Long Grove, IL: Waveland.

Mains, Daniel. 2012. Young Men's Struggles for Adulthood in Urban Ethiopia: Unemployment, Masculinity, and Migration. In *Young Men in Uncertain*

Times, ed. Vered Amit and Noel Dyck, 111–32. New York, Oxford: Berghahn Books.

Mann, Michael. 1993. *The Rise of Classes and Nation-States, 1760–1914*, vol. II. Sources of Social Power. New York: Cambridge University Press.

Marcus, George. 1995. Ethnography in/of the World System: The Emergence of Multi-Sited Ethnography. *Annual Review of Anthropology* 24 (1): 95–117. http://dx.doi.org/10.1146/annurev.an.24.100195.000523.

Marcus, George. 2008. The End(s) of Ethnography: Social/Cultural Anthropology's Signature Form of Producing Knowledge in Transition. *Cultural Anthropology* 23 (1): 1–14. http://dx.doi.org/10.1111/j.1548-1360 .2008.00001.x.

Marcus, George, and Michael Fischer. 1986. *Anthropology as Cultural Critique: An Experimental Moment in the Human Sciences*. Chicago: University of Chicago Press.

Masia, Michelina. 1992. *Il controllo sull'uso della terra. Analisi socio-giuridica sugli usi civici in Sardegna*. Cagliari: CUEC Editore.

Mastino, Attilio. 2006. La Sardegna Romana. In *Storia della Sardegna I: Dalle Origini al Settecento*, ed. Manlio Brigaglia, Attilio Mastino, and Gian Giacomo Ortu, pp. 33-57. Rome: Laterza.

Mattone, Antonello. 1976. Gramsci e la Questione Sarda. *Studi Storici* 17 (3): 195–222.

Matvejević, Predrag. 1999. *Mediterranean: A Cultural Landscape*. Berkeley: University of California Press.

Meloni, Benedetto. 1984. *Famiglie di Pastori: Continuità e Mutamento in una Comunità della Sardegna Centrale 1950–1970*. Torino: Rosenberg & Sellier Editori.

Meloni, Benedetto. 1996. *Ricerche Locali: Comunita, Economia, Codici e Regolazione Sociale*. Cagliari: CUEC Editrice.

Meloni, Piero. 1990. *La Sardegna Romana*. 2nd ed. Sassari: Chiarella.

Merton, Robert K. 1957. *Social Theory and Social Structure*. Glencoe, IL: The Free Press.

Mientjes, Antoon C. 1998. Pastoral Perceptions: Some Geographical Reflections on Pastoral Land Use in Sardinia. *Europaea* 4 (1): 133–47.

Mientjes, Antoon C. 2004. Modern pastoral landscapes on the island of Sardinia (Italy). Recent pastoral practices in local versus macro-economic and macro-political contexts. *Archaeological Dialogues* 10 (2): 161–90. http:// dx.doi.org/10.1017/S1380203804001230.

Ministero dell'Interno. 2013a. Elezioni 2013 Politiche e Regionali del 24 e 25 Febbraio. Scrutini: Provincia di Nuoro.

Ministero dell'Interno. 2013b. Elezioni 2013 Politiche e Regionali del 24 e 25 Febbraio. Scrutini: Comune di Orgosolo.

Morin, Edgar. 1998–1999. Penser la Méditerranée et Méditerranéiser la Pensée. *Confluences Méditerranée* 28:33–47. http://www.revues-plurielles.org/ _uploads/pdf/9_28_5.pdf.

Moss, David. 1979. Bandits and Boundaries in Sardinia. *Man (N.S.)* 14 (3): 477–96. http://dx.doi.org/10.2307/2801870.

Murru-Corriga, Gianetta. 2000. The Patronymic and the Matronymic in Sardinia: A Long-standing Competition. *History of the Family* 5 (2): 161–80. http://dx.doi.org/10.1016/S1081-602X(00)00034-8.

Needham, Rodney. 1975. Polythetic Classification: Convergence and Consequences. *Man (N.S.)* 10 (3): 349–69. http://dx.doi.org/10.2307/2799807.

Niceforo, Alfredo. 1898. *L'Italia Barbara Contemporanea*. Milan: Remo Sandron.

Niceforo, Alfredo. 1977 [1897]. *La Delinquenza in Sardegna*. Cagliari: Edizioni Della Torre.

Olwig, Fog. Karen. 1997. Cultural Sites: Sustaining Home in a Deterritorialized World. In *Siting Culture: The Shifting Anthropological Object*, ed. Karen Fog Olwig and Kirsten Hastrup, 17–38. London: Routledge.

Olwig, Kenneth. 2002. *Landscape, Nature, and the Body Politic: From Britain's Renaissance to America's New World*. Madison: University of Wisconsin Press.

Oppo, Anna. 1990. "Where There's No Woman There's No Home": Profile of the Agro-Pastoral Family in Nineteenth-Century Sardinia. *Journal of Family History* 15 (4): 483–502. http://dx.doi.org/10.1177/036319909001500127.

Ortner, Sherry B. 1974. Is Female to Male as Nature is to Culture? In *Woman, Culture, and Society*, ed. Michelle Rosaldo and Louise Lamphere, 68–87. Stanford: Stanford University Press.

Ortner, Sherry B. 1978. The Virgin and the State. *Feminist Studies* 4 (3): 19–35. http://dx.doi.org/10.2307/3177536.

Osborne, Thomas, and Nikolas Rose. 1999. Governing Cities: Notes on the Spatialisation of Virtue. *Environment and Planning D: Society & Space* 17 (6): 737–60. http://dx.doi.org/10.1068/d170737.

Paine, Robert. 1989. High-Wire Culture: Comparing Two Agonistic Systems of Self-Esteem. *Man (N.S.)* 24 (4): 657–72. http://dx.doi.org/10.2307/2804293.

Papataxiarchis, Evthymios. 1991. Friends of the Heart: Male Commensal Solidarity, Gender, and Kinship in Aegean Greece. In *Contested Identities: Gender and Kinship in Modern Greece*, ed. Evthymios Papataxiarchis and Peter Loizos, 156–79. Princeton: Princeton University Press.

Papataxiarchis, Evthymios. 2000. Dealing with Disadvantage: The Construction of the Self and the Politics of Locality. In *L'Anthropologie de la Mediterranée/Anthropology of the Mediterranean*, ed. Dionigi Albera, Anton Blok, and Christian Bromberger, 179–95. Paris: Maisonneuve et Larose.

Pardini, Andrea, and Michele Nori. 2011. Agro-silvo-pastoral Systems in Italy: Integration and Diversification. *Pastoralism: Research, Policy and Practice* 1:26. http://www.pastoralismjournal.com/content/1/1/26.

Pausanias. 1961. *Description of Greece*, vol. IV, books VIII–X. Trans. W.H.S. Jones. Cambridge, MA: Harvard University Press.

Peristiany, John. 1966. *Honour and Shame: The Values of Mediterranean Society*. Chicago: University of Chicago Press.

Pigliaru, Antonio. 2000 [1959]. *Il Banditismo in Sardegna: La Vendetta Barbaricina*. Nuoro: Il Maestrale.

Pinna, Gonario. 1992. *Il Pastore Sardo e la Giustizia*. Milano: Giuffrè.

Pira, Michelangelo. 1978. *La Rivolta dell'Oggetto: Antropologia della Sardegna*. Milan: Giuffrè Editore.

Pira, Michelangelo. 1979. *La festa, la farina, la forca (3a puntata, Su balente e sa 'emina)*, 16mm, directed by Giuseppe Mantovani. Italy: Radiotelevisione Italiana (RAI).

Pisano, Giorgio. 2005. *Lo Strano Caso del Signor Mesina*. Nuoro: Il Maestrale.

Pitt-Rivers, Julian, ed. 1963. *Mediterranean Countrymen*. Paris: Mouton.

Pitt-Rivers, Julian. 1968. The Stranger, the Guest, and the Hostile Host: Introduction to the Study of the Laws of Hospitality. In *Contributions to Mediterranean Sociology: Mediterranean Rural Communities and Social Change*, ed. John Peristiany, 12–30. Paris: Mouton.

Pitt-Rivers, Julian. 1977. *The Fate of Shechem, or the Politics of Sex. Essays in the Anthropology of the Mediterranean*. Cambridge: Cambridge University Press.

Pitzalis, Acciaro M. 1978. *In nome della madre: Ipotesi sul matriarcato barbaricino*. Milan: Einaudi.

Polanyi, Karl. 2001 [1944]. *The Great Transformation: The Political and Economic Origins of Our Time*. Boston: Beacon Press.

Principe, Ilario. 1985. Storia, ambiente, e società nell'organizzazione del territorio in Sardegna. In *Storia d'Italia, Annali 8: Insediamento e territorio*, ed. Cesare de Seta, 562–625. Torino: Einaudi.

Pungetti, Gloria. 1995. Anthropological Approach to Agricultural Landscape History in Sardinia. *Landscape and Urban Planning* 31 (1-3): 47–56. http://dx.doi.org/10.1016/0169-2046(94)01035-7.

Putnam, Robert D. 1993. *Making Democracy Work: Civic Traditions in Modern Italy*. Princeton: Princeton University Press.

Ravis-Giordani, Georges. 1990. La "casa" et la "piazza,"ou la leçon de Grossu Minutu. *Terrain* 15 (15): 41–8. http://dx.doi.org/10.4000/terrain.2981.

Ravis-Giordani, Georges. 2001 [1983]. *Bergers Corses: Les Communautés Villageoises du Niolu*. Ajaccio: Albiana/PNRC.

Redfield, Robert. 1955. *The Little Community: Viewpoint for the Study of a Human Whole.* Chicago: University of Chicago Press.

Reed-Danahay, Deborah. 1999. Friendship, Kinship and the Life Course in Rural Auvergne. In *The Anthropology of Friendship*, ed. Sandra Bell and Simon Coleman, 137–54. Oxford, New York: Berg.

Regione Autonoma della Sardegna. 2009a. Elezioni 2009: Risultati per Comune. http://www.regione.sardegna.it/argomenti/attivita _istituzionali/elezioni2009/risultati_comune.html.

Regione Autonoma della Sardegna. 2009b. Elezione del Quattordicesimo Consiglio regionale, 15 e 16 febbraio 2009. A: Circoscrizioni provinciali. http://consiglio.regione.sardegna.it/Manuale%20consiliare/XIV _Legislatura/Tomo%20II/02a%20-%202009%20Quattordicesimo.pdf.

Regione Autonoma della Sardegna, 2013. Parti e nascite in Sardegna: Informazioni di carattere generale. http://www.regione.sardegna.it/j/v/ 25?s=193885&v=2&c=1250&t=1.

Riegelhaupt, Joyce. 1984. Popular Anti-Clericalism and Religiosity in pre-1974 Portugal. In *Religion, Power, and Protest in Local Communities*, ed. Eric R. Wolf, 93–116. New York, Amsterdam: Mouton.

Rosetti, Carlo Giuseppe. 1982. The Ideology of Banditry. *Man* 17 (1): 158–60.

Ruffini, Julio. 1978. Disputing Over Livestock in Sardinia. In *The Disputing Process: Law in Ten Societies*, ed. Harry F. Todd and Laura Nader, 209–46. New York: Columbia University Press.

Ruju, Sandro. 2006. L'economia e la Societa nel Duemila. In *Storia della Sardegna 2: Dal Settecento a Oggi*, ed. Manlio Brigaglia, Attilio Mastino, and Gian Giacomo Ortu, 162–75. Rome: Laterza.

Sahlins, Marshall. 1972. *Stone Age Economics*. Chicago: Aldine-Atherton.

Satta, Gino. 2001. *Turisti a Orgosolo. La Sardegna pastorale come attrazione turistica.* Napoli: Liguori Editore.

Satta, Salvatore. 1987. *The Day of Judgement*. Trans. Patrick Creagh. New York: Farrar, Strauss, Giroux.

Scarcella, Gaspare. 2001. *Il Brigantaggio in Sicilia dagli Antichi Romani ai Nostri Giorni.* Palermo: Antares Editrice.

Schneider, Jane. 1971. Of Vigilance and Virgins: Honor, Shame, and Access to Resources in Mediterranean Societies. *Ethnology* 10 (1): 1–24. http://dx.doi .org/10.2307/3772796.

Schneider, Jane, and Peter Schneider. 1976. *Culture and Political Economy in Western Sicily*. New York: Academic Press.

Schwartz, Barry. 1967. The Social Psychology of the Gift. *American Journal of Sociology* 73 (1): 1–11. http://dx.doi.org/10.1086/224432.

Schweizer, Peter. 1988. *Shepherds, Workers, Intellectuals: Culture and Centre-Periphery Relationships in a Sardinian Village.* Stockholm Studies in Social

Anthropology, 18. Stockholm: Department of Social Anthropology, University of Stockholm.

Scott, James C. 1998. *Seeing Like a State: How Certain Schemes to Improve the Human Condition Have Failed*. Princeton: Princeton University Press.

Scott, James C. 2009. *The Art of Not Being Governed: An Anarchist History of Upland Southeast Asia*. New Haven, London: Yale University Press.

Sorge, Antonio. 2009. Hospitality, Friendship, and the Outsider in Highland Sardinia. *Journal of the Society for the Anthropology of Europe* 9 (1): 4–12. http://dx.doi.org/10.1111/j.1556-5823.2009.00002.x.

Sorge, Antonio, and Andrew Roddick. 2012. Mobile Humanity: The Delocalization of Anthropological Research. *Reviews in Anthropology* 41 (4): 273–301.

Sotgiu, Giovanna. 1980. *Per la diffusione del culto di Sabazio. Testimonianza della Sardegna*. Leiden: Brill.

Stacul, Jaro. 2003. *The Bounded Field: Localism and Local Identity in an Italian Alpine Valley*. New York, Oxford: Berghahn Books.

Stacul, Jaro, Christinia Moutsou, and Helen Kopnina, eds. 2005. *Crossing European Boundaries: Beyond Conventional Geographical Categories*. New York and Oxford: Berghahn.

Stade, Ronald, and Gudrun Dahl. 2003. Introduction: Globalization, Creolization, and Cultural Complexity. *Global Networks* 3 (3): 201–6. http://dx.doi.org/10.1111/1471-0374.00057.

Strabo. 1906. *Geography*, vol. I, books I-VI. Hans Claude Hamilton and William Falconer, trans. London and New York: G. Bell and Sons.

Tiragallo, Felice. 2001. To Stay, To Go: Pathways Open to Youth in Southeastern Sardinia. *Europaea* 1/2:131–43.

van Dommelen, Peter. 2001. Ambiguous Matters: Colonialism and Local Identities in Punic Sardinia. In *The Archaeology of Colonialism*, ed. Claire L. Lyons and John K. Papadopoulos, 121–47. Los Angeles: Getty Research Institute.

van Gennep, Arnold. 1960. *The Rites of Passage*. Trans. Monika Vizedom and Gabrielle Caffee. Chicago: University of Chicago Press.

Vargas-Cetina, Gabriela. 2000. From Handicraft to Monocrop: The Production of Pecorino Cheese in Highland Sardinia. In *Commodities and Globalization: Anthropological Perspectives*, ed. Angelique Haugerud, Margaret Priscilla Stone, and Peter D. Little, 219–38. Boston: Rowman and Littlefield.

Vargas-Cetina, Gabriela. 2011. Corporations, Cooperatives, and the State: Examples from Italy. *Current Anthropology* 52 (S3): S127–36. http://dx.doi.org/10.1086/656784.

Wiener, Martin J. 1998. The Victorian Criminalization of Men. In *Men and Violence: Gender, Honor, and Rituals in Modern Europe and America*, ed. Pieter Spierenburg, 197–212. Columbus: Ohio State University Press.

Wikan, Unni. 1984. Shame and Honour: A Contestable Pair. *Man (N.S.)* 19 (4): 635–52. http://dx.doi.org/10.2307/2802330.

Wilson, Roger J.A. 1996. Sicily, Sardinia, and Corsica. In *Cambridge Ancient History*, vol. X: *The Augustan Empire, 43 B –AD 69*, ed. A.K. Bowman et al., 434–49. Cambridge: Cambridge University Press.

Wilson, Stephen. 1988. *Feuding, Conflict, and Banditry in Nineteenth-Century Corsica*. New York: Cambridge University Press.

Wolf, Eric. 1982. *Europe and the People without History*. Berkeley, Los Angeles: University of California Press.

Wolf, Eric. 2001. *Pathways of Power: Building and Anthropology of the Modern World*. Berkeley, Los Angeles: University of California Press.

Wolf, Eric. 1957. Closed Corporate Peasant Communities in Mesoamerica and Central Java. *Southwestern Journal of Anthropology* 13 (1): 1–18.

Wolf, Eric. 1986. The Vicissitudes of the Closed Corporate Peasant Community. *American Ethnologist* 13 (2): 325–9.

Zene, Cosimo. 2005. Done e Vendetta nella Sardegna Centrale. *LARES* 71 (3): 683–717.

Zene, Cosimo. 2007. *S'Imbiatu:* Gift and Community in Central Sardinia. *Culture and Religion* 8 (3): 291–312. http://dx.doi.org/10.1080/14755610701660064.

Zolo, Danilo. 2007. La Questione Mediterranea. In *L'alternative Mediterranea*, ed. Franco Cassano and Danilo Zolo, 13–77. Milan: Feltrinelli.

Index

agrarian society, 4–9, 39, 51–7, 77–8
alcohol, 91, 103, 133–4, 139, 144,
150–1; overconsumption of, 91, 93,
95–6, 115, 150–1. *See also* bars
Angioni, Giulio, 121
Angius, Vittorio, and Goffredo
Casalis, 34
Appadurai, Arjun, 12–13, 21–2, 127,
137, 153
Assmuth, Laura, 75–6, 115, 172n6

balentia, xiii–xix, 9–10, 20, 24, 48–51,
56–83, 90, 99, 115, 157–9, 166n5;
and the life course, 10, 57–8; and
women, 57, 115
banditry, 18–19, 34–5, 40–3, 50–1,
61–3, 165n12. *See also* legal
self-help
Banfield, Edward, 130–1
Barbagia, xiii, 13–14, 38, 40–2;
stereotypes of, xii–xiv, 51. *See also*
Civitates Barbariae
Barbarism, xiii, 20, 49–70; as a
political construct, 30–1
bars, 17, 58, 64, 88–90, 91–8. *See also*
sociality; hospitality
Blok, Anton, 33, 52, 61–2, 69, 165n12

Bourdieu, Pierre, 9, 79, 166n5
Braudel, Fernand, 28, 31, 164n3

Cagliari, 25, 96, 117
Cagnetta, Franco, 33, 42–3, 67, 164n7
campanilismo, 119–22
cars, 15, 58, 85–6, 95, 103, 134
Circolo Giovanile, 123–6
Civitates Barbariae, xiii, 31
Clastres, Pierre, 6, 9, 28, 50–1
codice barbaricino, xiv, 9–10, 50–1. See
also *balentia*
Cohen, Anthony, 147, 153
Commissione Parlamentare d'inchiesta, 43
community, x–xi, xiii–xiv, 8–12, 13–22;
customary laws of, 50–2, 78; and
localism, 102–5, 118, 123ff; social
cohesion and fragmentation within,
83, 128–49. *See also* hospitality
consumerism, 75–6, 79, 118
cosmopolitanism, 13, 21–2, 76, 79,
100–3; aspirations to, 110–17;
and women, 74–7, 79, 84, 115–17;
vis-à-vis localism, 111–27. *See also*
localism
criminology, 19, 37–9. *See also*
policing

Deledda, Grazia, 39, 165n10
demographics, 172n7, 172n9
dialects, 37, 110, 119–22, 165n9;
    pastoral, 21, 24, 31, 39–40, 83–4,
    85–91; tertiary sector, 13, 73, 85,
    168n6

education, 54, 59, 106–9, 120
egalitarianism, 147–8
Elias, Norbert, 55–6

Family, 8, 22, 69, 77–8, 129–3; and
    household, 50, 75–6, 131–41, 172n5
Fentress, James and Chris Wickham,
    124
festivals: Assumption of the Virgin,
    16, 89–90, 105; *Sa Candelaría*, 139–
    40; carnival, 90 136–7, 140, 172n11;
    Festa del pastore, 105–6; Saints Peter
    and Paul, 16, 89–90
food, 76, 106, 119, 144, 151–2, 172n10,
    172n13; provisioning of, 136–8. *See
    also* pastoral production
friendship, 69, 141–9, 151–3; and
    enmity, 46, 75; and individualism,
    145–6

Gellner, Ernest, xiv, 5, 28, 52–4, 77–8,
    163n1
gender: customary roles, 135–6; and
    honour, 57–8, 136, 140–1; local
    binary models of, 108; relations
    between the sexes, 97, 108, 115–16,
    131–42; segregation, 6, 11, 16,
    163n4
Giddens, Anthony, 54
Gilmore, David, 6, 16, 131, 152
Giordano, Christian, 11–12, 69, 128,
    155, 157, 167n6
Goody, Jack, 102-103, 105

gossip, 22, 46, 83, 92–7, 115, 128–9,
    138–40, 143ff
Gramsci, Antonio, 61, 77, 123
Great Tradition, 54, 55. *See also* Little
    Tradition

habitus: rural, 112–13; transforma-
    tions of, 55
Hannerz, Ulf, 13, 102, 117, 170n11
Hayek, Friedrich, 54
Heatherington, Tracy, 36, 44, 48, 75,
    89, 122, 137
Herzfeld, Michael, 72, 77–8, 163n3,
    171n4, 173n15
history: Giudicati di Arborea, 32;
    landscape, 23–49; land tenure,
    33–5; Nuragic, 28–31; post-Italian
    unification, 36–46; Roman 29–31;
    Spanish, 32–3
Hobsbawm, Eric, 61–2, 165n12
honour, xiii, 6–11, 20, 24, 38–9, 49ff,
    57–70, 121, 158, 163n2, 163n3,
    166n3, 167n6, 171n1; and the
    family, 129ff, 152; and violence, 74,
    80ff, 158–9. See also *balentia*
Horden, Peregrine and Nicholas
    Purcell, xiii, 6, 7–8
hospitality, 92, 149–53; in the
    domestic sphere, 133–4; and the
    outsider, 150–1

identity: family and household,
    129–41; localists and cosmopolitans,
    100–27; the stranger, 150–1; shep-
    herds, 57ff, 73–9, 88–9, 94–9, 108–11

kidnap for ransom, 40, 43, 61–3, 148–9

Lai, Franco, 9, 34
Lambek, Michael, 153

land tenure: commons, 4, 35, 85–6, 122; General Enclosures Act, 33, 35–6, 101; Law on the Commons, 35; pastures, 8, 43–4, 58ff, 85–6, 107. *See also* Parco Nazionale del Gennargentu e del Golfo di Orosei

landscape: coasts, 25; highlands and lowlands, 25–8, 164n3; history, 23–49; tenure history, 33–7

law enforcement, 15, 18–19, 41–3, 63–6

Le Lannou, Maurice, 25, 27, 33, 34, 164n6 (chap. 2), 165n8

Ledda, Gavino, 109

legal self-help, 6ff, 28, 45–6, 66–7, 71–2, 158–9. *See also* violence, *codice barbaricino*

legitimation of authority, 39, 45–6, 52–4

Lilliu, Giovanni, 170n9

Little Tradition, 101–11, 127. *See also* Great Tradition

Livy, 29–30

localism, 13, 100ff; vis-à-vis cosmopolitanism, 111–27. *See also* community; cosmopolitanism

Macdonald, Sharon, 11

masculinity and male identity, 8–10, 57–8, 73ff, 115; crisis of, 57–8, 73–9, 116, 168n10. *See also* gender

Mediterranean region, xii–xiv, 28, 51, 57ff, 128–31, 155–8; anthropology of, 6–16

Mesina, Graziano, 62–3

modernity: entrenchment of, 52–7; national, 19–2, 35, 53–5, 83–4, 106ff; neoliberal, 73, 77–9, 83–5. *See also* Great Tradition; nation-state

nation-state, 13, 18ff, 36–48, 101, 157–9

Niceforo, Alfredo, 36–9, 124

Nuoro, 95, 113, 116, 118–19, 170n10

outlawry. *See* banditry

pacifism, 81–3, 114–15

Parco Nazionale del Gennargentu e del Golfo di Orosei, 4, 44, 122

pastoralism: as a problem requiring remedy, 39–46; as occupational identity, 57ff, 73–9, 88–9, 94–9, 108–11; transformations of, 58, 85–9; sartorial styles, 17, 89, 97–8

Pausanias, 29

Pigliaru, Antonio, xiii, 50–1, 78, 108, 149, 166n1

Pira, Michelangelo, 78, 106–10, 148

Pitt-Rivers, Julian, xiii, 7–8, 39, 151, 163n2

Polanyi, Karl, 83–4

politics: electoral, 46–8, 75, 122; Sardinian nationalism, 46–7. *See also* Circolo Giovanile; gossip; nation-state

Provincia Sardiniae et Corsicae, 29ff

Redfield, Robert, 14

religion, 16–17, 41–2, 89, 123, 136; anticlericalism, 16

Satta, Gino, 68, 152, 169n12

Schneider, Jane, 8–9

Scott, James C., 5, 20, 24, 28, 49–53, 77

secrecy, 67–9, 83, 148–9

sex. *See* gender

social memory, 19, 122–7

spaces: countryside, 59–61, 77, 113–14, 142, 149; and gender, 91–9, 107–8, 116, 133–7, 143, 148–9; legible and non-legible, 27, 50, 77;

village, 15–18, 20, 58–9, 88–90, 105, 151
status: with age, 10, 57–8, 80; familial, 129, 132, 136; of guests, 150–3; and reputation, 143, 167n; social, 75–6, 83, 95, 99, 107, 11–16; women in Orgosolo, 133
su connottu, 35–6, 66, 108ff. *See also* legal self-help

tourism, 87, 88, 143
traditionalism, 13, 57ff., 76-78, 99, 105–11, 113, 159; rejection of, 113ff
travel, 103, 112, 117, 126,
trust, 66, 69, 145, 146–9, 151, 170n11

Vargas-Cetina, Gabriela, 39, 88
violence: against the state, 5–6, 9, 28, 34-35, 45, 53, 70; legacies of, 11, 69, 159; in agrarian society, 8–9, 39, 77–8, 158–9; blood feud, 28; 50–1, 62-63, 67, 71–2, 74–5, 78,

79–83, 149; and "pacification," 18–19, 54–5; raiding, 34–5, 38, 40; the Roman conquest, 29–31; and the state, 41–3, 67; state monopoly over means of, 45, 52, 54–5, 69, 158–9; sublimation of, 55–6. *See also balentia*; banditry; *codice barbaricino*; honour; pacifism

Wolf, Eric, 10, 14, 156
women: and family honour, 57–8, 140–1; life aspirations of, 21, 73–6, 84, 115–16; sociality among, 134, 136–8

youth: dating, 115–16, 141; education, 107–9; opportunities open to, 48, 82, 84, 110. *See also* Circolo Giovanile

Zene, Cosimo, 140

ANTHROPOLOGICAL HORIZONS

Editor: Michael Lambek, University of Toronto

Published to date:

The Varieties of Sensory Experience: A Sourcebook in the Anthropology of the Senses /
Edited by David Howes (1991)

Arctic Homeland: Kinship, Community, and Development in Northwest Greenland /
Mark Nuttall (1992)

*Knowledge and Practice in Mayotte: Local Discourses of Islam, Sorcery, and Spirit
Possession* / Michael Lambek (1993)

*Deathly Waters and Hungry Mountains: Agrarian Ritual and Class Formation in an
Andean Town* / Peter Gose (1994)

Paradise: Class, Commuters, and Ethnicity in Rural Ontario / Stanley R. Barrett
(1994)

The Cultural World in Beowulf / John M. Hill (1995)

Making It Their Own: Severn Ojibwe Communicative Practices / Lisa Philips
Valentine (1995)

*Merchants and Shopkeepers: A Historical Anthropology of an Irish Market Town,
1200–1991* / Philip Gulliver and Marilyn Silverman (1995)

Tournaments of Value: Sociability and Hierarchy in a Yemeni Town /
Ann Meneley (1996)

Mal'uocchiu: Ambiguity, Evil Eye, and the Language of Distress /
Sam Migliore (1997)

Between History and Histories: The Production of Silences and Commemorations /
Edited by Gerald Sider and Gavin Smith (1997)

Eh, Paesan! Being Italian in Toronto / Nicholas DeMaria Harney (1998)

Theorizing the Americanist Tradition / Edited by Lisa Philips Valentine and
Regna Darnell (1999)

Colonial 'Reformation' in the Highlands of Central Sulawesi, Indonesia, 1892–1995 /
Albert Schrauwers (2000)

The Rock Where We Stand: An Ethnography of Women's Activism in Newfoundland /
Glynis George (2000)

Being Alive Well: Health and the Politics of Cree Well-Being / Naomi Adelson
(2000)

Irish Travellers: Racism and the Politics of Culture / Jane Helleiner (2001)

*Of Property and Propriety: The Role of Gender and Class in Imperialism and
Nationalism* / Edited by Himani Bannerji, Shahrzad Mojab, and Judith
Whitehead (2001)

An Irish Working Class: Explorations in Political Economy and Hegemony, 1800–1950 / Marilyn Silverman (2001)

The Double Twist: From Ethnography to Morphodynamics / Edited by Pierre Maranda (2001)

The House of Difference: Cultural Politics and National Identity in Canada / Eva Mackey (2002)

Writing and Colonialism in Northern Ghana: The Encounter between the LoDagaa and the 'World on Paper,' 1892–1991 / Sean Hawkins (2002)

Guardians of the Transcendent: An Ethnography of a Jain Ascetic Community / Anne Vallely (2002)

The Hot and the Cold: Ills of Humans and Maize in Native Mexico / Jacques M. Chevalier and Andrés Sánchez Bain (2003)

Figured Worlds: Ontological Obstacles in Intercultural Relations / Edited by John Clammer, Sylvie Poirier, and Eric Schwimmer (2004)

Revenge of the Windigo: The Construction of the Mind and Mental Health of North American Aboriginal Peoples / James B. Waldram (2004)

The Cultural Politics of Markets: Economic Liberalization and Social Change in Nepal / Katherine Neilson Rankin (2004)

A World of Relationships: Itineraries, Dreams, and Events in the Australian Western Desert / Sylvie Poirier (2005)

The Politics of the Past in an Argentine Working-Class Neighbourhood / Lindsay DuBois (2005)

Youth and Identity Politics in South Africa, 1990–1994 / Sibusisiwe Nombuso Dlamini (2005)

Maps of Experience: The Anchoring of Land to Story in Secwepemc Discourse / Andie Diane Palmer (2005)

Beyond Bodies: Rain-Making and Sense-Making in Tanzania / Todd Sanders (2008)

We Are Now a Nation: Croats between 'Home' and 'Homeland' / Daphne N. Winland (2008)

Kaleidoscopic Odessa: History and Place in Post-Soviet Ukraine / Tanya Richardson (2008)

Invaders as Ancestors: On the Intercultural Making and Unmaking of Spanish Colonialism in the Andes / Peter Gose (2008)

From Equality to Inequality: Social Change among Newly Sedentary Lanoh Hunter-Gatherer Traders of Peninsular Malaysia / Csilla Dallos (2011)

Rural Nostalgias and Transnational Dreams: Identity and Modernity among Jat Sikhs / Nicola Mooney (2011)

Dimensions of Development: History, Community, and Change in Allpachico, Peru / Susan Vincent (2012)

People of Substance: An Ethnography of Morality in the Colombian Amazon / Carlos David Londoño Sulkin (2012)

'We Are Still Didene': Stories of Hunting and History from Northern British Columbia / Thomas McIlwraith (2012)

Being Māori in the City: Indigenous Everyday Life in Auckland / Natacha Gagné (2013)

The Hakkas of Sarawak: Sacrificial Gifts in Cold War Era Malaysia / Kee Howe Yong (2013)

Remembering Nayeche and the Gray Bull Engiro: African Storytellers of the Karamoja Plateau and the Plains of Turkana / Mustafa Kemal Mirzeler (2014)

In Light of Africa: Globalizing Blackness in Northeast Brazil / Allan Charles Dawson (2014)

The Land of Weddings and Rain: Nation and Modernity in Postsocialist Lithuania / Gediminas Lankauskas (2015)

Milanese Encounters: Public Space and Vision in Contemporary Urban Italy / Cristina Moretti (2015)

Legacies of Violence: History, Society, and the State in Sardinia / Antonio Sorge (2015)

Looking Back, Moving Forward: Transformation and Ethical Practice in the Ghanaian Church of Pentecost / Girish Daswani (2015)

www.ingramcontent.com/pod-product-compliance
Ingram Content Group UK Ltd.
Pitfield, Milton Keynes, MK11 3LW, UK
UKHW032119310125
454513UK00001B/46